A SPY LIKE NO OTHER

A SPY LIKE NO OTHER

THE CUBAN MISSILE CRISIS, THE KGB AND THE KENNEDY ASSASSINATION

ROBERT HOLMES

Biteback Publishing

First published in Great Britain in 2012 by
Biteback Publishing Ltd
Westminster Tower
3 Albert Embankment
London SE1 7SP
Copyright © Robert Holmes 2012

ISBN 978-1-84954-415-3

10 9 8 7 6 5 4 3 2 1

A CIP catalogue record for this book is available from the British Library.

Set in Baskerville and Steelfish by Namkwan Cho
Cover design by Namkwan Cho

Printed and bound in Great Britain by
CPI Group (UK) Ltd, Croydon CR0 4YY

For Nancy and all my family, present and departed; remembering especially my first wife, Margaret, who was with me in Moscow in 1961–2, and my sister, Alice, who died at far too young an age.

CONTENTS

ACKNOWLEDGEMENTS

When I began writing this book three years ago, it was going to be about Oleg Penkovsky, his relationship with the CIA and MI6, and the part he played in the outcome of the Cuban Missile Crisis. In the course of my research, however, I came across references to someone called Ivan Serov. At first I tried to ignore him but he became so persistent that I had to incorporate him into the story. As my research continued I became intrigued by this relatively unknown anti-hero who had been largely removed from the record by the obsessive Communist machine when he fell into disfavour shortly after Penkovsky's trial and execution in 1963. Then I began to research the creation of Castro's Cuba and became fascinated by the Mafia's and CIA's involvement in it. This inevitably led me to extend the story to include the assassination of President Kennedy. My further research led me to some startling and, to me, unexpected conclusions that might just help to bring a flicker of light into the dark corners that have yet to be illuminated by incontrovertible evidence of the truth.

While I have used my experience in the British Diplomatic Service to describe the story, virtually all of the information is drawn from open sources rather than from specific knowledge gained while I was employed there.

My infinitely patient wife, Nancy, has been a tower of strength and encouragement to me. All of our loving and much loved children have had faith in my ability to complete this task – or so they said – and have also given me much encouragement.

I do not speak Russian, and am accordingly most grateful to Professor Geoffrey Swain (Alec Nove Chair in Russian and East European Studies, University of Glasgow) for his guidance on where Nikita Petrov's book *First Chairman of the KGB: Ivan Serov* (published only in Russian) either supplemented or contradicted the content of my original draft.

My thanks also to the several family members and friends who bravely volunteered, or were conscripted, to read and comment upon my early drafts. Their suffering, hopefully, has not been in vain.

However, my efforts would undoubtedly have come to nought had it not been for the encouragement and expert guidance of Michael Smith, Hollie Teague, Reuben Cohen and everyone else at Biteback Publishing.

I am also grateful to the US Department of State and the CIA for publishing so much information on their websites. All of the quoted parts of Penkovsky's debriefing were taken from the CIA.

Stalin originated the concept *'enemy of the people'*. This term automatically made it unnecessary that the ideological errors of a man or men engaged in a controversy be proven. It made possible the use of the cruellest repression, violating all norms of revolutionary legality, against anyone who in any way disagreed with Stalin, against those who were only suspected of hostile intent, against those who had bad reputations.

Excerpt from Nikita Khrushchev's 'secret speech' delivered during the 20th Congress of the Communist Party of the Soviet Union (24–25 February 1956)

The KGB's exclusive concern was to be absolutely certain of its non-involvement in the assassination.

KGB Chairman Vladimir Semichastny answering a question years after the assassination of President Kennedy

GLOSSARY

ÁVH: Hungarian State Security (the secret police agency).

BOB: Berlin Operation Base. The name given to the CIA's station in West Berlin.

CIA: Central Intelligence Agency. A United States government agency responsible for providing national security intelligence to senior US policymakers.

CPSU: Communist Party of the Soviet Union.

DRE: Cuban Student Revolutionary Directorate (an anti-Castro organisation).

FBI: Federal Bureau of Investigation. The organisation that protects and defends the United States against terrorist and foreign intelligence threats and enforces the criminal laws of the United States.

FPCC: Fair Play for Cuba Committee. A pro-Castro organisation based in the United States.

FRD: Revolutionary Democratic Front. An anti-Castro Cuban exile organisation that combined a number of smaller groups of like mind.

G-2: Cuban intelligence organisation.

GKKNIR: The Soviet Union's State Committee for the Coordination of Scientific Research Work. This organisation was formed in 1961 following the reorganisation of the GNTK.

GNTK: The Soviet Union's State Committee for Science and Technology.

GRU: An acronym for the Russian for 'Main Intelligence Directorate', being short for the Main Intelligence Directorate of the General Staff of the Armed Forces of the Soviet Union. (It still exists under the same name but now relating only to Russia.)

HVA: Hauptverwaltung Aufklärung, or General Reconnaissance Administration: the foreign intelligence section of the Stasi.

ICBM: Intercontinental Ballistic Missile.

IRBM: Intermediate-Range Ballistic Missile.

JCS: United States 'Joint Chiefs of Staff' body.

JM/WAVE: The CIA's station in Miami.

KGB: Committee for State Security. The most important Soviet Union national security agency covering internal security, intelligence, and the secret police. It operated from 1954 until 1991. See also 'KGB History'.

KGB History

The Cheka (All-Russian Extraordinary Committee to Combat Counter-Revolution and Sabotage) was established after the October Revolution in 1917. It was under the control of the NKVD (People's Commissariat for Internal Affairs).

In February 1922 the Cheka was replaced by the State Political Directorate (GPU), which was the secret police of the Russian Soviet Federative Socialist Republic (RSFSR). In November 1922, when the Soviet Union proper was formed, the GPU had to be reorganised to exercise control over state security through-out the new union. The new organisation was called the Joint State Political Directorate (OGPU) and control of it passed from the NKVD (still an organisation of the RSFSR) to the Council of People's Commissars.

In 1934 the NKVD was transformed to encompass all of the Soviet Republics (not just Russia) and the OGPU was incorpo-rated into this new NKVD as the Main Directorate for State Security (GUGB).

In February 1941 the sections of the NKVD responsible

for military counterintelligence became part of the People's Commissariats of Defence and the Navy (RKKA and RKKF). The GUGB was separated from the NKVD and renamed the People's Commissariat for State Security (NKGB). Five months later, after the German invasion, the NKVD and NKGB were reunited. The military counterintelligence sections were returned to the NKVD in January 1942.

In April 1943 the military counterintelligence sections were again transferred to the RKKA and RKKF, becoming SMERSH (an acronym of the Russian for 'Death to Spies'). At the same time, the NKGB was again separated from the NKVD.

In 1946 all Soviet commissariats were made into ministries. The NKVD became the Ministry of Internal Affairs (MVD) and the NKGB was renamed as the Ministry of State Security (MGB).

On 5 March 1953 – the day Stalin died – Lavrentiy Beria merged the MGB back into the MVD, and in a subsequent reorganisation in 1954 Khrushchev once more split the police and security services to make them:

The Ministry of Internal Affairs (MVD), responsible for the criminal police and correctional facilities; and,

The Committee for State Security (KGB), responsible for the political police, military counterintelligence, intelligence, personal protection of the leadership, and confidential communications.

KPD: Communist Party of Germany.

MDA: The Soviet Union's Military-Diplomatic Academy.

MDP: Hungarian Workers' Party.

MECAS: The British-run 'Middle East Centre for Arabic Studies' based in the Lebanon.

MGB: Ministry for State Security. See also 'KGB History'.

MI5: Originally 'Military Intelligence 5', but the title lingered on to become the popular short title of the United Kingdom's Security Service – the national security intelligence agency that protects the UK against threats to national security from espionage, terrorism and sabotage, against the activities of foreign agents, and against actions intended to overthrow or undermine parliamentary democracy.

MI6: Originally 'Military Intelligence 6', but the title lingered on to become the popular short title of the United Kingdom's Secret Intelligence Service. See 'SIS'.

MRBM: Medium-Range Ballistic Missile.

MVD: Soviet Ministry of Internal Affairs.

NASA: The United States' National Aeronautics and Space Administration.

NATO: North Atlantic Treaty Organisation.

NKGB: People's Commissariat for State Security. See also 'KGB History'.

NKVD: People's Commissariat for Internal Affairs. See also 'KGB History'.

OVIR: The Soviet Union's Visa and Registration Department.

RD: Revolutionary Directorate. A Cuban anti-Communist organisation.

SAM: Surface-to-air missile.

SGA: Special Group Augmented. A United States group of senior military, political and CIA personnel with the task of overseeing the activities of *Operation Mongoose*.

SIS: Secret Intelligence Service. Also commonly known as MI6. The United Kingdom agency that provides a global covert capability to promote and defend the national security and economic well-being of the United Kingdom.

SMERSH: An acronym of the Russian for 'Death to Spies'. It was the nickname given by Stalin to his new security organisation, the 'Main Counterintelligence Directorate'.

Stasi: East German Ministry for State Security. In essence, the East German secret police.

UB: Polish Military Intelligence organisation.

USSR: The Union of Soviet Socialist Republics.

WWI, WWII, WWIII: First World War, Second World War, Third World War.

PROLOGUE

Most readers with even a passing interest in Cold War-era espionage will recall the names of some of the more celebrated spies implicated in passing Western secrets to the Soviet Union during the 1940s, 1950s and 1960s. The inglorious list would include such names as Klaus Fuchs, the executed nuclear whistle-blowers Julius and Ethel Rosenberg, the 'Cambridge Five' (Kim Philby, Donald Maclean, Guy Burgess, Anthony Blunt and John Cairncross), the Portland spy ring (Ethel Gee, Harry Houghton, Konon Molody (a.k.a. Gordon Lonsdale), Lona and Morris Cohen (a.k.a. the Krogers)), and George Blake, the KGB's mole inside the British Secret Intelligence Service (MI6).

The actions of these people impacted on the Cold War, at times 'heating' or speeding it, at others 'slowing' or cooling the global stand-off, depending on one's perspective. Few would claim, however, that any of these individuals ultimately changed the course of history. This book is not about the aforementioned traitors and double agents, though George Blake did play a part in certain key events described in it. It concerns, instead, some of the spies and senior members of the security services of the United States, the United Kingdom and the Soviet Union whose personal decisions and actions *did* change the course of history during the 1950s and early 1960s. People such as Ivan Serov, who throughout this period was, first, the head of the KGB and then the GRU (the Soviet military intelligence organisation);

Oleg Penkovsky, the GRU officer who passed invaluable military secrets to the West; Bill Harvey, the larger-than-life, gun-toting CIA officer who played a part in most of the major CIA Cold War operations throughout the period.

The story records how this exotic but, to most Westerners, obscure cast of characters, and others in their orbit, influenced events leading up to the Cuban Missile Crisis of October 1962 and the assassination of President John F. Kennedy just over a year later.

Given the limited period of time covered by the book it might be useful for the reader to have some background information about one particular – and particularly elusive – character: Ivan Serov.

One has to look closely at the canvas of history to spot Ivan Serov. He deserves a more prominent position in accounts of the Cold War, for he left his indelible mark on many important events in his thirty-year career as a senior Soviet intelligence officer. One of the twentieth century's great unsung anti-heroes, Serov played an essential part in establishing and consolidating Stalinist totalitarianism in the USSR and beyond.

Born of peasant stock in the Russian village of Afimskoe in 1905, General Ivan Aleksandrovich Serov joined the Red Army in 1923 and the Communist Party in 1926. For the next fifteen years, his military training and experience were varied and testing, but his native talents and instincts saw him perform with sufficient distinction to rise through the ranks of both the army and party. His knack for being close to the right people at the right time, a crucial skill for successful espionage officers serving at the whim of dictatorial regimes, came to the fore during Stalin's Great Purge of 1936–8, which saw more than 1.5 million people arrested and 700,000 of them executed. Serov not only survived the purge but played a part in implementing it: he was responsible for the execution of Marshal Tukhachevski and other leading figures of the Red Army.

His success in the army won him a place at the prestigious

Frunze Military Academy. Serov graduated in 1939 and within a few months was appointed the Ukrainian Commissar of the People's Commissariat for Internal Affairs (NKVD), which brought him into close contact with the Head of the Ukrainian Communist Party, Nikita Khrushchev.[†] Khrushchev became known as 'the butcher of the Ukraine', for his enthusiastic policy of 'annihilating all agents of fascism, Trotskyites, Bukharinies and all other despicable bourgeois nationalists in Ukraine' in 1938. Yet this title was soon forgotten when he rose to be First Secretary of the Communist Party (1953–64) and Soviet Premier (1958–64).

In 1941 Serov was promoted to Deputy Commissar of the NKVD, working directly under the notorious Lavrentiy Beria. He wrote the *Procedure for carrying out the Deportation of Anti-Soviet Elements from Lithuania, Latvia, and Estonia*, also known simply as 'the Serov instructions'. These specified, in chilling detail, the procedure to be followed in executing Stalin's programme of mass deportations from the Baltic and Caucasian states to Siberia during the Soviet occupation of the Baltics in the early years of the Second World War.

Historians record that Serov and Khrushchev were responsible for the deaths of perhaps 500,000 'enemies of the people' in the Ukraine and the Baltic and Caucasian states, and for the deportation of multitudes more to the freezing wastelands of Siberia, where many soon died from lack of shelter, food and adequate clothing.[‡]

Joseph Stalin (effectively leader of the Soviet Union 1922–53) created a new security organisation – the Main Counter-intelligence Directorate – in 1943 and personally nicknamed it 'SMERSH', which is an acronym of the Russian for 'Death to

---

[†] The NKVD (People's Commissariat for Internal Affairs) was reorganised and renamed several times during the 1940s. See 'NKVD' and 'KGB History' in the glossary.

[‡] Khrushchev's participation was in the Ukraine only.

Spies'. Serov was head of the SMERSH operational group that entered Poland with the advancing Red Army in 1944. He stayed there until May 1945 weeding out and punishing – often with the death penalty – everyone suspected of involvement with counterintelligence activities. He also established the Polish secret police organisation – the Ministry of Public Security or MBP (Ministerstwo Bezpieczeństwa Publicznego) – with operational rules based tightly on Stalinist principles.

A report by a United States Central Intelligence Agency source in Poland in 1944–5 describes Serov as hard-working, strict, determined to get results by any means, and a good staff manager:

He was exceedingly active in all security matters. He personally planned, directed, and was informed of all security cases of significance. No operations were run, or prominent individuals arrested, without his knowledge or approval and all security actions were under his personal supervision and personal care. He saw all interesting documents and reports and attended portions of the most interesting interrogations. He had his hand in almost every case and knew most details of everything that was being done in counterespionage in Poland. He personally recruited many agents.

An insight into Serov's operational mentality can be had from the following incident. Serov was asked for his views regarding the future of a certain case. The case was that of the Warsaw district leader of the anti-Communist underground Home Army, Colonel 'Aleksander', who had been arrested by the MO (Citizens Militia). The MO's leader wanted to liquidate him on the spot. Serov rejected this proposal and ordered the case to be taken over by the Soviets, pointing out that 'Aleksander' could and should be made to talk, thereby being much more useful in the investigation than if he were dead.

The source has very great respect for Serov, considering him extremely intelligent, a very hard worker, with great experience and knowledge in the field of intelligence work, capable of making decisions whenever necessary and not afraid to accept responsibility. Serov was not only highly respected by his subordinates for his ability, but was very well liked for his human treatment of subordinates – knowing, for example, when they had earned a rest from the intense pace of operations at that time, and showing appreciation when work was well done.

The source believes that Serov must have had a high protector in Moscow because of his complete self-confidence and willingness to assume responsibility in the direction of these operations.

When the war ended the Soviet military headquarters moved from Poland to Berlin and Serov's SMERSH group went with them, staying until 1947. Berlin was in a mess. It had been split into four sectors, each of which was controlled by one of the Allied countries (France, United States, United Kingdom and Soviet Union). Serov thrived in these conditions, which required the imposition of discipline and organisation.

One of his first duties in Berlin was to manage the search for Adolf Hitler's remains; but there was never any definitive proof that the bodies he produced were those of Hitler and his wife, Eva Braun. In February 1946 Serov ordered the remains to be buried in the grounds of a Soviet military site near Magdeburg, East Germany. That sufficed in 1946, but as time passed and the science of postmortem examinations improved, there was a growing risk that the bodies might be exhumed and proven not to be those of Hitler and Braun. It was not surprising, therefore, that in 1970 Yuri Andropov, head of the KGB, ordered that the remains be exhumed and destroyed.[†] They were burned, ground to powder and thrown in a river.

Another incident involving Serov in Berlin was an investigation into the death of Stalin's son, Yakov, who had been shot

---

† Andropov and Serov were close colleagues and friends for many years, as will be seen in the body of this book.

and killed in 1943 by a German guard while a prisoner of war in Sachsenhausen SS camp. Serov personally carried out the investigation and, in a typically thorough manner, wrote a six-page report for the personal attention of his boss Sergei Kruglov, head of the NKVD. The report stated that he had interrogated the two German officers in charge of Sachsenhausen at the time of Yakov's death:

> When we got charge of them from the Americans, they asked us to turn them over to the court. For this reason, we are not able to apply the full measure of physical intervention to them. But we did organise to have a mole in their cells.[†]

There are two interesting points in this excerpt. First, Serov would have tortured the Germans to extract the truth had he not been forced to hand them over to US forces. Second, this may be the earliest example of the use of the word 'mole' in the context of having a spy inside the enemy camp.[‡] It was normal NKVD practice to have a 'stukach' (an informer) in prison cells.

Serov's other activities in Berlin followed much the same course as in Poland, which included establishing the dreaded East German Ministry for State Security (the secret police force known as the Stasi).

With the establishment of the Ministry of Public Security in Poland and the Stasi in East Germany – both of them following the practices and procedures of Beria's NKVD – Serov had introduced the most feared elements of Stalinism into the two most populated East European countries.

But unlike his master, Stalin, Serov was not a mirthless, merciless killer and sadist. Indeed, he enjoyed a happy family life

---

[†] Paul R. Gregory, *Lenin's Brain and Other Tales from the Secret Soviet Archives* (Hoover Institution Press Publication No. 555).

[‡] The author John le Carré popularised the word in *Tinker, Tailor, Soldier, Spy* and other novels.

with his wife Valya and his daughter Svetlana. Furthermore, he could be personable and had a sense of humour. Sergo Mikoyan (historian, writer and son of senior statesman Anastas Mikoyan) described Serov as 'short, balding, always joking ... a nice man'.[†]

Ilya Dzhirkvelov, on the other hand, despised him:

> The man appointed to be Chairman of the KGB was Army General Ivan Serov, notorious for having carried out the deportation of whole peoples (the Ingushi and Chechens and other peoples of the North Caucasus) and other large-scale military operations. He was short in stature and limited in outlook, a cruel man with little education, with little understanding of the finer points of operational and intelligence work, which is why he did not enjoy the authority he should have had among us operatives. We knew all about his ruthless character and his fondness for bossing people about and punishing them.[‡]

This, then, was the complex man who became deputy to Lavrentiy Beria. Beria, as head of the NKVD/NKGB and Stalin's first lieutenant, was the personification of all the evils of Stalinism, terrorising the citizens of the Soviet Union and haunting public imagination in the West.

After leaving Berlin in 1947, Serov was shunted sideways into the GRU. Perhaps it was because his experience with SMERSH made him better qualified for service with the GRU than with the MGB, but it is more likely to have been the result of a serious ongoing feud between Serov and the brutal Viktor Abakumov, head of SMERSH from 1943 until 1946 and subsequently appointed as Minister of the MGB. Abakumov, who was Serov's boss in SMERSH, was either afraid or jealous of Serov's ability.

[†]   William Taubman, 'Chapter 14', *Khrushchev: The Man – His Era* (London: Free Press, 2003)

[‡]   Ilya Dzhirkvelov spent thirty-seven years in the KGB and its predecessors before defecting to the United Kingdom in 1980; Ilya Dzhirkvelov, 'Chapter 6', *Secret Servant* (New York: Harper & Row, 1987).

He informed Stalin that Serov had been involved in embezzle-
ment in Berlin in the context of his (Serov's) responsibility for
finding and making proper arrangements for the disposition of
wartime 'trophies'. One particular accusation was that Serov
had stolen the crown of the King of the Belgians.

Being appointed to the GRU rather than the MGB was bad
enough, but Serov must have been hurt even more when the
shadowy General Mikhail Shalin was appointed chief of the GRU
in 1953, rather than himself.

Serov's exploits from 1953 onwards, when he became first
chairman of the KGB and later chief of the GRU, are an inte-
gral part of the events recorded in this book.

Why has the world in general heard so little about one of the
most important people in the history of the Soviet Union?

In 1963 he was disgraced, removed from his position as head
of the GRU, and later expelled from the Communist Party. It was
Soviet practice in those days to conceal and cover up the records
of such 'apostates', even to expunge them from the history books
and destroy all official records of their service. That distinctly
non-dialectical, but undeniably material, approach to sanitising
official history accounts for some but not all of Serov's obscurity.

Mystery surrounds Serov's life from 1963 onwards. He simply
disappeared and many people assumed he had committed
suicide or drank himself to death. However, he lived on for
another twenty-seven years, dying of natural causes on 1 July
1990 at the age of eighty-four.

His paymasters may well have had their reasons for generating
the rumours of his early demise.

1

MOSCOW 1953

Joseph Stalin died a slow, miserable and painful death: no more, it could be said, than he deserved. As effective ruler of the USSR from 1928, he had governed through a mixture of persuasive propaganda, shrewdly identifying himself with his predecessor, Lenin, and building a vicarious cult of personality through his presentation of himself as Lenin's natural and loyal successor. Where propaganda failed, he turned to cruder methods, eliminating all sources of opposition with a massive and ruthless array of secret police forces. Estimates of the numbers killed under his regime range from 3 to 60 million. There were undeniable advances made under his rule, but his regime remains a watchword for the most paranoid and brutal forms of murderous authoritarianism.

By early 1953 the 73-year-old had become more paranoid and unpredictable than ever so that those closest to him, including his doctors, household staff and family, lived in fear for their very lives.

On Saturday 28 February 1953 Stalin invited Lavrentiy Beria (head of the secret police, NKVD), Georgy Malenkov (Deputy Prime Minister and heir apparent), Nikolai Bulganin (Defence Minister) and Nikita Khrushchev (head of the Communist Party in Moscow) to dinner at his Kuntsevo dacha. They consumed large quantities of excellent Georgian white wine, Stalin's favourite drink, over the course of a long night that saw Stalin in excellent spirits. It was after five o'clock in the morning before his guests departed, leaving Stalin preparing himself for bed. In the morning, a maid knocked quietly on his bedroom door and, hearing no response, returned to the kitchen. She and other household staff tried once more to raise their master a little later, again to no effect. No one dared to enter Stalin's bedroom uninvited until after midnight. When, approaching midnight, concern for his well-being overwhelmed fears of the potential consequences of awakening a hung-over supreme leader, some brave soul ventured to open the door. They found Stalin lying on the floor, soaked in his own urine. He had suffered a stroke.

There are various accounts of what happened next, but what seems undeniable is that Stalin received no medical attention for quite some hours following his stroke, which minimised the possibility of any meaningful recovery. This led to conjecture that Malenkov, Khrushchev and the others may have had little interest in keeping Stalin alive, and seized the opportunity to leave him, at best, weakened and incapable of continuing as Soviet leader.

All of his final visitors had made the appropriate gestures of sorrow and respect, save for one: the man who had the most to gain from Stalin's death, Beria. Whatever their true feelings, Khrushchev and the other senior members of the leadership had the sense to weep and grieve in public, while Beria could neither summon tears nor conceal his delight at the possibility for career advancement created by the top man's death.

Stalin died a choking, agonising death on the evening of 5 March 1953 and the new leadership was announced the next day. Nominated by Beria, Malenkov became the new Prime Minister, and in turn appointed Beria first deputy. Khrushchev was relieved of his duties as head of the Moscow branch of the Communist Party and was appointed one of the Communist Party secretaries.

Beria, canny enough to understand that he could not, as a fellow Georgian in a multi-ethnic federation of Republics, follow Stalin into the Kremlin, seems instead to have reached an understanding with Malenkov that made Beria very much the power behind the throne. He quickly re-merged the MVD and MGB, establishing himself in a powerful position as head of all Soviet internal affairs.[†] He immediately took the initiative by tabling a series of proposed reforms, some of which, such as the release of hundreds of thousands of gulag inmates, would, in essence, have passed all of the blame for past atrocities onto Stalin, working wonders for Beria's image. Some of his other proposals were quite extraordinary and controversial. One in particular was to allow East Germany to unite with West Germany to form a new, single, neutral Germany in exchange for massive Western financial and technical assistance to boost the Soviet Union's ailing economy. (It should be remembered that, in spite of the growing mutual mistrust between East and West, the Soviet Union, United States, United Kingdom and France were at that time still allies and jointly responsible for the future of Germany.)

Premier Malenkov was generally considered to be weak, his only strong card being the self-serving support he had received from Beria. The latter, on the other hand, was now all-powerful, particularly with regard to his control of the MGB. The ever-alert Khrushchev warned the other leading politicians that if Beria engineered a coup, which would not be difficult in the present situation, he would become even more powerful than Stalin had been. They needed to do something to stop him – and soon. If they could develop a strong enough case against Beria, Khrushchev argued, they might be able to turn Malenkov against him.

The Berlin Uprising of 17 June brought them the pretext they needed. It was evidence, they said, of what would happen if Germany were to be reunified. They now needed to plan Beria's downfall and Ivan Serov played a key role in this.[‡]

[†]   See 'KGB History' in the glossary.
[‡]   See the Prologue for background information about Serov.

Serov, barely five feet tall (152cm), was a man of serious temperament and intense appearance. He dressed well, but could hardly be described as dapper. He had a Kirk Douglas-dimpled chin and strong jaw-line, but neither could he be described as handsome. His heavy, dark eyebrows were invariably furrowed, which drew attention to his steely grey eyes, and his lips were mostly held straight and tight. His high forehead led to neatly combed black hair. He looked the quiet, contemplative part of a philosopher, but was decisive and uncompromising when moved to action.

The perceptive Serov, although never a true insider, scented trouble brewing at the top level of Soviet politics. As a true disciple of Stalin, he was incensed by Beria's vilification of him and the proposed reunification of Germany. One of Serov's strongest beliefs was that the Soviet Union should never relinquish its domination of a country or territory. He offered to assist the Khrushchev faction that wanted to remove Beria and was able to bring with him the support of other senior GRU officers.

Khrushchev and Serov had worked effectively as colleagues in pre-war Ukraine, though there is no evidence of great personal warmth between them. Nonetheless, here they were again, presented with a common cause. Serov's task was to produce a litany of offences purportedly committed by Beria, while Khrushchev would convene an extraordinary meeting of the Politburo to try Beria on Serov's charges.

The physical side of this operation – the arrest and imprisonment of Beria – was arranged by Deputy Defence Minister Georgy Zhukov, Khrushchev's long-time friend and ally. Marshal Zhukov was the Soviet Union's most decorated soldier. He, like Serov, had been accused by Abakumov and Beria of plundering German war booty for his own personal gain. This was Zhukov's opportunity to take his revenge on Beria.

Zhukov arranged the arrest as a precision miniature military operation. He assigned a small special force and allocated to them two special VIP cars with darkened glass to enable them to enter the Kremlin covertly. He also ordered the Moscow Military Zone's Guard to replace the usual NKVD Guard.

The Politburo meeting was arranged for 26 June within the historic, powerful building of the Kremlin. Beria was uneasy as he had not been told the purpose of the meeting, and knew that his powerful ally Vyacheslav Molotov had abandoned him over the German issue. Nonetheless, he must have been startled when Khrushchev opened the proceedings by reading the list of offences that had been prepared by Serov. He was accused of treason (spying for British Intelligence), terrorism, and counter-revolutionary activities. Molotov and others followed Khrushchev's lead with scathing verbal attacks. Khrushchev proposed a motion to dismiss Beria from his position in the government, and even his erstwhile friend Premier Malenkov supported the motion.

When given the signal, Zhukov's small force rushed in and arrested Beria on the spot. Many of his subordinates and associates were arrested later. He and six accomplices were tried at a special session of the Supreme Court of the Soviet Union on 23 December 1953. All were found guilty and shot the same day. Not for the first time, Serov had chosen his side wisely. Had he not betrayed Beria he would undoubtedly have been executed along with the others.

☦

At the end of July 1953 – a month after the fall of Beria – an exceptional officer, Colonel Oleg Penkovsky, was appointed to a senior position in the GRU with responsibility for the Near East. At thirty-four years of age, he was of medium height, athletic, and commanded attention with his natural air of self-confidence and ruggedly handsome face, and receding fair hair with a few rogue streaks of grey. He had just completed a three-year course in Military Espionage and English at the Military Diplomatic Academy.

Oleg Vladimirovich Penkovsky was born in Ordzhonikidze

in the Caucasus on 23 April 1919, when Eastern Europe was in turmoil in the aftermath of the 1917 October Revolution. He completed his secondary education at the age of eighteen and went as a cadet to the 2nd Kiev Artillery School. His training there finished just as WWII started, in 1939, and he was immediately appointed a battery political officer. He had what soldiers might describe as a good war; seeing active service on several fronts and also having spells as an instructor, mostly in Moscow.

He was wounded in 1944 when he was an artillery battalion commander in a Tank Destroyer Regiment. After hospitalisation in Moscow he was appointed liaison officer to Lieutenant-General Sergei Varentsov, Artillery Commander of the 1st Ukrainian Army Group, who was also recovering in hospital following a tank accident. Their closeness turned into a lifelong friendship, with Varentsov becoming Penkovsky's mentor and, to some extent, a father-figure.

The brilliant Penkovsky rose to the rank of colonel by the age of twenty-six. He had been awarded two Orders of the Red Banner, the Order of Alexander Nevsky, the Order of the Fatherland War (First Class), the Order of the Red Star, and eight medals. At the end of the war he went to the Frunze Military Academy, graduating top of the class in 1948.

Penkovsky, as a new member of the GRU, may have been introduced to Serov in the summer of 1953. Neither of them could have known that within a few years their lives would be inexorably thrown together with disastrous results for both of them.

2

BERLIN 1953

By 1953, eight years after the end of WWII, Berlin had become the espionage capital of the world. West Berlin, under the Allied control of France, the United States and the United Kingdom, was a highly vulnerable virtual island surrounded by East Germany and the Eastern sector of Berlin. The Eastern sector was controlled by the Soviet Union. People could, however, pass freely between the sectors with only a cursory inspection of identity papers. It would be another eight years before the Soviet Union and the East Germans built the Berlin Wall, but by then nearly three million East Germans had escaped to the West through Berlin.

For years, particularly since 1948 when the Soviet Union had blocked the rail and road routes used by the Western allies to reach West Berlin, the West's political and military leaders had been desperate for reliable intelligence on Soviet political intentions and military strength in East Germany.[†] America's Central Intelligence Agency (CIA) and Britain's Secret Intelligence Service (SIS, or MI6) had proven unable to ascertain the strength and deployment of Soviet military power in the so-called 'Democratic Republic' of East Germany. This represented

---

†   The blockade was lifted in less than a year because the amazingly success-ful Berlin Airlift brought in ample supplies of food, fuel and other items to sustain the population.

a serious weakness, as Berlin remained a likely flashpoint for confrontation across the Iron Curtain.

In 1951, Frank Rowlett, America's greatest code-breaker, approached his friend Bill Harvey with the suggestion that the CIA should try to locate and tap communications cables used by the Soviet Union's civil and military authorities. Rowlett was a highly respected, capable cryptologist who knew from wartime experience that the ability to record and analyse Soviet telephone and telegraphic traffic would reap huge dividends. He was in charge of the National Security Agency's National Cryptographic School, while Harvey was the Chief of Staff C (counterintelligence) in the CIA's Office of Special Operations.

William King Harvey was a striking personality and made few concessions to the expected norms of behaviour for CIA agents. Though widely respected for his dedication and success, many fellow agents found the man insufferable in person. He was rotund, unfit, uncouth and short-tempered. A heavy drinker, Harvey often downed a three martini lunch only to snooze away the afternoon at his desk. His earlier career in the FBI had come to an abrupt end owing to his drunk driving. He was prone to insubordination when he disagreed with senior officers, including Attorney-General Robert Kennedy, a man known for making snap judgements and bearing lifelong grudges. Harvey was probably best known for carrying a loaded pistol in a shoulder holster, often laying it on the table or playing with it at meetings. His darting, bulging eyes only came to rest when they stared, unblinking, at an adversary.

Astute and a fine judge of character, Harvey was the first agent to raise security concerns regarding the British traitor Kim Philby, after working alongside him at the British Embassy in Washington, while Philby served at the MI6 station. Harvey enjoyed his work as Chief of Staff C, but could not resist the challenge of a project based on Rowlett's idea of tapping Soviet cables. He set to work on it with fierce determination.

Walter O'Brien, an accomplished recruiter, was transferred

from Zurich to the CIA's station in Berlin, known as the Berlin Operations Base (BOB), and soon had a useful group of agents, some of them inside the East German Ministry of Post and Telecommunications. He was later assisted by Hugh Montgomery, a counterintelligence expert.

Rowlett was transferred from the National Security Agency to the CIA and effectively became the Washington controller of the cable-tapping project, with responsibility for overseeing the protocols governing collection of ciphered communications by covert surveillance. He reported directly to Richard Helms, the CIA's chief of operations.

Harvey was posted to Berlin, arriving there towards the end of 1952. Although the central reason for his posting was to lead the top-secret cable-tapping project, so few agents were aware of its existence that his appointment as chief of BOB provided both internal and external cover.

By January 1953, O'Brien and Montgomery had amassed enough comprehensive data concerning Soviet communications that Harvey was able to recommend the placement of secret permanent taps on three specific cables used by senior Soviet personnel.

Most important were the long-distance cables used by the huge Soviet military complex at Karlshorst, which housed the USSR's Berlin garrison, the KGB's German headquarters and some GRU units. These cables lay close to the American sector, below the busy Schönefelder Chaussee highway in the Soviet-controlled sector.

It would take a long tunnel to reach them.

The CIA's Berlin base was subordinate to the 1,000-strong station in Frankfurt commanded by General Lucien Truscott, empowered with overall control of CIA activities throughout West Germany and Berlin. Truscott received Harvey's assessment with enthusiasm and agreed that feasibility studies and detailed planning should proceed. Truscott appointed one of his senior officers – whom Harvey nicknamed 'Fleetfoot' – as his linkman with Harvey on tunnel matters. Harvey was in the habit of giving apposite or humorous nicknames to people with whom he worked. 'Fleetfoot' was awarded the name because of his many journeys between Frankfurt and Berlin on tunnel business.

There were, however, major practical and technical problems to resolve before submitting the proposal to the Director of Central Intelligence, and thence to the President, for approval.

Berlin's sub-soil, much of it sandy, was a treacherous medium for tunnelling, and stood above a water table that could rise almost to the surface after a wet winter. Thus construction would be hazardous, and the practicalities of conducting the excavation in secret were a further complicating factor. One thousand two hundred feet (360 metres) of the tunnel would lie beneath Soviet territory, and spies were everywhere, monitoring American, British and French activity. The transportation and disposal of vast quantities of earth was likely to attract attention.

Once the tunnel was dug, there remained the issue of installing the hidden taps and providing amplification that would produce high quality recordings. The three cables carried over eighty speech circuits, each of which would have to be wired to an individual tape recorder. Placing the taps was an incredibly difficult task, even for the most skilled and experienced of technicians. A chamber had to be constructed below the cables to place the taps, house the pre-amplifier and other equipment necessary to boost the intercepted signals and transmit them to the tape recorders. The cables lay a mere 28 inches (70cm) below the surface of the Schönefelder Chaussee, so the erection of the chamber in precarious soil prone to being waterlogged presented an engineering challenge every bit as complex as the placement of the taps.

They considered many options before deciding to start the tunnel at Rudow in the American sector. They would erect three large buildings to be used ostensibly as military equipment storage and distribution warehouses. One of the warehouses would be deep and large enough to hold all of the excavations from the tunnel.

In Washington, Rowlett and Helms knew that the British would also be seeking to penetrate Soviet intelligence defences, and were the West's greatest experts when it came to building such tap-tunnels, having constructed a network of three in Vienna. Lacking the technical expertise and experience of the British, Rowlett and Helms thus approached MI6 for assistance.

In the spring of 1953 O'Brien from Berlin and 'Fleetfoot' from Frankfurt flew to London to brief MI6 on the Berlin tunnel project. MI6 endorsed the idea and from then on it was a joint CIA/MI6 project.

‡

Peter Lunn arrived in Berlin in the early summer of 1953 to take up his duties as head of the MI6 station. He was delighted with this appointment because it enabled him to add to his reputation for effective work in Western Europe as head of the MI6 stations in Vienna (1948–50) and Berne (1950–53). Eton-educated and the grandson of the famous Sir Henry Lunn, founder of the Lunn Travel Agency, Peter Lunn appeared the epitome of the mild-mannered English gentleman, but his soft tones and slight lisp belied his determination and the mental and physical capacities of an international athlete. As captain of the British skiing team in the 1936 Winter Olympics, he had finished twelfth in the alpine combined skiing event, but castigated himself for attaining only a lowly fifteenth place in the slalom. He had not, he insisted, tried enough, as evidenced by the fact he had stayed on his skis and not fallen!

His resolve to make a success of the Berlin tap operation may well have been reinforced by the location of MI6's offices in the very Olympic Stadium complex that played host to Hitler's infamous 1936 summer Olympic Games. This time Lunn would not fail to do his very best. His 100-strong MI6 team shared these premises with other departments of the British Military Administration in Berlin.

While in Vienna in 1949 Lunn had pounced on intelligence findings concerning the location of Soviet Army telephone cables. He brought in tunnelling and cable-tapping experts to build three short tunnels in different parts of Vienna to install taps and the results were so successful that MI6 had to set up a new section – Section Y – to analyse the vast amount of information gathered. Section Y was housed in a mansion house at 2 Carlton Gardens, near Buckingham Palace and the gentlemen's club district of St James.

Lunn's posting to Berlin was, of course, a direct result of the CIA's approach to MI6. Soon after he arrived in Berlin he reassembled all of his Vienna tunnel team, some of them coming directly to Berlin while others remained in England for specialist training and to design, sometimes by trial and error, prototypes for the taps and chamber. Although totally different by way of temperament and bearing, Harvey and Lunn, respective heads of the CIA and MI6 stations, established an effective working relationship and appear to have enjoyed each other's company. Both were skilled, experienced and dedicated, sharing not just a common objective in the limited shape of the tunnel project, but the worldview of avowed and loyal cold warriors.

Piecemeal planning and liaison for the tunnel continued in Berlin, Frankfurt, London and Washington throughout the summer and autumn of 1953. Comprehensive proposals were prepared and submitted to Allen Dulles, the director of the CIA, who approved them in October. Harvey and Lunn now had official sanction – and a budget – to move forwards. Regular meetings were scheduled to discuss and approve the process of building the tunnel and analysing intelligence garnered from the cable taps. The first such meeting was scheduled for 15 December 1953, to be held in MI6's Section Y offices at 2 Carlton Gardens.

‡

Roderick Chisholm – always called by the Scottish Gaelic name 'Ruari' rather than Roderick – was one of Lunn's best officers in Berlin. At 5ft 10in. (178cm) tall, Ruari looked strong and fit, with an easy, wide smile that incorporated bright and friendly eyes. His glasses were almost unnoticeable, seeming somehow to be a natural part of his face. His hair was light-ginger and slightly wavy, with a neat parting. He was not involved with the tunnel and, in the typical operation of strict MI6 security, did not even know of its existence until it was eventually 'discovered' by the Soviets.

Chisholm's Scottish schoolmaster father had ensured he had a solid primary education and the excellent marks recorded in his school leaving certificate earned him a place in the Army Intelligence Corps in 1941 at the age of just sixteen. He spent much of the war interrogating German prisoners, thus acquiring fluency in the language. During the advance through north-western Europe, he served with a forward group of the Intelligence Corps, later assisting in the search for war criminals. His career in the Intelligence Corps continued for a few years, mostly in Hanover, before his invitation to join MI6.

Janet Deane, an MI6 secretary, was posted to Berlin at about the same time as Lunn: the early summer of 1953. She was typical of many of the young MI6 secretaries of those days. Her father, an officer in the Royal Engineers, was of aristocratic English stock. Janet was born in India in 1929 during her father's service there, and was educated at the top-ranking independent boarding schools of Wycombe Abbey and Queen Anne's, Caversham, in England.

She worked hard, taking her duties and security responsibilities incredibly seriously. It was a quality for which she became renowned, even in her later life when others allowed some secrets to emerge and several of her erstwhile colleagues even published details of their MI6 escapades.

But life in Berlin was not all work and no play for she was soon attracted to the charming Ruari Chisholm.

Chisholm was equally taken with the attractive, slim 24-year-old Janet who always dressed impeccably, smiled readily, and soon grew more self-assured after an understandably nervous first few weeks.

✝
✝

Janet Deane's early nerves were not due entirely to her recent arrival at her first overseas post, but to an event that tested the nerves of everyone in Berlin.

After Stalin's death, the people of East Germany and East Berlin hoped there would be some relaxation of the Stalinist-Soviet policies imposed by Walter Ulbricht's Communist Party of Germany (KPD). But the opposite transpired: soon there was *still greater* emphasis on state control of industry and the collectivisation of farming. Unhappiness with the regime's policies and the depressed state of the economy saw ever-increasing numbers of East Germans and East Berliners fleeing to the West.

A new ruling imposing a wage freeze coupled with a 10 per cent increase in work norms was due to come into effect on 30 June and this caused the frustration to boil over. On 16 June, 300 East Berlin road workers went on strike in response to a pay cut attributed to 'poor productivity'. News of the strike spread fast and a general strike was called for the next day.

Growing unrest overnight turned into strikes and protests in every major East German town and city. By 11 a.m., strikers in East Berlin had occupied some government buildings. Sixteen Soviet divisions, totalling some 20,000 troops, and a further 8,000 members of the National People's Army were used to quell the uprising. Approximately 500 people were killed and over 100 executed or later condemned to death. There were more than 5,000 arrests.

The speedy, brutal and uncompromising Soviet intervention crushed the uprising, bringing home to West Berliners just how precarious their situation remained. Such Soviet actions became the customary approach of Ivan Serov, and, later, Yuri Andropov, towards dissent in any Soviet satellite country. Serov was deputy head of the GRU at the time of the Berlin uprising, which served him as a master class in the efficient, ruthless extinguishing of resistance to his master's rule. It was a lesson he would not forget.

3

LONDON 1953

At 2 Carlton Gardens, MI6's Section Y took up residence in a subdivided former ballroom and lounge, in which royalty, celebrities and the wealthy had once danced, chatted and lolled through pleasant afternoons and evenings. Still resplendent with crystal chandeliers and exquisite plasterwork, the room now overflowed with fluent Russian speakers, from White Russian émigrés to British merchants who had fled St Petersburg after the revolution and Polish army officers unable to return to their occupied homeland. With such a motley crew of operatives at work on demanding and tedious translations that required total concentration, it is hardly surprising that the office atmosphere was sometimes fraught. The dry heat of the London summer was a daily aggravation. There were inevitable disagreements, frayed tempers, verbal scuffles and occasional tears. Yet Tom Gimson, a former commanding officer of the Irish Guards, managed this huge operation with a potent mixture of strict discipline, encouragement and understanding.

His staff transcribed a relentless succession of tapes filled with recorded telephone conversations from the three Vienna tunnels. The written records were passed to Russian-speaking army and air force officers for evaluation, and the more important items of intelligence then extracted, summarised and passed to the Foreign Office and War Office.

In the summer of 1953 an MI6 'celebrity' was assigned to help Gimson. His name was George Blake.

This was Blake's first job since his return to the UK that April in a blaze of publicity as one of six British civilians captured by the Communist North Koreans in June 1950 when they over-ran Seoul. Blake had borne the title of vice-consul at the British legation in Seoul as cover for his MI6 duties, and was returned to the UK, alongside other British officials, by the Royal Air Force.

Blake was born in Rotterdam, Holland, in 1922 of a Dutch mother and a Turkish/Jewish father called Albert. His name at birth was George Behar. His father, who became a naturalised British citizen after serving with the British Army in the First World War, named his son George after the King. The family lived in Holland until Albert's death in 1936 when the thirteen-year-old George was sent to live with Albert's sister's family in Egypt. Another uncle in Egypt (not Albert's sister's husband) was a leading member of the Egyptian Communist Party and may have influenced George. Four years later, at the age of seventeen, he returned to the Netherlands and became a courier in the Dutch Resistance. He soon left for England to escape compul-sory internment by the Germans, which would have been an automatic consequence of his reaching the age of eighteen. In England he changed his surname to Blake and worked variously for the Royal Navy and the security services, mostly translating captured German documents and assisting with the interrogation of German prisoners. After the war he was officially recruited by MI6.

At the end of 1945 he was sent to Germany to spy on the Soviet forces in East Germany. While there, he faced the robust counterintelligence work of the SMERSH unit led by Ivan Serov.

Blake's performance in Germany was exceptional and he was rewarded with a career development sabbatical at Cambridge University, where he studied Russian. His tutor was an English woman whose Russian mother had lived in St Petersburg before the revolution. She had a great love of Russia, though not of Communism, and inspired her students with her lyrical patriotism. This made a considerable impression on the youthful Blake and it stirred in him something of a romantic outlook towards Russia and all things Russian.

Early in 1950 Blake was posted to the British Embassy in Seoul, Korea, entrusted with building a network of agents. He had made little progress before the outbreak of the Korean War rendered his task impossible. When Seoul was overrun by the North Korean Army, Blake was taken captive, along with two other British and four French diplomats. They were interned in a small village in North Korea, fed frugal rations and held in prison-like accommodation by their North Korean captors.

At some point they were moved from one prison site to another and, in the course of this two-day journey, they saw the devastating results of the bombing of villages and towns by the huge US Fortress aircraft. This led to extensive soul-searching on Blake's part as to the human cost of military conflict and the legitimacy of war itself – any war.

As a concession to their status as internees rather than prisoners, the diplomats were allowed to correspond with the Soviet Embassy in Pyongyang. They protested that their captivity was unjust and a violation of international law. The Soviets countered that they were in no position to set them free, but Soviet Embassy staff sent them books, including Marx's *Das Kapital*, which Blake read several times. He seems to have found it persuasive, undergoing a secret conversion to Communism as the means to achieve world peace, freedom and social justice.

As time went on – they were interned for three years – the diplomats were allowed to meet regularly and individually with Soviet Embassy officials for thirty-minute interviews. Blake's half hour was always spent with a particular Soviet official, a colonel in the MGB. Together, they made plans for Blake's new life as a double agent.

Following his release and triumphant return to London, Blake was granted some recuperation leave. He spent his break in Holland, where a secret meeting was arranged in The Hague with Nikolai Rodin, the MGB's London *Rezident*. They agreed upon arrangements for future contacts in London. Blake was now established as a double agent.

By the time Blake met Rodin again in London – after Blake had started to work at Section Y in Carlton Gardens – it was already clear just how valuable Blake could be; so valuable that, even in the chaos in Moscow following Stalin's death and the imprisonment of Lavrentiy Beria, the MGB sent a new man to London for the specific purpose of running Blake as a double agent.

The new man was Sergei Kondrashev, a bright thirty-year-old officer, rising rapidly through the ranks of the MGB's counter-intelligence personnel. He arrived in London in October with cover as First Secretary, Cultural Relations, to replace Rodin as the *Rezident*.

Throughout the autumn and early winter Blake was able to give Kondrashev comprehensive details of the intelligence picked up by the British on the Vienna tunnels tapes, in addition to the names of, and personal information about, increasing numbers of MI6 personnel.

But all of that faded into relative insignificance when Blake started to make the administrative arrangements for the arrival of CIA and MI6 representatives for the first formal meeting about the proposed Berlin tunnel, to be held at 2 Carlton Gardens on 15 December.

The CIA's delegation was headed by Frank Rowlett. Accompanying him were William Wheeler, his personal assistant, Carl Nelson from the CIA's Office of Communications, and Vyrl Lichleiter, Bill Harvey's technical man from Berlin.

MI6's delegation was headed by Stewart Mackenzie (one of MI6's senior operations managers), George Young (MI6's Director of Requirements) and Tom Gimson (the head of Section Y). Supporting MI6 on the technical side were Colonel Balmain (a mining consultant), and John Taylor from the Post Office Special Investigations Unit who was an expert in signal strength and the prevention of moisture penetration in telephone cables.

Blake was appointed secretary for the meeting.

It had already been agreed that the US would largely fund the project and build the tunnel, while Britain would supply the sophisticated equipment and technical experts for the critical removal of the sandy soil for the chamber immediately below the cables, and placing the tap connections.

For three days they discussed the technical details of building the tunnel, making the taps and processing the data they transmitted. Rowlett estimated that they would need teams of over 150 people to edit, translate, transcribe, index and type up the data.

The Christmas break slowed Blake's progress and it was early January before he produced the minutes of the meeting. Photocopying, or xerography, was still in its infancy and such machines were not available in government offices, so Blake had to insert an extra sheet of paper and carbon paper into his manual typewriter and bash the keys hard. Even so, the typeface on the extra copy handed to Kondrashev must have been faint, if more than worth the eyestrain for its contents.

4

MOSCOW 1954

The Supreme Soviet of the USSR – the bicameral Soviet parliament – was the highest legislative body in the Soviet Union. It was responsible for electing members of the Politburo (also known as the Presidium from 1952 to 1966), which was invariably made up of the top members of the Central Committee of the Communist Party of the Soviet Union (CPSU).[†] The Politburo made all major policy decisions, which it then passed down through the Central Committee, the Supreme Soviet and the Party Congress. Its control extended from the party and into government because party personnel held all key government posts, thus ensuring that Politburo policy was implemented by all government organisations. In short, the Politburo was the most powerful body in the Soviet Union, with control over virtually all parliamentary and executive decisions.

Although Khrushchev had been the architect of Beria's downfall, he was still relatively low in the Kremlin hierarchy: tenth out of the ten members of the Politburo and one of several secretaries of the Central Committee of the Soviet Communist Party. He was not rated as a strong contender to replace Premier Malenkov. No one, therefore, saw any danger in promoting him to First Secretary of the party in September 1953. They were mistaken. He stealthily and cleverly contrived to move power

---

†   For ease of reference and to reflect general practice, 'Politburo' is used throughout the book in preference to using its new name of 'Presidium'.

away from the Premier to his own post of First Secretary, with such success that by February 1954, it was Khrushchev who took the seat of honour at Politburo meetings instead of the weak Malenkov.

Khrushchev's influence continued to increase. On 13 March 1954 the Politburo appointed his nominee as chairman of the KGB.[†] That nominee was Ivan Serov.

One of the earliest papers to land on Serov's desk was the Russian translation of the minutes of the joint CIA–MI6 Berlin tunnel meeting that Blake had supplied to Kondrashev in London.

---

† Khrushchev detached the MGB (Ministry for State Security) from the Ministry of Internal Affairs and renamed it the Committee for State Security (KGB).

5

BERLIN 1954

The physical work of digging the Berlin tunnel started in February 1954 with the construction of a building complex designated as military equipment storage and distribution warehouses, a large part of which would be filled in with the tunnel diggings. The work was completed just over a year later, in March 1955.

But building the tunnel was only part of the espionage activities in the Berlin of 1954. It would be another six years before the East Germans and the Soviets built the Berlin Wall, so movement between East and West Berlin was still relatively easy. The migration of East Germans to West Berlin continued apace, eventually reaching a total of 3.5 million – nearly 20 per cent of the East German population – before the erection of the Wall. Thus it was simplicity itself for Soviet and East German secret agents to infiltrate West Berlin.

The intellectually brilliant spymaster Markus Wolf – tall, handsome and ruthless – was in charge of the Stasi side of these operations. His Jewish-Communist parents had fled from Hitler's Germany in 1932 when Markus was just nine years old. They eventually settled in Moscow and Markus became a notable young Communist while still at school. After the war they moved back to what had become East Berlin, and Markus found a job with Berlin Radio. His main task was to report on the trials at Nuremburg of Nazi war criminals and this strengthened his hatred of fascism and his dedication to Communism. In the early 1950s he joined the Stasi, working in the new foreign intelligence section known as the HVA (Hauptverwaltung Aufklärung, or General Reconnaissance Administration). In 1954, still only thirty-one, he was head of the HVA and well on the way to establishing what ultimately became an impressive and successful network of 4,000 spies.

The HVA worked within the Stasi's operational framework, originally set out by Serov. Wolf perfected some of Serov's concepts and became one of the greatest exponents of the use of orthodox and deviant sexual activities to ensnare and blackmail the enemy. This, together with torture and killing, made him a truly formidable opponent.

The CIA and MI6 saw and suffered the results of Wolf's strong leadership of the HVA, yet they were unable to identify him.[†] They had no idea what he looked like, making it virtually impossible to target him in any kind of undercover operation. He became known in Western intelligence circles by the unimaginative label of '*the man with no face*'.

The Western agencies had to work much harder to plant agents in the Eastern sector. MI6 made their own job in this respect much harder by observing a self-imposed rule that effectively kept one hand tied behind their backs. British forces personnel and government civilian staff were allowed to enter East Berlin, where there were a few attractions surpassing those of West Berlin, such as orchestral concerts, ballet and opera, and inexpensive gramophone records of classical music. MI6 officers, on the other hand, were forbidden by their own internal regulations from entering East Berlin for fear of being discovered by the KGB or Stasi. This caused some awkward and embarrassing situations in general conversations with non-MI6

---

† Markus Johannes 'Mischa' Wolf was head of the HVA for thirty-four years, spanning most of the Cold War and beyond it. He was not identified as such to Western intelligence agencies until 1978 when he was photographed by Sweden's National Security Service during a visit to Sweden and was later identified from the photograph by Werner Stiller, an East German defector.

friends when they had to manufacture excuses for not crossing the border. More importantly, this internal regulation meant that virtually all of MI6's espionage work in East Berlin had to be carried out through locally recruited agents in both East and West Berlin.

MI6 still keeps details of the work performed by its agents strictly secret. We do not know, therefore, what duties occupied Ruari Chisholm during his time in Berlin, but he or one of his colleagues would, for example, almost certainly have been trying to identify the elusive head of the HVA.

One can imagine Chisholm cultivating a young man – let us call him Dominik Stecher – who worked for the HVA.[†] Perhaps Stecher offered his services to the West for money to help support his wife and young child. Maybe he or his wife had elderly parents who refused to defect, but still needed support.

Espionage, especially where deep-cover, high-risk operations are concerned, is never a restful or simple profession. Many covert operatives live and work in circumstances that pose constant threats not only to their own lives and safety, but often those of their families. Some agents thrive in this environment, their metabolisms becoming dependent, like a cocaine or amphetamine addict's, on the accompanying surges of adrenalin. Others, perhaps equipped with a lesser love of danger and more powerful survival instincts, must be pushed to their limits by handlers, a difficult and unenviable task.

At this time Markus Wolf's identity would have been kept secret, even from his own low- and middle-level staff within the HVA, and Chisholm would have had to push Stecher to take considerable risks to discover the identity of the *man with no face*. If Stecher were caught asking too many questions, or found in corridors where he had no business, the consequences would have been dire for him.

[†] This is an entirely hypothetical case. Dominik Stecher did not exist nor is his name a substitute for the name of any other person who did exist.

Stecher would probably have had to meet Chisholm in West Berlin, maybe on a Saturday afternoon after he (Stecher) had finished work, increasing the danger of being caught. Chisholm would have been embarrassed about the meagre amount of money he could offer Stecher, as Lunn (the head of MI6) was renowned for being tight-fisted with the public funds at his disposal.

Janet Deane's relationship with Ruari Chisholm flourished in the six short months since she had arrived in Berlin and they agreed to marry. It would not have been an easy decision: he was from a working-class Roman Catholic family and she was from a traditional upper-class Church of England (Protestant) family.

Nevertheless, they married at Corpus Christi Roman Catholic Church, Wokingham, Berkshire, England, on 19 June 1954. He was twenty-eight and she was twenty-five. There was a good turnout of family, friends and colleagues. The witnesses were Chisholm's father (William Andrew Chisholm), and Deane's father (Geoffrey Ronald Hawtrey Deane) and sister (Sylvia Deane).

Chisholm recorded his profession on the marriage certificate as 'Foreign Office Clerical Officer', which was either intended as a joke, or an overeager attempt to cover up his true profession. Family and friends who did not know he worked for MI6 – and the secret services strongly discourage agents from revealing their identities to even close relatives – could not possibly have believed a man of his calibre was in the most junior grade in the Foreign Office. Perhaps they had their suspicions, but thought better of giving voice to them.

6

BERLIN 1955

By some kind of perverse justice – or injustice – George Blake was removed from his job with Section Y and posted in West Berlin, arriving on 14 April 1955. In a historically delicious irony, his new appointment carried the priority task of recruiting Soviet military and civilian personnel as double agents, and, with it, license to *pose* as a double agent himself. Blake was officially empowered to pass low-level information and misinformation to his Soviet recruitment targets, in order to bolster his credibility. This licence both served as perfect cover for his own treachery, and brought with it the danger of a slip-up that could result in his unmasking. The double agent known to both his paymasters as a double agent: but only in his fullness by one of them. Truly, this was the stuff of spy fiction. Blake concentrated his efforts on KGB and GRU officers based in the Soviet Karlshorst Headquarters, source of the communication cables tapped through the Berlin tunnel project. One imagines he had little by way of spare time.

In Berlin, Blake continued to collect and pass secrets to his designated KGB contact. These secrets would no longer include reports on the progress of the tunnel, for he was not one of the few who were privy to such information. Blake relentlessly sought out and photographed other intelligence from within the MI6 station, using a Minox 'spy' camera. This was particularly dangerous because he shared an office with a colleague. He later confessed that he tried to take great care over this but on occasion took risks that could have been disastrous for him.

Blake, unlike most of the staff at MI6's West Berlin station, was allowed to cross the border into East Berlin. He and his wife, Gillian, were regular shoppers at the large East Berlin branch of the Kaufhaus store, where he would hand over the film cassettes from his Minox camera to a member of staff who doubled as his Soviet contact.

The secrets passed over included details of German agents who had been recruited by MI6 as well as information about everyone working at MI6's West Berlin station. This, of course, included the Chisholms.

It was Blake who first betrayed Lieutenant-Colonel Pyotr Popov, a GRU officer who had been spying for the CIA for several years before he was posted to East Berlin from Vienna. His CIA case officer in Vienna had been George Kisevalter, who was later one of the four case officers for Oleg Penkovsky.

Popov had no CIA contact when he arrived in East Berlin, so he wrote a letter to Kisevalter and gave it to a member of a British military mission visiting East Berlin, asking him to see that it got to the CIA station in Vienna. The letter arrived on Blake's desk. Blake photographed it before passing it to an acquaintance at the CIA's West Berlin station for onward transmission.

In all, Blake was to betray more than 400 undercover agents, forty-two of whom were killed by the KGB, the Stasi, or other Soviet or satellite country agencies.

Thinking of Dominik Stecher, our hypothetical agent run by Chisholm: he would have been betrayed by Blake and, in all likelihood, killed either by the KGB or Wolf's HVA arm of the Stasi. There was no thought or compassion for Stecher's young family or elderly parents. That was one of the risks of becoming involved in espionage.

In spite of all of Blake's dangerous and time-consuming work for his Soviet masters he performed his legitimate work to a standard that prompted Peter Lunn, the head of the station, to tell a visiting colleague that Blake was one of his best officers.

✝

Bill Harvey, as head of the CIA's Berlin base, took an overall interest in Berlin's maelstrom of espionage activity, as did Peter Lunn, his opposite number in the MI6 station. But both were preoccupied with the building of the tunnel as it moved into its final and most critical stage.

On 11 May 1955, John Wyke, MI6's chief technical communications engineer, led his small team of British technicians along the completed tunnel to where the three Soviet telephone and signals communications cables stood exposed. A neat and impressive array of coloured wires, connectors and signal boosters had been installed in the chamber during the previous three weeks, along with a microphone to detect any sounds of possible human interference. The team conducted a final examination of this facility before reaching up to remove the bottom and one side of the boxed area that housed the Soviet cables.

They knew the cables would be pressurised with nitrogen to keep them dry and that a cable monitoring system would detect any loss of pressure. A short blip on the monitor would probably go unnoticed or be ignored, but accidental damage to the circuits would be a disaster. The taps onto the cables had to be made and the joins resealed with the precision of a surgeon and the speed of a grand prix pit team changing the wheels of a racing car. The team had practised this operation repeatedly in England in a mocked-up version of the chamber.

A room in the bogus store at the beginning of the tunnel contained hundreds of signal-activated tape recorders. David Stafford records that 'the three cables being tapped carried some 1,200 communications channels, with the maximum number of channels being used at any one time amounting to 500. On average, twenty-eight telegraphic and 121 telephone circuits were continuously recorded on Ampex tape recorders, using about 50,000 reels of magnetic tape.'[†]

There were cheers from everyone in the tape-recorder room when each bank of recorders burst into life as the experts connected the taps at the other end of the tunnel.

The technical success of the taps exceeded expectations, soon amassing a staggering amount of material in need of analysis. Over the next eleven months, more than 30,000 two-hour reels of voice recordings – two-thirds of them in Russian and the rest in German – were sent to London where a team of more than 200 exiles – mostly Russian-speaking Poles from the Polish Resettlement Corps – transcribed and translated them. MI6's Section Y were busy enough with the Vienna tapes, so a new operation was set up in a similar Georgian building, this time in Chester Terrace overlooking Regent's Park. This arrangement also satisfied security worries about too many people having knowledge of the operations in both Vienna and Berlin.

Telegraphic and coded signals were sent to Washington for deciphering and analysis. The CIA's team of 350 people were secretly housed in a prefabricated building in Washington Mall. They worked in shifts around the clock. In all, they transcribed 20,000 six-hour teletype reels, most of them in Russian and the rest in German. A surprisingly large number of the conversations recorded were not coded. The cyphered signals were sent to the National Security Agency for deciphering.

$$\ddagger$$

Shortly after the tunnel became operational the Chisholms returned to London. Ruari was assigned to the East European and Soviet section in MI6's headquarters office in Broadway Buildings, near to St James's Park Underground Station.

---

†   David Stafford, 'Chapter 11', *Spies Beneath Berlin* (London: John Murray, 2003).

7

MOSCOW 1955

Chief Marshal of Soviet Artillery, Sergei Varentsov, was head of the Soviet tactical missile forces, which included nuclear weapons. His friendship with Colonel Oleg Penkovsky of the GRU went back to WWII, when Penkovsky had served as his personal liaison officer.

Varentsov had a daughter, Nina, by his beautiful first wife, Anya, who died quite young of tuberculosis. Nina inherited her mother's looks and Varentsov doted on her, though he did not approve of her choice of husband.

In January 1944 Varentsov's car was involved in a collision with a tank, resulting in a serious hip injury. He was confined to hospital in Moscow for three months with his hip and leg in plaster, suspended by traction pulleys.

During this time Penkovsky shuttled backwards and forwards between Varentsov's hospital bed and his current command at the First Ukrainian Front. He also visited Varentsov's family (his mother, second wife Ekaterina, and two daughters by Ekaterina) in Lvov, also the home city of Nina and her husband. Times were hard and there was very little food or new clothing.

When news came through to Varentsov that Nina's husband and two of his associates had been shot for dealing in the black market he asked Penkovsky to check in on Nina and assess her state of mind. Penkovsky arrived to find Nina dead: she had killed herself the previous day. He sold his watch to pay for a coffin and a black dress for her body, and made sure she was buried in a proper grave. When he reported to Varentsov on these events, the latter embraced and kissed him, telling Penkovsky he was like his own son.

✝

Now, in 1955, their friendship was closer than ever. Varentsov regularly invited Penkovsky and his family to visit, particularly when he threw family parties at his dacha just outside Moscow, such as when his daughter Yelena and her husband – a nephew of General Ivan Kupin – took leave from his assignment in East Germany.

Penkovsky had risen rapidly through the officer ranks during the war and later joined the GRU, winning promotion to the rank of colonel. At thirty-six he was in excellent physical condition and passably handsome, though he registered some concern over his receding hairline. To those who knew him well he was considered vain, but this was not always obvious on first acquaintance. He adored his wife, Vera, and their young daughter Galina who was now eight. Vera was the daughter of General Dmitri Gapanovich, who had died in 1952. Galina was in the same class at school as Varentsov's third daughter, Natasha.

After dinner at the dacha parties the ladies would withdraw, leaving the men to discuss military matters. Emboldened by the liberating effects of good wine, the men would talk openly and often critically about the views and lifestyles of the most senior politicians and military personnel.

In this way, and in the course of other occasional meetings with Varentsov in Moscow, Penkovsky got to hear much about Soviet political and military thinking at the highest levels. In these informal seminars, he learned of Khrushchev's concepts for Soviet military strategy, and the more he heard, the more he feared that Khrushchev would lead the Soviet Union into a disastrous war with the West.

Penkovsky's growing interest in international politics made

the news of his posting to Turkey all the more welcome and exciting. The appointment was as acting military attaché at the Soviet Embassy in Ankara. He was informed at the outset that someone else would eventually be appointed military attaché, at which time he would be demoted to assistant military attaché. This hurt Penkovsky, who felt he had, by this point, served long enough as a colonel to warrant promotion to major-general. He had always received glowing performance appraisals from his superiors, and was an earnest and longstanding member of the Communist party, having joined in 1938. This slight by way of temporary promotion seems to have marked the beginning of Penkovsky's dissatisfaction with his unappreciative superiors and the system behind them.

The other disappointing aspect of the posting was that he and Vera would have to leave their daughter Galina behind in Moscow. The reason given for this was that there was no suitable education available for Galina in Ankara, but in truth it was normal practice for Soviet officials sent to Western countries to be required to leave a close family member behind, reducing any risk of defection.

Turkey was a member of the powerful Western military alliance, the North Atlantic Treaty Organisation (NATO), and stood right on the border with the Soviet Union. It was thus a strategically important place to both East and West.

On 9 May 1955, West Germany joined NATO, which greatly improved the organisation's ability to defend Western Europe from Soviet invasion. In direct response, on 14 May, the Soviet Union created the Warsaw Pact, a similar alliance for mutual defence, comprising the USSR, East Germany, Hungary, Czechoslovakia, Bulgaria, Romania and Albania.

It was all quite perplexing for Penkovsky, who had expected Khrushchev to use the strength of the opposing alliances as a justification to expedite plans for a nuclear attack on the West. With these thoughts churning round in his mind, Penkovsky completed the briefing for his posting to Ankara.

✝
✝

The year 1955 was a busy but unspectacular one for Ivan Serov as he strove to find an effective operational formula for his KGB in the post-Stalin era. He was determined that the KGB would retain the power of its predecessor, the MGB, to stamp down hard on anyone who dared to question or tried to undermine the supreme power of the Communist Party in the Soviet Union. This applied to the representatives of foreign countries as well as to Soviet citizens.

His problem was that Khrushchev, who had appointed him the first chairman of the KGB, sought to rehabilitate the public image of the secret police. No longer 'the butcher of the Ukraine' Khrushchev was not Stalin, who had once accused him of 'populism', and seems to have been aware of the necessary limits of even totalitarian state power – or, as the Soviets preferred to call it, 'centralised democracy'. Serov reluctantly accepted his orders but was determined to continue his fight against the enemies of the people in his own remorseless style.

Serov stepped up the KGB's efforts to harass the staff of Western embassies. Security offensives on embassy staff, offices and residences, together with severe travel restrictions and intentionally clumsy administrative procedures sapped morale. Electronic scans by various embassies' technical staff uncovered more hidden microphones than ever. Members of staff were followed more closely, both on foot and in vehicles. Requests to travel outside the ten-mile restriction zone in Moscow took up to two weeks for approval and, even once granted, approval was often withdrawn at the last minute on the slightest pretext. Even the use of a different car from the vehicle listed on the original request could result in the cancellation of an approved travel permit.

Serov gave instructions to redouble action to compromise and blackmail staff in foreign embassies and these met with some success. John Vassall worked as a clerk in the British Embassy

Naval Attaché's office. The KGB discovered that he was homo-sexual and, in 1955, invited him to a gay party where he was photographed in some highly compromising positions. He succumbed to blackmail and started to spy for the Soviet Union when he returned to the UK in 1956. For the next seven years Vassall passed thousands of highly classified documents and photographs to the KGB. These included information about British radar, torpedoes and anti-submarine equipment.

Vassall was arrested on 12 September 1962, following a lengthy investigation begun by warnings from Soviet defectors Anatoliy Golitsyn and Yuri Nosenko of his 'turning' by the KGB. Sentenced to eighteen years' imprisonment, Vassall was released in 1972, having served only ten years. This relative leniency on the most serious of Cold War-era charges reflected, in part, a degree of public and governmental sympathy, as Vassall was widely thought to have been a victim of circumstances. Despite his attempt to explain and justify himself in a 1975 autobiog-raphy, Vassall felt compelled to change his name, and died in obscurity in 1996.

8

ANKARA 1955-6

Penkovsky arrived in Ankara in the summer of 1955 accompanied by his wife Vera.

As acting military attaché he was invited to numerous official receptions and made courtesy visits to senior defence personnel in other embassies. His pay and allowances were decent by Eastern European standards and he soon started to enjoy his new lifestyle. His engaging personality made it easy for him to establish an easy rapport with Western representatives.

He struck up a particularly warm relationship with Colonel Charles Peeke, the United States military attaché. He may also have had conversations with Anthony Parsons, First Secretary at the British Embassy, who was then on his first overseas posting as a diplomat, having previously spent fourteen years in the army, culminating in his tenure as military attaché at the British Embassy in Baghdad.[†]

Diplomatic niceties aside, Penkovsky worked diligently at his prime task of managing the small network of part-time agents and informants with access to intelligence on United States and NATO personnel and military establishments in Izmir and other parts of Turkey. He excelled at this work, building strong personal

---

[†]   Anthony Derrick Parsons, later Sir Anthony Parsons, was awarded the Military Cross as an artillery officer during WWII. His career as a diplomat, spent mostly in the Middle East, was equally successful. He became Prime Minister Margaret Thatcher's foreign policy adviser after retiring from the Diplomatic Service.

relationships with contacts he had inherited from his predecessor and winning over additional talent. His attention to detail in arranging dead-letter drops and other secret communications was of the highest professional standard. However, the more he learned about military transportation, weapons, deployment and plans for defence and attack, the more he grew to question the overall direction of the Cold War.

It could well have been about this time that the first thoughts of helping the West to understand the full dangers of Khrushchev's hawkish attitude entered Penkovsky's head. If he made any tentative approaches to Peeke, Parsons or anyone else they were not taken seriously enough to attract follow-up action, or they may have suspected him of being an *agent provocateur*.

Penkovsky contrived to have his photograph taken with Colonel Peeke at a social gathering and later used this photograph as evidence of his friendship with the West.

✝
✝

General Nicolai Petrovich Savchenko and Lieutenant-Colonel Nicolay Ionchenko arrived in Ankara together on 20 January 1956. The 63-year-old Savchenko used the pseudonym 'Rubenko'. He was the new GRU chief in Ankara, with Penkovsky assuming the second-in-command position. Ionchenko was also GRU and ranked below Penkovsky.

It was natural that Penkovsky would be upset that his comfortable situation as the acting GRU *Rezident* in Ankara had come to an end, but Savchenko soon proved to be – at least in the eyes of Penkovsky – not up to the task, while Ionchenko, in turn, resented Penkovsky's seniority. Savchenko and Ionchenko had become good friends in Moscow and en route to Ankara; so much so that Penkovsky felt they often conspired against him, trying to find fault in the way he toed the party line.

Despite the deteriorating office atmosphere, Penkovsky focused on executing his professional duties to the best of his ability. He was not a man to lower his standards or neglect his work.

As Penkovsky's subordinate, Ionchenko was obliged to submit requests for operational funds and expenses to his office. As such, in April, Penkovsky realised that Ionchenko was buying military manuals and other confidential information from Turkish soldiers with a distinct lack of subtlety. This was, to say the least, an unprofessional means of collecting intelligence as Ionchenko could easily have been caught red-handed by the host counter-intelligence agency. Penkovsky made this point to Savchenko, who promised it would not happen again.

This incident stirred Penkovsky to write to headquarters, requesting a transfer. Anywhere would do, as long as it freed him from Ankara and Savchenko. An unsympathetic official reply instructed him to remain in post and await a later transfer. Penkovsky would later confess that it was this incident that finally triggered his decision to offer his services to the Western powers.

✝
✝

The Shah of Persia and his wife were scheduled to make an official visit to Turkey during the second week in May 1956. As Turkish security would be on high alert the GRU headquarters sent instructions to Savchenko not to participate in any espionage-related activities during the visit.

On 10 May Penkovsky was in Savchenko's office on routine business when an embassy official knocked on the door and came in. He reported that the Turkish police had called to say that Ionchenko was being held on a charge of buying a classified military manual from a Turkish soldier.

Savchenko shouted at Penkovsky, trying to blame him for the incident, and instructed him to arrange for Ionchenko's release. Penkovsky argued that he had not advanced Ionchenko any money and denied all responsibility. In the end Savchenko had to acknowledge that *he* had, in fact, authorised Ionchenko's operation. An almighty row erupted between the embarrassed Savchenko and Penkovsky, who had, after all, drawn his boss's attention to the problem.

Penkovsky rescued Ionchenko from the clutches of the Turkish authorities, but they declared him *persona non grata* and he returned to Moscow. His Turkish accomplice, a lieutenant in the Turkish Army, was found guilty of selling state secrets to an enemy and executed.

Savchenko sent a report of the incident to Moscow. It claimed that Ionchenko had been the victim of a conspiracy hatched by US and Turkish intelligence. He was, Savchenko claimed, innocently buying some fruit in the market when he was pounced upon by the Turkish police and accused of spying. Savchenko also sent a telegram accusing Penkovsky of 'gross insubordination' over the matter.

Savchenko had full control over the content of all GRU signals sent from the embassy to Moscow, so Penkovsky could not report his side of the story directly to GRU headquarters. It was not in his character to accept this situation, so he took the drastic step of reporting his side through Colonel Yerzin, the KGB *Rezident* in the Soviet Embassy. In spite of the normal mistrust between the GRU and the KGB, Penkovsky and Yerzin had become good friends over the preceding six months.

In official parlance the GRU referred to the KGB as 'our neighbours' and the KGB referred to the GRU as 'our military neighbours'. There were strong jealousies between the two, sometimes boiling over into hostility. It was virtually unheard of for one of them to send a report through the other.

Yerzin addressed the cable directly to Ivan Serov, the head of the KGB. Serov reported the incident to Khrushchev, since all cases of compromised intelligence officers were brought to the attention of the Politburo. Savchenko's cable arrived about the same time. Khrushchev demanded an investigation to find out which of the two (Penkovsky or Savchenko) was telling the truth, or, at least, approximating it.

General Savchenko was given a severe reprimand by the Minister of Defence, Georgy Zhukov. Penkovsky received no such official chastisement. The two men tolerated each other, mostly in silence, for the next few months.

In October and November of that year the abortive anti-Soviet revolution in Hungary dominated headlines and news broadcasts around the world. Penkovsky was an avid fan of the BBC Overseas Service programmes beamed to Turkey through a powerful relay station on Cyprus. Through those chaotic weeks he also enjoyed access to the embassy's mail, much of it made up of government telegrams explaining the official stance of the USSR regarding events in Hungary, a stance that shifted several times before an eventual military crackdown. The bully-ing tactics of the Soviet Union and the repression of the new Communist government it imposed on Hungary (still nomi-nally a sovereign state) distressed him and further reinforced his intention to work for the West. He was sorry for the people of Hungary but pleased, in the interests of world peace, that the West's denunciation of the Soviet Union's aggressive action was muted.

A week before he left Ankara, Penkovsky tried to contact Colonel Peeke, only to be told that he had returned to America with his wife for the funeral of his mother-in-law and could not be contacted.

Penkovsky left on 6 November 1956. Savchenko was removed shortly afterwards and was later discharged from the service.

‡

Penkovsky had an interview with General Smolikov, the GRU's chief of personnel, on his return to Moscow. Smolikov told him he was right, in principle, to denounce Savchenko. In practice, he pointed out, the price of such principled action was high:

Savchenko was a general and not many generals would be prepared to trust or work with him after such action.

Penkovsky was put on the reserve list and given temporary assignments at headquarters pending a suitable vacancy arising. He was disappointed at the outcome, but not surprised. He went to see Marshal Varentsov, told him about his recent differences with the GRU, and said he would like to return to a regimental command in the artillery. Varentsov claimed he would try to intercede on his behalf.

9

MOSCOW 1956

In the early morning hours of 25 February 1956, Khrushchev addressed a closed session (limited to Soviet delegates) of the 20th Party Congress. It became known as his 'Secret Speech', though news of it leaked out quickly and spread like wildfire.

Congress sat in stunned silence for four hours, as Khrushchev condemned Joseph Stalin and all his works. The speech vilified Stalin for his murderous brutality, intolerance, repression of Soviet peoples, abuse of power, the persecution of millions of innocents, and much more. In one of its most striking passages, he said:

> Stalin originated the concept *'enemy of the people'*. This term automatically made it unnecessary that the ideological errors of a man or men engaged in a controversy be proven. It made possible the use of the cruellest repression, violating all norms of revolutionary legality, against anyone who in any way disagreed with Stalin, against those who were only suspected of hostile intent, against those who had bad reputations.

It was an incredibly brave speech to deliver, not only because all senior members of the Communist Party, the very highest group that composed his audience, still professed allegiance to Stalinism, but because he, himself, was a product of it. Khrushchev had, as his daughter once put it, 'risen to power on the crest of the Stalinist wave'. He had himself implemented some of Stalin's cruellest policies with apparent relish, most notoriously when working with Ivan Serov in the Ukraine from 1939 to 1941. Admitting his own, and the party's, history of error took great moral courage, and brought huge political risk.

Khrushchev had not always been a devout supporter of Stalin – in the early 1920s he supported Trotsky against Stalin over the question of party democracy – and now he was openly challenging the basic concepts of Stalinism at the highest levels of the party.

The gamble paid off: most party members threw their hats into the ring with Khrushchev, who held power for another eight years, until his ousting by Leonid Brezhnev and Alexander Shelepin in October 1964. It is now widely accepted that the Secret Speech and Khrushchev's traducement of Stalin were seeds that would germinate, in time, into the liberal reforms of Mikhail Gorbachev. Eventually, their spread across the nations of the USSR and Eastern Europe would culminate in the disintegration of the Soviet Union and reunification of a wholly capitalist Germany.

Serov was never a political animal. He possessed neither the ability nor the will required to hold one of the top party offices. His appointment as KGB chairman came about solely owing to the recommendation of Khrushchev to the Politburo – the ultimate Soviet authority. It left him subordinate to overall Politburo control, and his office did not bring him membership in the Politburo.

It is possible that Khrushchev had warned Serov of his plans to recant his previous support of Stalin, but Serov was still shocked and angered by the severity and manner of the denunciation. He would have joined any organised group strong enough to oust Khrushchev, had there been one.

The majority of Politburo members gave overt – though in some cases uncomfortable – support to Khrushchev's new anti-Stalinist strategy, and Serov was subservient to the Politburo. This would have left a lesser operator impotent, but Serov had the conviction, strength and determination to continue promoting his own brand of Stalinist action and discipline in the KGB's activities, regardless of the Politburo's dictat. From this point onwards there was a discernible cooling of the close relationship between Khrushchev and Serov.

✝

At the beginning of April 1956, just a few weeks after the Secret Speech, Serov left for the United Kingdom as the advance man for arranging security on a nine-day goodwill visit by First Secretary Khrushchev and Premier Marshal Bulganin. Stalin himself could not have created a worse impression than Serov in his most officious mode.

A senior British police officer who was coordinating arrangements for the visit said: 'It was totally impossible to deal with him. He ranted and raved and demanded the impossible everywhere we went. On one occasion he shouted instructions to the Soviet Ambassador and the Ambassador felt obliged to accede to his demands.'

The British media branded Serov 'Ivan the Terrible' and 'The Butcher'. The Foreign Office requested that Serov not return to the United Kingdom for the goodwill visit itself. No political animal, Serov clearly had his limits as a diplomat, as well.

Khrushchev and Bulganin arrived in the UK on 18 April on the prestigious new cruiser *Ordzhenikidze*, which docked at Portsmouth together with an escort of two Soviet warships.

The day after the boat came into harbour, the officer on watch reported seeing what appeared to be a diver under the water near the cruiser. The ship's commanding officer consulted the senior KGB officer on board, who just happened to be Ivan Serov – who had in fact returned to the UK with the General Secretary and Prime Minister, though he did not venture ashore. He was at hand for exactly such eventualities as this, and dealt with the potential security issue simply by ordering the immediate execution of the diver.

Serov's suspicions were correct: the diver was none other than the heroic Commander Lionel 'Buster' Crabb, at that time in the employ of MI6. He had been sent to inspect and photograph the Soviet cruiser's hull and propellers, with the particular aim of investigating how the ship, given its impressive size, had proven so remarkably manoeuvrable.

Khrushchev was furious upon learning of the incident. He was furious both that Britain had dared to perpetrate such an act during a goodwill visit, and appalled that the diver had been summarily executed rather than captured. A captured spy, after all, could prove a useful bargaining chip.

However, Khrushchev was enjoying his visit – his first official visit to a Western country – and decided not to embarrass his hosts in public. He and Bulganin took British Prime Minister Sir Anthony Eden aside at a reception to register their protest. Eden was horrified. He apologised profusely and, with unfeigned sincerity, told his guests he had given no instructions to spy on the Soviet vessels. He promised to discover who had authorised the deed and take the strongest possible disciplinary action against him.

Crabb's disappearance – initially there was no body and no evidence that a diver had died, let alone been murdered – made front page news. However, there were so many different stories and theories about the incident that it cast only a small shadow over the visit. *The Times* came closest to the truth with its coverage of the event, but – strongly identified with and supportive of Eden's Conservative Party – the newspaper mysteriously backed away from the story the next day. There was certainly a successful exercise in damage limitation that lasted until after the Soviet visitors had departed.

It was almost a year later that a body in a frogman suit was found floating near Pilsey Island in Chichester Harbour. The head and both hands were missing, making identification impossible using the technology of the time, but the coroner was satisfied that it was the body of Crabb. Rumours that Crabb lived on, becoming a Soviet secret agent or possibly a double agent, still persist.

As a direct result of this incident, Eden forced Major-General John Sinclair, the Director-General of MI6 to resign, replacing him with Sir Dick White, previously the Director-General of MI5.

‡

Just three days after the diving incident, on 22 April, another near-disaster came close to scuppering the 'goodwill' visit. This time, Serov was responsible.

Serov had never approved of allowing the West's Berlin tunnel continued operation. His Stalinist instinct was to take immediate action to terminate any espionage activity as soon as it was discovered, but Sergei Kondrashev – now back in Moscow after being Blake's spymaster in London – prevailed upon him to allow the cable-tapping to continue, in order to protect Blake's identity as a double agent.

Conditions towards the end of April were right for the fortuitous 'discovery' of the tunnel and Serov gave instructions to proceed. Someone – it may have been Kondrashev – suggested that, in the light of the goodwill visit by Bulganin and Khrushchev, all of the blame for the tunnel should be placed on the Americans and none on the British. This saved the day – and the face of Her Majesty's government.

‡

In spite of the two near-disasters, Khrushchev and Bulganin enjoyed their nine days in the United Kingdom. The highlights for Khrushchev in particular were the incredible performance of Margot Fonteyn in a ballet at Covent Garden, and the visit to Edinburgh. He was overwhelmed with the rugged beauty and history of Edinburgh Castle, and so taken with the library in

Edinburgh University that he arranged for the chief librarian to go to Moscow for six months and set up something similar in the Moscow State University library.

As goodwill visits go, it had been a civilised diplomatic success. Talks were 'constructive'. The resulting joint communiqué pledged both nations to seek peace in the Middle East through the United Nations, to give guarantees not to use nuclear weapons, to reach agreement on disarmament, to make a significant increase in cultural exchanges, and to record a Soviet 'aim' to spend £1,000 million on British goods and services over the next five years. Eden accepted an invitation from Bulganin to visit the Soviet Union and publicly thanked Bulganin and Khrushchev for their 'patience and perseverance' during their stay in Britain.

The most unsavoury parts of the visit, according to later writings and reports, were obligatory meetings with leading members of Britain's opposition Labour Party. The uncouth, heavy-drinking George Brown, a future deputy leader of the party and Foreign Secretary, was particularly obnoxious.

The afterglow of the visit soon faded as the Suez Canal crisis developed through the summer and into the autumn of 1956, when the Soviet Union sided with and assisted Egypt against Britain, France and Israel. In the end, it was the non-participation and veiled criticism of the United States, rather than Soviet support for Egypt, that caused France and Britain to back down.

10

BUDAPEST 1956

Created in December 1922 and dissolved in December 1991, the Soviet Union – the Union of Soviet Socialist Republics (USSR) – was a federation of fifteen republics ruled centrally from Moscow by the Marxist–Leninist Communist Party.[†] After WWII, a number of East European countries, pleased to be liberated from the Nazis by the Soviet Army, formed their own Marxist–Leninist Communist parties, but they soon fell into the clutches of Stalinist-controlled bodies and became subservient to Moscow. The West called these nations the 'satellite' countries.[‡] Failure by their governments to kowtow to the wishes of Moscow could be costly, as several of them discovered over the years.

It is difficult, after the passage of over half a century, to comprehend how sovereign nations in Eastern Europe allowed themselves to be controlled by the Communist Party of the Soviet Union (CPSU). Yet the satellite countries, and Communist regimes that governed them, were utterly subservient to the Politburo. Their leaders were appointed on the recommendation of the Politburo. Although the parliaments of the satellite

---

[†]   The fifteen republics were: Russia, Georgia, Ukraine, Moldova, Belarus, Armenia, Azerbaijan, Kazakhstan, Uzbekistan, Turkmenistan, Kyrgyzstan, Tajikistan, Estonia, Latvia and Lithuania. From the international perspective, there were doubts as to whether the last three (the Baltic States) were legally part of the Soviet Union.

[‡]   The Communist-ruled satellite countries were: Poland, Hungary, Romania, Bulgaria, Czechoslovakia, Yugoslavia, Albania and East Germany.

countries did not, legally, have to accept these 'recommendations', the consequences of not accepting them could be disastrous.

In Poland, Hungary, Czechoslovakia and Yugoslavia there were individual politicians, intellectuals, workers' leaders, teachers and students who *did* kick against the pricks. These dissidents' cause was boosted when they learned that parts of Khrushchev's Secret Speech had proposed some relaxation of Moscow's dogmatic central control. They could now think out loud and even discuss the possibility of alternative policies, provided they were intended to support and further the aims of Communism.

Polish Communists took the lead in this refreshing development, pressing for the reinstatement of Wladyslaw Gomulka, a fervent party member who, in 1948, had opposed the introduction of collectivised farming and strict adherence to other policies laid down by the party's Central Committee in Moscow. He was removed from his position of First Secretary of the Polish Communist Party and placed under house arrest.

The movement to reinstate Gomulka led to a revolt by workers at the Poznan Stalin Works – a locomotive manufacturing plant – on 23 June 1956 in which at least seventy-three people died after the confused and inept intervention of the Poznan civil and military authorities. This revolt prompted further development of Polish national Communism with the dismissal of some Stalinist elements in the government, the mushrooming of workers' councils, the reassessment of the Polish government's relationship with Moscow and finally, in August, the reinstatement of Gomulka.

These developments were watched closely in Hungary, particularly by members of the Petöfi Circle who, in a similar manner, sought to assert their sovereignty. The circle supported the establishment of a new Communist government, independent of Moscow, under Imre Nagy.[†]

[†]   The Petöfi Circle was an organisation of mostly young intellectuals led by
    István Lakatos, a non-party member and poet. It was established in 1954
    by members of the Hungarian National Museum.

The leadership in Moscow were ambivalent towards Nagy. There was no doubt about his Communist credentials, for he had spent fourteen years (1930–44) in Moscow, during which time he was involved with agricultural research and also served as an NKVD informant. He returned to Hungary in 1944 and became Minister of Agriculture. Many Soviet officials considered him a relatively harmless lightweight, while others expressed concern over his anti-collectivisation – and therefore anti-Soviet – stance on agriculture.

Ivan Serov closely monitored events in Hungary with the benefit of a continuous stream of intelligence from the KGB's agents. The (mostly overt) intelligence provided by Ambassador Yuri Andropov and his team was supplemented by reports from undercover agents in Budapest and across the country about the secret plans of anti-Soviet groups and individuals.

Serov had already made up his mind about Nagy. In July 1956 – a month after the Poznan revolt in Poland and three months before the Hungarian Revolution – he wrote that 'the young people of the Petöfi Circle say they are also communists but they do not want to copy Russian methods'. They wished – he wrote – to be led by Imre Nagy, just as the Hungarians were led by Lajos Kossuth against the Austrians and Russians in 1848.[†] Serov's knowledge and understanding of what motivated Nagy's supporters belied the claims by many in Moscow that Serov was an uneducated oaf.

The Hungarian leader, Mátyás Rákosi, was a staunch Stalinist; a man after Serov's own heart. In the years 1948–56 he had purged about 350,000 Hungarian officials and intellectuals. On 30 May 1949 he ordered the arrest of Foreign Minister Lászlo Rajk, whom he saw as a threat to his own leadership: falsely accusing him of supporting the Yugoslavian leader, Marshal

---

†   See Johanna Granville, 'Chapter 1', *The First Domino* (Texas: Texas A&M University Press, 2004) p. 4.

Tito. Rajk was found guilty and executed. Rákosi later admitted he had been wrong.

In fact, Rákosi had been so zealous that, in June 1953, Moscow reprimanded him for excessive persecution and for grossly increasing the size of the Hungarian Army. He was then forced by Moscow to share government leadership with the liberal Communist Imre Nagy, who was appointed Prime Minister.

But Nagy went too far in resisting land reform, even encouraging farmers to leave the collective farms. He was strongly censured in April 1955 and when he refused to recant he was dismissed as Prime Minister, leaving Rákosi back in sole charge. This made Nagy something of a hero in a nation that felt an historic antipathy to Russia. Rákosi, who referred to himself as Stalin's best Hungarian disciple, was extremely unpopular.

Khrushchev and senior members of the Politburo made the mistake of thinking they could control events in Hungary by manoeuvring and manipulating senior politicians, as exemplified by the dismissal of Nagy. The Soviets did not realise, until it was too late, that politicians appointed from Moscow were not the force behind the forthcoming counter-revolution. It came from the grass roots.

By early 1956, peaceful demonstrations against Rákosi increased in frequency and attracted ever-larger crowds. László Rajk, who had been executed under Rákosi in 1949, was rehabilitated on 28 March 1956. This had profound consequences for Rákosi, undermining his authority, and telegraphing in the rubric of Soviet rehabilitations and condemnations that he was out of favour.

Telegrams from Soviet Ambassador Andropov and from Soviet Embassy Third Secretary Vladimir Kryuchkov (both of them KGB officers) multiplied as Rákosi's ability to govern waned. Andropov – himself a hard-liner – recommended that Rákosi should be replaced by the strict disciplinarian Ernö Gerö, who had been an active NKVD agent during the twenty-odd years he spent in the Soviet Union between the two world wars.

Gerö took office as First Secretary of the Hungarian Workers' Party (MDP) on 18 July. András Hegedüs was appointed Prime Minister. Rákosi was exiled to the Soviet Union and never returned to Hungary.

Ernö Gerö's appointment was ill-conceived, as the Kremlin readily admitted some weeks later. Either János Kádár or Imre Nagy, both of whom attracted some measure of support from the Hungarian populace, would have made better candidates, if only because their appointment would have pacified the demonstrators and possibly prevented revolution.

After Gerö's appointment, Serov's undercover agents reported hearing many conversations among teachers, intellectuals and underground organisations, all concluding that Gerö would not last long as leader. Moscow would then have no other hard-liner to lead Hungary on their behalf.

On 6 October a crowd of more than 100,000 attended a service for the reburial of Rajk's body. This was the watershed for the events of the following four weeks.

Nagy's qualities and beliefs were similar to Rajk's, so it was inevitable that Rajk's rehabilitation and reburial would herald Nagy's readmission to the MDP and, consequently, his ability to participate in high-level political power. He was formally reinstated in the MDP on 13 October.

The Petöfi Circle met virtually every day during the first three weeks of October, debating economic and political solutions to Hungary's many problems. This culminated in a peaceful demonstration by 10,000 students on 23 October demanding, among other things, the dismissal of Gerö, the return of Imre Nagy, the withdrawal of Soviet troops from Hungary, and true political independence from Moscow.

That evening, Gerö made a radio speech condemning the demonstration and stressing Hungarian friendship with the Soviet Union: sentiments that could only serve to enrage the demonstrating students.

Observing the growing unrest after his speech, Gerö consulted senior members of the MDP and then made a telephone call to the Soviet military attaché in Budapest asking for Soviet military assistance to break up any future demonstrations. The military attaché spoke to Ambassador Andropov who asked the leader of the Soviet Army's Special Corps in Hungary, Pyotr Laschenko, to intervene. Laschenko said he could only do so on orders from the Soviet Politburo. The Politburo insisted it could not authorise intervention without a formal request from the Hungarian leadership. Andropov phoned Khrushchev and Khrushchev phoned Gerö asking him to submit a written request. Gerö replied there was no time for such bureaucratic niceties.

This merry-go-round resulted in the Politburo convening late on the evening of 23 October. They authorised Minister of Defence Marshal Zhukov to mobilise five divisions of the Soviet Army. Khrushchev immediately dispatched First Deputy Premier Anastas Mikoyan and Politburo member Mikhail Suslov to Budapest.

Ivan Serov also went to Budapest, probably at his own insistence. It was not in his nature simply to analyse the intelligence he received and send reports and recommendations to the Kremlin: he wanted to have a stronger, and active, influence over events. He was appalled by evidence that certain members of the Politburo wanted to take a soft line on Hungary and was determined to enshrine a policy of painful repercussions for everyone who opposed, or even questioned, the Soviet Communist Party's line.

An all-night meeting of the Central Committee of the MDP led to an early morning (24 October) announcement that Imre Nagy was to replace András Hegedüs as Prime Minister, but that Gerö would remain First Secretary of the MDP.

There was a peaceful demonstration by 25,000 Hungarians outside the parliament building on the morning of 25 October. They were calling for Gerö's resignation.

At about eleven o'clock members of the ÁVH (Hungarian State Security: the secret police agency) opened fire on the demonstrators. The shooting continued for close to twenty minutes and resulted in the deaths of nearly 200 demonstrators. That day became known as 'Bloody Thursday'.

Mikoyan and Suslov immediately castigated Gerö for the inflammatory speech he had made on the evening of 23 October and instructed him to resign. János Kádár replaced him as First Secretary of the MDP.

The same day, Nagy promised to disband the hated ÁVH and replace it with a regular civilian police force. Two days later he started to restructure the government. Within a week he had formed a new coalition, including members of the Smallholders' Party, the National Peasant Party and the Social Democratic Party, as well as the Communist Party.

In the days following Bloody Thursday, bands of Hungarian insurgents carried out violent acts against Communist targets and particularly against members of the ÁVH. It was ÁVH members, after all, who had killed the peaceful demonstrators. In one particularly nasty instance, they hanged some members of the ÁVH outside the Communist Party committee building in Budapest. There were reports of lynchings elsewhere in Budapest and throughout Hungary, while insurgents were claimed to have stormed prisons, releasing scores of inmates.

Andropov and other Soviet Embassy staff and their families witnessed some of the hangings. Andropov's wife was physically ill and required hospital treatment to deal with the trauma. This had a profound influence on Andropov and Third Secretary Vladimir Kryuchkov, both of whom adopted a lifelong policy of supporting immediate and decisive action against any signs of insurrection in Soviet and satellite countries.

A ceasefire ordered by Nagy on 28 October was only partially successful. Its purpose was not just to stem the violence; Nagy saw it as an essential precursor to opening negotiations for the withdrawal of Soviet troops from Hungary.

Nagy's tolerant disposition led to confusion. He was opening doors for non-Communist political and religious organisations while at the same time trying to develop an independent (non-Soviet) Communist government. New or resurrected political organisations each had their own, often conflicting, agendas which they publicised on radio and in print. Some of these – particularly the radio broadcasts – criticised Nagy and Kádár for their links to Communism.

Sittings of Nagy's new all-party government were chaotic. The chamber was packed with delegates all clamouring for attention, while members of the public milled around in hallways. In Moscow, the Politburo decided it would be better to accept the creation of Nagy's unity government than to risk a bloodbath and the total alienation of the Hungarian people. On 30 October they agreed to withdraw Soviet troops from Hungary, but that decision was reversed the next day when Khrushchev argued, in effect, that Hungary would be lost to the West if Soviet troops did not move in to restore order. Mikoyan, Marshal Zhukov and others continued to support troop withdrawal, but they were outvoted.

At this time, Britain and France were heavily engaged in the Suez Canal crisis, which seriously reduced the possibility of Western military intervention in Hungary.

Serov had set his own agenda. Throughout the week since his arrival in Budapest he had sent graphic descriptions of the fast-moving scene to Khrushchev. These cables were not designed to tell Khrushchev what he wanted to hear; nor were they replicating the content of Ambassador Andropov's diplomatic communications. They were slanted to highlight evidence supporting the need to come down hard on the perpetrators of acts of violence and subversion against the 'legitimate' rule of the Communist government; that is, the government installed by the Soviet Communist Party's Central Committee.

On 27 October, for example, Serov reported that proclamations were appearing around Budapest declaring Imre Nagy a traitor. Hungarian activists were also, he claimed, proposing

Béla Kováks (a non-Communist and former general secretary of the Independent Smallholders' Party) as Prime Minister.[†]

On 29 October he reported:

> The situation in several cities can be characterised in the following way: the population has been mobilised against the Communists. In several regions the armed people search in the apartments of Communists and shoot them. In the factory town of Csepel (near Budapest) there were eighteen Communists killed. The bandits check the buses travelling between cities; prominent Communists are pulled out and shot.[‡]

These telegrams gave Khrushchev a clear warning that even the acceptance of the Nagy government – as the only alternative to Soviet invasion – was not going to work.

Soon after Moscow's initial decision on 30 October to withdraw Soviet troops, Nagy received reports that although the troops were withdrawing from Budapest, more were crossing the borders from other Soviet satellite countries into Hungary and massing beyond the capital.

Nagy confronted Ambassador Andropov, who at first tried to deny it and then made excuses about the extra troops being required to ensure a safe withdrawal in the light of possible attacks by insurgents.

The influx of troops infuriated Nagy and he was moved to a fateful decision. On 1 November he withdrew Hungary from the Warsaw Pact and declared it a neutral country. He sought help from the United Nations by appealing to the Security Council. The majority of the council voted to debate the Hungarian crisis, but the Soviet Union, one of the five permanent members of the

---

[†]   See Johanna Granville, 'Chapter 6', *The First Domino* (Texas: Texas A&M University Press, 2004) p. 175.

[‡]   See Johanna Granville, 'Chapter 3', *The First Domino* (Texas: Texas A&M University Press, 2004) p. 88.

council empowered with a right of veto, opposed the resolution. Hungary was on its own.

✝
✝

The Politburo's decision on 31 October to send troops into Hungary to restore order was kept secret from Nagy. As far as he was aware, the Soviet troops would be withdrawn in accordance with an agreement to be negotiated by a mixed commission led on the Hungarian side by Pál Maléter.

However, also on 1 November – the same day that Nagy withdrew Hungary from the Warsaw Pact and declared it neutral – a Politburo inner circle group secretly flew János Kádár to Moscow with a view to grooming him for the leadership of a new, pro-Soviet post-invasion government. Kádár was accompanied by Ferenc Münnich, the Minister for Internal Affairs in Nagy's short-lived administration.

Nagy wanted Poland to host the mixed commission negotiations between Hungary and the Soviet Union over the withdrawal of Soviet troops. That, however, would have taken control of the situation away from Serov, who used all of his skills to persuade Nagy that it would be quicker and easier to arrange for the negotiations to take place at the Soviet Military Command at Tököl on Csepel Island, at the southern edge of Budapest. This was vital to the overall outcome of the cunning deception, and to Serov's specific role in it.

Early negotiations seemed to have made good progress and the mixed commission agreed to reconvene at Tököl at 10 p.m. on 3 November.

Nagy was aware of the continuing movement of Soviet troops just outside the Hungarian borders but could only rely on the result of the negotiations to prevent an invasion and to have existing troops in Hungary removed. It would have been futile to disrupt the negotiations and make separate attempts to remove the troops by force.

At midnight on 3 November Serov himself entered the room where Pál Maléter's Hungarian delegation were in deep negotiation with the three generals of the Soviet delegation. He told the surprised group – the Soviet generals had been under the impression that the negotiations were genuine all along – that there would be no agreement concerning the withdrawal of troops. The Soviet troops already in Hungary would be reinforced by as many additional troops as were required to restore law and order, or obedience, in Hungary.

Five hours later, Ferenc Münnich announced the establishment of a new Revolutionary Workers' and Peasants' Government, to be led by Kádár. It would initially be based in Szolnok, about fifty-five miles (ninety kilometres) south-east of Budapest.

Nagy knew, then, that he had been betrayed and, together with a dozen or more of his closest supporters and their families, sought refuge in the Yugoslav Embassy in Budapest.

In the early hours of 4 November twelve divisions of Soviet tanks and troops crossed the borders into Hungary to join forces with the five divisions already there and set about destroying all opposition to Soviet control.

The Hungarian Army had been under orders from Nagy not to fight the Soviet Army during the so-called negotiations. They were now permitted to fight. The overpowering Soviet force took eight days – five days longer than they expected – to overcome Hungarian resistance. The Hungarians suffered some 2,500 dead with a further 20,000 wounded. The Soviet Army emerged with fewer casualties: 670 dead and 1,500 injured.

Support for Nagy and condemnation of Soviet actions by the Western powers was understated, even muted.

Mass arrests and denunciations continued for several months under Serov's local direction. This caused some consternation in Moscow and, at one point, the Ministry of Internal Affairs complained to Khrushchev that the KGB were going too far with their policy of arresting on vague charges and little evidence. Serov responded to Khrushchev:

In my own opinion, we should not make any concessions to the insurgents. Experience shows that the least concession you make, the more demands and threats they make. The arrests are being made only when there is concrete data about the accuseds' hostile activities, confirmed by evidence.

He went on to say:

The experience of the investigatory work shows that at present the active enemies and organisers under arrest persist for a long time and do not admit their guilt. Even those arrested persons who were caught at the scene of the crime with weapons in their hands deny their guilt. This is how we can explain the declarations of innocence by the arrested persons.[†]

Khrushchev and his Politburo colleagues were unhappy about Yugoslavia giving asylum to Nagy and his followers. In practice, it put President Tito of Yugoslavia in a difficult position: he did not wish to be seen yielding to pressure from Moscow but neither did he wish to be seen supporting an 'enemy' of the Soviet Union.

As living conditions in the Yugoslav Embassy for the thirty or so people in the Nagy group (supporters and their families) were becoming unbearable, it was agreed that they would move out to some Yugoslav diplomatic apartments on 22 November. The bus to be used for the move had a Russian driver. When the party boarded the bus a Yugoslav diplomat and the Yugoslav military attaché joined them to ensure that the passengers arrived safely at their new homes. But an uninvited Soviet official also boarded. The driver stopped the bus after it rounded the first corner and the Soviet official demanded that the diplomat and the military attaché leave it. The bus was then driven to the KGB compound

---

[†]   See Johanna Granville, 'Chapter 5', *The First Domino* (Texas: Texas A&M University Press, 2004) p. 151.

in Mátyásföld and then on to the Romanian Embassy where the party were granted 'asylum'.

The next day, they were flown to Romania where they lived in secluded, guarded accommodation for nearly six months. Throughout Nagy's asylum in both the Yugoslav Embassy and in Romania, he was asked on numerous occasions to resign as Prime Minister and to declare that he accepted the Kádár government as legitimate. He always refused.

On 14 April 1957 Nagy was arrested and sent back to Budapest to stand trial. The question of his trial and execution (which was by now a foregone conclusion) became a political hot potato in a series of difficult situations that arose between the Soviet Union, Poland and Yugoslavia.

Nagy was eventually executed by hanging on 16 June 1958 after a secret trial.

‡

Whatever one's views about Serov's devotion to the legacy of Stalin and Stalinism it is difficult to argue against the quality of his work and his achievements in Hungary in October and November 1956. In a practical sense he, probably more than anyone else, was responsible for bringing Hungary safely back into the fold after Imre Nagy had all but freed it from Soviet domination.

Serov did it, first of all, by getting himself into the centre of the action in Budapest. Then he sent carefully and expertly drafted telegrams back to Moscow; telegrams that persuaded Khrushchev that the only solution to the crisis was to send in large numbers of tanks and troops to retake Hungary by force. Having established that position, he deceived Nagy into believing that he could negotiate the withdrawal of Soviet troops. Throughout his time in Budapest he demanded tough action by his KGB officers against any and all people who might be insurgents.

One consequence of Serov's time in Hungary was his meeting

and becoming friends with two kindred spirits at the Soviet Embassy in Budapest: Ambassador Yuri Andropov and Third Secretary Vladimir Kryuchkov, both of whom would eventually become, in turn, the chairman of the KGB. Andropov went on to become the leader of the Soviet Union. In June 1989 Kryuchkov did everything in his power to prevent the rehabilitation of Imre Nagy by sending a dossier of incriminating KGB documents, both genuine and bogus, to Soviet General Secretary Mikhail Gorbachev.[†]

Kryuchkov was a leading member of the August 1991 coup that temporarily ousted Gorbachev from power, leading to Boris Yeltsin's dramatic if not always coherent defence of democracy, and the eventual dissolution of the USSR itself.

Before Serov returned from Budapest to Moscow, he relived his glory days with SMERSH in Poland and East Germany at the end of WWII: he set about organising a new internal security organisation for Hungary and left recommendations for the reorganisation of the police force.

---

† On Friday 16 June 1989, several hundred thousand Hungarians gathered in Heroes' Square in Budapest to witness the ceremonial reburial of Nagy and several other leaders of the 1956 revolt who had been tried and executed in 1958.

11

BERLIN 1956

Berlin was important to Serov. He had spent two fruitful years there, leading his SMERSH team, at the end of WWII. He had, among many other things, established the East German secret police: the Stasi. Now, in the mid-1950s, Berlin was the hub of the espionage world and a politico–military gunpowder keg in East–West relations. It was natural for him to consult regularly there with Lieutenant-General Yevgeny Pitovaranov, the head of the large KGB unit at Karlshorst. He also needed to liaise with the Stasi's brilliant Markus Wolf.

The existence of the Berlin tunnel must have perplexed Serov. The thought of all those secrets about Soviet military strength, disposition and strategies being picked up by the West was ideologically repellent to him. His Stalinist inclination was to destroy the tunnel at the earliest possible moment and use its existence as an excuse to take some kind of revenge on the Americans. (Although the Soviets knew about the British involvement in the tunnel they chose to ignore it.) He knew, also, that Khrushchev wanted the tunnel to be discovered and a big song-and-dance made about it. The 'Secret Speech' had weakened Khrushchev in the eyes of the satellite countries and he needed a moral or political victory over the West, or at least the perception of one.

At the same time, Serov was well aware of the need to protect Blake. He had demonstrated this from the very beginning when, in September 1953, he purposefully withheld from the Soviet Defence Minister details about the Vienna tunnels that Blake had given to Kondrashev. But Blake was now in West Berlin, where his work was not even remotely connected with the tunnel. It was highly unlikely, therefore, that its 'discovery' would light a path to Blake's doorstep.

Sergei Kondrashev – Blake's controller in London – had returned to Moscow and was now serving as head of the German section of the Counterintelligence Department of the KGB, which gave him responsibility for the tunnel. He urged Serov to be patient until they could concoct a suitable circumstance that would not cause suspicion.

That moment came in the spring of 1956. The end of the winter had been particularly wet and the rising water table was damaging some of the telephone cables, underground junction boxes and repeater stations.

A few months earlier, Serov had sent a team of communications technical specialists to Karlshorst with the underlying purpose of 'finding' the tunnel and dealing with its contents when the time was ripe. They were under the leadership of Vadim Goncharev who gave orders to tighten the communications security of Soviet forces in Berlin, including the inspection of cables. He was not told specifically about the tunnel, but part of his brief was to check for possible tapping of cables. Goncharev and his team worked diligently throughout the late winter and eventually discovered the existence of the tunnel. He told the KGB's General Pitovaranov – who already knew about the tunnel, the taps and the need to protect Blake – and Pitovaranov instructed him not to take any action without direct orders from Moscow.

‡

The store complex that housed the beginning of the tunnel incorporated an observation room from which there were continuous day and night watches along the busy Schönefelder Chaussee to the spot directly above the tap chamber.

Shortly after midnight on the night of 21/22 April 1956 the

duty officer saw some trucks stopping near the tap area, and disgorging nearly fifty men. It was Goncharev's team, though only Goncharev knew what they would find. It would look much better if the team, led by Captain Bartash, showed natural incredulity over the discovery.

Bill Harvey was the first to be called. He pulled on some clothes, called Hugh Montgomery – who would be needed as an interpreter – and rushed to Rudow to take control of the unfolding events.

Montgomery listened in to telephone conversations on the tapped lines to detect any evidence that the taps had been discovered. He also listened to the noises, and eventually the voices, picked up by the microphone in the tap chamber.

For a variety of reasons, it took an eternity for the Soviet team – now helped by East German engineers – to understand the enormity of what they had found. At first they thought they were simply looking for a fault caused by flooded cables. The cables, assumed at first to be standard equipment reaching down to relay equipment, aroused no initial suspicion. When it became clear that the cables were tapped, work ceased as engineers awaited orders based on this discovery. When orders were sent to remove the taps, it was natural to assume they might have been booby-trapped, thus work proceeded gingerly as the crew made the first hole in the frame of the tap chamber, uncovering the door leading to the pre-amplification chamber. So strong was this door that it necessitated an attack on the neighbouring wall with drills and pickaxes to break into the room. Only when that hole was large enough to allow a person through did they discover the tunnel that led all the way to the American sector.

In all, Captain Bartash and his men took fourteen hours to get to the tunnel from the time the trucks originally arrived in Schönefelder Chaussee. As they progressed to the tap chamber, into the pre-amplifier chamber and eventually into the tunnel, Harvey and Montgomery listened to the exclamations of astonishment picked up by the microphone which, surprisingly, the Soviets failed to disconnect until the exercise was all but complete.

At one point Harvey sent a message to General Charles Dasher, the US commander in Berlin, asking for permission to detonate charges that had been laid in the tunnel. The answer was negative, on the grounds that if any Soviets were killed 'it could start World War III'. Instead, a three-quarter height wall of sandbags was built at the border point between the American and Soviet sectors and a handwritten notice placed on it saying – in German and Russian – 'You are now entering the American Sector'. Harvey sat behind this wall with an unloaded heavy machine gun (again, to reduce the risk of casualties and retribution). When the first of the Soviets ventured along the tunnel, Harvey pulled the bolt noisily and the Soviets retreated.

‡

Although the team working under Captain Bartash did not know what to expect when they started to investigate the 'flooded cables', KGB leader General Pitovaranov back in Karlshorst *did* know and had made appropriate preparations. Shortly after the operation got under way he sent a photographer to record everything as it happened.

The CIA assumed the Soviets would not wish to publicise the West's espionage prowess as manifested by the tunnel. They were quite mistaken. A few hours after the discovery of the tunnel, the Soviet Ambassador in East Berlin delivered a strongly worded protest to the Americans.

Two days later, the Soviets invited the world press to inspect and photograph the site so that they could report on the devious treachery of the Americans. In spite of ample evidence – such as the manufacturers' name plates – that most of the equipment in the tunnel was British, the Soviets never once mentioned British involvement. This was, in all probability, because Khrushchev and Bulganin were on an enjoyable and successful visit to the United Kingdom at the time the tunnel was discovered.

Unfortunately for the Soviet and East German authorities, the Western media did not see the tunnel as an insulting act of espionage but hailed it as an outrageously brilliant and successful US project. The British government was happy to keep a low profile, allowing the Americans to handle the propaganda aspects and to take all of the glory and any brickbats that came out of it. Peter Lunn did, however, call the whole of his MI6 West Berlin station staff together, told them about the part the British had played, and said how proud he was about this successful joint venture with the Americans.

There was massive television coverage and front page headlines throughout the world, as East and West exchanged claim and counterclaim in a noisy propaganda battle.

Behind the scenes there was considerable embarrassment and annoyance on the Allied side that the tunnel had been discovered. Bill Harvey was beside himself with anger for weeks.

After the best joint efforts of the world's pre-eminent Western intelligence agencies, the tapping of Soviet communications had remained operative for eleven months and eleven days. Impressive as the technical 'triumphs' involved must have seemed, they had not proven durable.

The KGB had been clever with their timing of the 'discovery' (and were also fortunate that there had been so much rain at the time). The Americans and the British set up a commission to study why the cable had been discovered and concluded, unanimously, that it was a technical fault in the line caused by the heavy rain. Sabotage – and thus Blake – was never suspected.

Blake passed all of this and much more to Kondrashev in Moscow through dead-letter drops and direct contact with several agents during his now frequent trips into East Berlin. Throughout his four years in Berlin he passed so many secrets to the KGB that he virtually destroyed the effectiveness of MI6's activities in Eastern Europe during that time.

It was he who, in 1959, exposed Pyotr Semyonovich Popov as a CIA informant from within the GRU. Popov was executed by the Soviets in 1960.

For all the pros and cons of the Western Allies successfully tapping the communications lines, and of the calculated Soviets response not to prevent it, it is perhaps fitting that neither side appears to have benefited or suffered unduly by the existence of the tunnel. Most of the 40,000 hours of recorded voice transmissions were composed mostly of dreary office gossip with occasional juicy allegations of infidelity among the army officer classes. The 6 million hours of telegraphic and coded signals were certainly classified confidential or secret. They contained some useful but limited information about Soviet orders of battle, force dispositions and the latest developments in Soviet atomic research. Ultimately, however, none of this turned out to be of great strategic importance, in part because of the delays inherent to processing such an immense volume of information. The processing, indeed, was not completed until two years after the tunnel's exposure. There was no evidence of any serious attempt by the Soviets to plant disinformation through the taps.

However, the existence and planned discovery of the tunnel undoubtedly brought espionage to the front line of the Cold War battlefield. In the end, it would be the outcome of the espionage battles that proved decisive in preventing nuclear war and ending the Cold War.

It is likely that both Khrushchev and Serov were frustrated by the outcome of the 'discovery' of the tunnel. It had not been the out-and-out propaganda success for which they had hoped. Khrushchev chose not to mention it in his memoirs. Serov was hurt by the CIA's gloating over their success in tapping secret Soviet communications for nearly a year. It was another step along the way to his hatred of America as the warmongering, capitalist enemy of the people.

12

MOSCOW 1957

Penkovsky was put on the GRU reserve list after returning from Ankara. He was given a series of temporary assignments during 1957 and most of 1958. His close friend Marshal Varentsov had promised to intercede on his behalf to get him out of the GRU and into a regular regimental command in the artillery, but this came to nothing.

It was a peculiar and frustrating interlude in Penkovsky's life. He still felt committed to helping the West understand and deal with Khrushchev's exaggerated claims of Soviet superiority in nuclear military capacity, but some of his earlier passion and urgency had drained away. Perhaps the result of the Savchenko and Ionchenko affair had taken the wind out of his sails. Or perhaps his remoteness from involvement with day-to-day work that could have an impact on world events simply led to a temporary loss of interest.

In any case, he did not make any serious attempt to contact British, American or any other Western officials during this time. What could he say to them? 'I really want to help you but at the moment I'm twiddling my thumbs in backwater offices.' That only devalued him, in Western eyes, as a source of intelligence. Penkovsky bided his time.

‡

Khrushchev's Secret Speech and the Hungarian Revolution had weakened his hold on power. There was open criticism of the soft line he had taken with Poland, Hungary and other satellite countries. The proposals he made in February 1957 to abolish national economic ministries and replace them with regional economic councils also attracted strong opposition in certain quarters. Throughout the spring and early summer his behaviour became erratic and some senior politicians began to question his ability to rule.

The canny Serov, recognising what might be afoot, had started to spy on Politburo members from early spring and warned Khrushchev of the burgeoning dissatisfaction with him.

In June, a group of Khrushchev's critics (Malenkov, Molotov, Bulganin, Shepilov, Voroshilov, Kaganovich, Saburov and Pervukhin) attempted a coup, with Malenkov taking the lead. These eight represented a majority of the Politburo's full membership of fifteen, and it was normal practice for politicians outvoted in the Politburo to resign even though, constitution-ally, Politburo decisions were subject to endorsement by the Central Committee. Khrushchev enjoyed support from Minister of Defence Marshal Zhukov and Serov, and also from Suslov, Mikoyan, Kirichenko, Brezhnev and Furtseva.

On 19 April, a majority of the Politburo voted for Khrushchev to leave office but he stubbornly refused to resign, calling for a special meeting of the Central Committee the next day.

Overnight, the military and the KGB marshalled their resources to fly and drive Central Committee members who supported Khrushchev – most of them, as he had appointed them to their positions in the first place – from all parts of the Soviet Union to Moscow for the crucial vote. Khrushchev had a comfortable majority and was able to continue to govern as First Secretary of the Central Committee of the Communist Party and Chairman of the Council of Ministers.

In the final event, the logistical efforts of the military and the KGB saved Khrushchev.

In 1953, Serov had played a leading part in organising support for Khrushchev in his battle to succeed Stalin. Now he had galvanised support to keep him in power. In both cases one could claim that, at the outset, the odds were against Khrushchev winning. Why did Serov join and stay in Khrushchev's camp? True, they had known each other for a long time, but they were not particularly close friends and they certainly had their differences. Serov had been badly shaken by Khrushchev's Secret Speech. Khrushchev had been unhappy with Serov over the killing of diver Commander Crabb during the visit to the United Kingdom, and the overzealous way in which he had put down the Hungarian uprising. Perhaps the shrewd Serov simply knew how to pick a winner.

✝
✝

Serov was working as hard as ever. His main priority was to improve the capability of the KGB 'Illegals' throughout the world, and particularly in America.

Unlike Western intelligence agencies that relied on 'turning' regular residents in foreign countries, the Soviet Union groomed its own citizens sometimes for several years, before sending them on long-term assignments to foreign countries where they lived illegally on false documents and spied for their masters.

13

MOSCOW 1958

Something of a break came for Penkovsky, at last, in September 1958. He was assigned to a course of the General Staff for the study of new technology. It was a high-grade, nine-month course at the Dzerzhinsky Military Artillery Engineering Academy, which specialised in rocket artillery. The students were trained in the use of rocket propelled weapons. Some were trained specifically as engineers to service the rockets on their testing pads prior to launching.

His initial disappointment on being assigned to a course rather than to active duty soon evaporated when he realised that this was the perfect opportunity to acquire up-to-date intelligence about Soviet weaponry to pass to the West.

‡

The deteriorating reputation of the KGB as a highly visible and unforgiving force did not sit comfortably with Khrushchev's desire to portray a friendlier and more accommodating image of the Soviet Union to the outside world. The manner in which Serov had taken the Hungarian situation by the scruff of the neck and meted out the strongest possible retributions had damaged the Soviet Union's global standing. It would not be possible to change the KGB's image while Serov remained its chairman.

First Deputy Premier Anastas Mikoyan suggested to Khrushchev that Serov should go. At first Khrushchev rejected the idea, both out of loyalty towards Serov for his support over the years, and because there was no obvious vacancy for him to fill.

At the same time, Khrushchev was preoccupied with the career of Georgy Zhukov who had supported him in the 1957 attempted coup. He had sacked him as Defence Minister just a few months later due to serious policy differences, and Khrushchev now feared Zhukov might lead an attempt to oust him. Sergei Shtemenko, the chief executive of the GRU, was a close associate of Zhukov. In December 1958, Khrushchev decided to remove Shtemenko – thus weakening Zhukov's position – and appoint Serov as his replacement.

14

CUBA 1958

Fulgencio Batista assumed leadership of a five-member Cuban presidency in 1933 following a successful coup. He continued in that position until 1940, when he was elected to the new office of President in his own right. He did not stand for re-election in 1944 but went, instead, to live in the United States, claiming to 'feel safer' there. This was unsurprising, as his immediate predecessor and successor as President, Dr Ramon Grau San Martin, had first held the office prior to Batista's coup, and been ejected from it unceremoniously barely three months later. Remaining active in Cuban politics, however, Batista was elected to the Senate in absentia in 1948. In a suicidal failure of judgement, President Grau granted Batista permission to return to Cuba in 1952. Batista, reverting to form, showed his gratitude by overthrowing Grau again. He was quick to establish himself not merely as President, but as a right-wing dictator with absolute power and above the rule of law.

During Batista's time in America he met Meyer Lansky, a leading member of the Jewish Mafia who held interests in casinos across the length and breadth of the United States. The two became close friends and business associates and agreed that if Batista returned to the Cuban presidency, Lansky and the Mafia could have control of the gambling industry in return for paying substantial kickbacks to Batista.

In 1946 Lansky organised a meeting in Havana of Mafia leaders from all over the United States and sold them the idea of investing heavily in the city. He argued it was a prime potential market, rampant as it was already with gambling, prostitution, extortion and drug trafficking, much of it opportunistic and disorganised.

During Batista's second term as President, from 1952 onwards, he duly encouraged investment in race tracks, hotels and casinos, and the Mafia moved in, led by Lansky, Frank Costello, Joe 'Bananas' Bonanno, Salvatore 'Sam' Giancana, Santo Trafficante (Jr), 'Lucky' Luciano and others.

✝

Fidel and Raúl Castro, Che Guevara (an Argentinian Communist) and about eighty other members of the Cuban rebel '26th of July Movement' sailed from exile in Mexico and arrived in a remote part of south-eastern Cuba on 2 December 1956 in the yacht '*Granma*'. They were attacked by Batista's army and only twenty of them survived to disperse into the inhospitable and virtually unpopulated Sierra Maestra Mountains. For the next year they built up and trained a small rebel guerrilla army comprised mostly of guajiros dissatisfied with their lot under Batista.

Guajiros were the peasants of Sierra Maestra. For most of the year, they scraped a bare subsistence living on land that did not belong to them, or in the small villages. They were illiterate and of black, white and mixed origins. In November each year many of them went to help with sugar cane harvesting to earn a miserable but nonetheless welcome supplementary income.

The poverty of these people, coupled with the remoteness and physical attributes of the territory, made the Sierra Maestra an ideal spawning ground for the revolution.

Che Guevara, the master of propaganda and motivation, took a number of initiatives to show the guajiros how the 26th of July Movement was committed to improving the lives of people like themselves. He built a small hospital, a school, an oven to bake bread enough for hundreds of people, a communal farm with chickens and pigs, another to grow vegetables, and even a small cigar factory to add value to the tiny tobacco crops grown by some guajiros. The last of these may have been inspired more by Fidel Castro than Guevara. The clandestine radio station, *Radio Rebelde* (Rebel Radio), was also one of Guevara's ideas. These activities were crucial in the campaign to convert guajiros to join the rebel cause.

There were occasional skirmishes with ill-disciplined Batista soldiers, but in most cases the rebels came out on top. Although Che Guevara was a self-confessed Communist, Fidel Castro insisted that the 26th of July Movement was a socialist organisation and definitely *not* Communist.

Castro's rebels were not alone in wanting to oust Batista. On 13 March 1957, the anti-Communist 'Revolutionary Directorate' (RD) attacked the Presidential Palace in Havana and tried to kill Batista. It was a desperate, foolhardy venture doomed to failure. The RD assault group was mostly made up of students. Many of them, including their leader, died in the fighting.

The United States government took note of the growing dissatisfaction of Cubans with Batista's corrupt, autocratic and brutal rule. It recalled its ambassador and imposed an economic embargo on Cuba.

Castro's rebels started to grow more confident about their chances of succeeding in overthrowing Batista. Although their numbers were still small – possibly numbering only 300 to 400 – they started to attack small Batista garrisons, first in the Sierra Maestra, later venturing into more populated areas. Large parts of the mountainous area of south-eastern Cuba soon fell under Castro's control.

Many United States businesses, and the Mafia, continued to support Batista. However, Santo Trafficante – one of the Mafia godfathers – also took note of the growing popular dissatisfaction with Batista and widespread support for Castro. He decided it would be wise to hedge his bets.

Trafficante was born in Tampa, Florida, on 15 November 1914. His father (also Santo) together with other Mafia leaders set up gambling operations in Cuba in the 1940s and he sent his son to Cuba to manage these in 1953. Santo Jr took full control of these operations after his father died in 1954.

Early in 1958, Trafficante sent a trusted messenger to find Fidel Castro in his secret location in the Sierra Maestra. He was to convey Trafficante's support and best wishes to Castro and to offer him a US$250,000 contribution towards the running costs of the rebel army, with a promise of further payments. Castro, always short of money, gladly accepted. This financial support helped the rebels to commence their advance towards Havana, gaining new recruits and support in rural areas before taking larger towns.

On 14 March 1958, the United States added an arms embargo to the economic embargo that they had imposed on Cuba almost a year earlier. This had serious consequences for Batista's forces, particularly the Air Force, as they were unable to replace or repair aircraft and weapons.

Castro's progress came to a shuddering halt at the end of July 1958 when a determined assault by Batista's troops almost destroyed the rebel army of some 300 men. They were surrounded and a ceasefire was called on 1 August to negotiate terms of surrender. The negotiations continued for a week, during which time Castro's men slipped quietly away between groups of the surrounding forces and escaped into the mountains.

A regrouped force of Castro's rebels launched an offensive on 21 August. They soon scored victories in villages and towns where the local populace were quick to give their support. Other groups, including the RD – now calling themselves the '13th of March Movement' – were also on the march.

The decisive Battle of Santa Clara took place on 31 December 1958. All of the groups who had been fighting in various parts of the country were involved, which caused some confusion but did not affect the outcome of victory for the rebels. They overran

Santa Clara, the capital city of Las Villas province and, led by Guevara, started the advance towards Havana.

Batista now feared the worst. He fled to the Dominican Republic with many of his associates by plane during the early hours of the morning of 1 January, taking with him his ill-gotten fortune, said to be about US$300 million.

The next day, the military commander in Cuba's second largest city, Santiago de Cuba, surrendered the city to Castro's forces without a fight. Much the same happened when Che Guevara led his men into the capital, Havana.

15

CUBA 1959

On 2 January 1959 Che Guevara conquered Havana, establishing rebel control of Cuba. Fidel Castro was six days behind, rallying support in the major towns before arriving triumphantly in Havana on 8 January.

Even before he reached the capital, Castro started to govern Cuba. One of his first directives was to close down the casinos and all other activities that had been controlled by the Mafia.[†]

Meyer Lansky, the head of the Mafia's operations in Cuba, had escaped with Batista on 1 January, but Santo Trafficante stayed on, expecting favours from Castro because of his donations to the fighting fund. It was an easy mistake for a Mafia godfather to make: everyone, after all, could be bought. He was arrested by the Cuban National Police on 3 January and sent to Tiscornia Prison along with other top Mafia men who had not been as nimble as Lansky.

Trafficante had been operating the Sans Souci and the Casino International gambling establishments in Havana and also had interests in other syndicate-owned Cuban casinos. He did not look like a Mafia godfather nor, when it suited him, did he talk or act like one. At forty-four he still looked slim and healthy. His hair was beginning to recede but it remained dark and always

---

[†] The casinos reopened a few weeks later under Cuban government control, but only for the use of foreigners. They were closed again in September 1961.

well groomed. His conventional clothes were expensive. Well educated, he spoke fluent Spanish. Trafficante was a thinker, almost an intellectual, and a meticulous planner. Had he not been born into his father's Sicilian family he might have become a doctor, politician, diplomat, or the director of a successful legitimate business corporation.

He used these abilities to gain access to the prison governor, with whom he negotiated a more civilised routine than that afforded to the other prisoners. He was given a single cell and allowed to receive visitors. Soon, he was having regular meetings with his beautiful wife, Josephine, in the prison gardens. On one occasion he was permitted to leave the prison to attend his daughter's wedding in Havana.

Trafficante was under no illusions: he knew he could be tried, found guilty of giving large sums of money to Batista, and executed. It had already happened to others. Guevara was responsible for the trial of senior military personnel in Batista's armed forces and ordered hundreds of them executed. In non-military courts, pimps, thieves, drug dealers and people involved in illegal gambling operations were sentenced to long prison sentences with hard labour. There were rumours that the leaders of major illegal operations might be executed.

One of Trafficante's visitors was his lawyer, whom he instructed to contact Castro's office to see if there was any way he could be released, bearing in mind that he had contributed so generously to Castro's fighting fund.

‡

The Soviet Union had shown little interest in Cuba until Castro came to power. Now, there were opportunities to do business with a country right on America's doorstep. But there was a problem: Fidel Castro still insisted his government was not Communist. Castro's foreign policy was that of a non-aligned nation.

On 12 June, Castro sent Guevara on a three-month tour of

fourteen countries. They were mostly countries that had attended the Bandung Conference in 1955; nations such as Morocco, Egypt, Pakistan and Burma. The aims of that conference had been to promote Afro-Asian economic and cultural coopera-tion and to oppose colonialism or neo-colonialism, whether by the United States, the Soviet Union or any other imperialistic nation. He would also be visiting Yugoslavia and Greece, but not the Soviet Union.

Castro saw the Soviet Union as a nation that dominated and oppressed the other Communist countries in Eastern Europe and was itself a forced union of republics that should have retained their own independence. On the other hand, he had no illusions about the dangers of Cuba's proximity to the United States and its distance from other friendly Communist and non-aligned countries. He had to be pragmatic. He knew he would have to come to some sort of an accommodation with the Soviet Union in the short term, until Cuba had the international stature and economic capability to stand on its own feet.

Castro had another motive for sending Guevara on the lengthy tour of foreign countries: it gave him the opportunity to press ahead with some aspects of internal policy on which they did not agree. Castro did not support the manner in which Guevara summarily meted out heavy punishment to people found guilty of working for the Batista regime. Many of these people would have been prepared to work equally hard for the new Castro government, but they were not given the chance. Castro thought Guevara was interpreting some of Karl Marx's teachings much too harshly, in much the same way that Stalin had. Stalinism was an abomination to him and he did not want it to have any part in Cuba.

‡

According to an article in the *Miami News* dated 8 June 1959, the government of Cuba approved the expulsion of Santo

Trafficante as an undesirable alien. This action may have been taken on direct orders from Castro, who was taking advantage of Guevara's preoccupation with his long overseas trip. Guevara would have wanted to punish Trafficante, possibly even execute him.

In the light of subsequent events, Trafficante's release might well have been conditional upon him spying for Castro. Castro would have been keen to gather intelligence on the United States' policy towards Cuba, possible military action against his government, and about any plans to kill or capture him. Trafficante would have been well placed, with his position in the Mafia, to spy for Castro. However, there would be no doubt about his fate should any of the other godfathers discover his treachery.

After his expulsion, Trafficante returned to Tampa, Florida, where he had interests in the Columbia Restaurant, the Nebraska, Tangerine and Sands Bars. He quickly resumed contact with his Mafia associates and befriended leaders of the Cuban exile community who were plotting to overthrow Castro and take back their 'nationalised' casinos.

16

MOSCOW 1959

Serov's move to the GRU, arriving there in January 1959, was seen as a demotion. The GRU was smaller than the KGB and in many respects subordinate to it. Both organisations were directed by the Central Committee and both of them carried out similar intelligence activities against military, political, economic and scientific targets in foreign countries. Both organisations also perpetrated acts of sabotage, terrorism, provocation and blackmail, and both were engaged in disseminating propaganda. The two main differences were that the GRU concentrated on collecting *military* intelligence in Western countries, while only the KGB had a mandate to spy on Soviet citizens *within* the Soviet Union.

As chairman of the KGB, Serov had held ministerial rank, but his new post as chief executive of the GRU made him a deputy chief of the General Staff, a lower status post than that of minister.

In spite of the rivalry between the two organisations, and the discomfiture of his own demotion, Serov was generally well accepted by GRU personnel. He brought with him the reputation of a man who worked hard, was fair to his staff and had considerable clout. He also retained respect, and even continued support, from his former colleagues and friends in the KGB. After his appointment to the GRU there was a noticeable improvement in the turnaround time for answers to enquiries the GRU had addressed to the KGB.

Perhaps surprisingly, Serov did not interfere to any great

extent with the normal chain of command. His deputies, Major-General Rogov and Major-General Mamsurov, respectively managed the day-to-day executive work of the organisation, and its general administration. Serov studied the most important intelligence reports that arrived on his desk, made decisions on where to place emphasis and resources, reported to, and received instructions from, the Politburo.

Oleg Penkovsky, the consummate professional intelligence officer, did not give Serov high marks for his ability as an intelligence officer. He described him, in 1961, as: 'not the most brilliant of men. He knows how to interrogate people, imprison them and shoot them. In more sophisticated intelligence work he is not so skilful.'[†]

✝

Penkovsky made the most of every day he spent on the advanced rocketry course at the Dzerzhinsky Military Artillery Engineering Academy. He had already decided to work for the West and was determined to bring something valuable from the course. It was mentally taxing, owing not to the high degree of technical detail associated with modern rocketry, but because he recorded all of it by hand, against the day he would start talking to the West.

The course started with the basic concepts of fuel and propulsion of free direction rockets before going on to guidance systems and then the different types of launching equipment.

With his seniority, his position in the GRU (known only to the course administrator) and his intellectual ability, he occupied a privileged position in his class of eighty students. He possessed a certain amount of authority which gave him the opportunity to study books and classified lecture papers from the secure classified library. He also had the opportunity to work independently. In the evenings he would go into the

---

[†]   See Oleg Penkovsky, 'Chapter 2', *The Penkovsky Papers* (London: Collins, 1965).

library and block the door by placing a chair-back under the handle while he laboriously copied full details into a notebook. On the rare occasions when anyone rattled the door handle he would quickly put his notebook into his briefcase and explain that he just wanted to study in silence.

Penkovsky graduated from the course, top of his class, on 1 May 1959, but he was not awarded a regimental command. He was assigned to the Fourth Directorate of the GRU, which dealt with Asia. He had already worked in this directorate, from 1953 to 1955, in his first active appointment in the GRU following initial schooling at the Military Diplomatic Academy.

Serov had followed his progress – just as Khrushchev had suggested – and, in the autumn of 1959, he called him in for a discussion about his future.

Serov was now 53. His hairline had been receding for the past twenty years, but his remaining hair was still naturally dark, and his encroaching forehead did not detract significantly from a pleasant, if slightly mousey, face that could express contentment without actually smiling. He did nothing to keep himself fit, yet he looked to be in good shape. This appearance complemented his always impeccable and expensive clothes. He was, by all accounts, a devoted family man. Only his steely grey-blue eyes gave any hint about the dark side of his nature and history.

Looking at him, Penkovsky wondered how this could possibly be the man who bore responsibility for the deaths of hundreds of thousands of peasants and other workers; the man who had ordered mass deportations from the Baltic States to Siberia; who was responsible almost single-handedly for enforcing the overthrow of the new Communist Hungarian government in 1956, killing hundreds of its supporters and deporting thousands of sympathetic youths; who still thought the best way to reach a Communist utopia was through the Stalinist methods of fear and suppression, and severely punishing – even with death – those who showed dissent.

Serov congratulated Penkovsky on graduating from the course

with distinction. He then moved on to recall how Penkovsky had blotted his copy-book in Ankara. Perhaps he told him that First Secretary Khrushchev saw an amusing side to that incident, but also saw merit in his courage to report it the way he did.

Finally, Serov told Penkovsky that in spite of how things ended in Ankara he had done a good job and, on the basis of that, he was to have a second chance at working overseas. This time he would go to India – to the Soviet Embassy in New Delhi – as military attaché.

Although New Delhi was a far more strategically significant post than Ankara, Penkovsky would not be promoted on taking up duty, but there was a possibility – Serov told him – that he would be considered for promotion after he had been there for a while.

Penkovsky was delighted with this unexpected news of his posting to India, but naturally disappointed with his standstill status. India was important to the Soviet Union. It declared itself to be neutral and therefore a place that the Soviets wished to cultivate. Strategically, it was exceptionally important and they aimed to conduct operations there in due course, perhaps by selling or giving them rocket-borne weapons. Penkovsky's knowledge of such arms would be an asset.

Pleased as he was about the posting, he nevertheless harboured a vexed conscience about helping the Soviet Union to promote military strategies against the West. It could, he thought, only increase tensions and bring the world ever closer to nuclear annihilation.

He put these thoughts to one side and entered into his training and briefing for the new post with enthusiasm.

‡

Lee Harvey Oswald was determined to make a success of this part of his life. He did not know how many different places he had lived in with his mother, but he was able to count twelve different schools before he left the last one, at the age of seventeen, to join the US Marine Corps. The Corps had accepted him in spite of his lack of educational qualifications and his history of psychiatric treatment.

His time in the Marine Corps had certainly been better than his earlier childhood. There had been no overpowering mother, for a start, and he had enjoyed his studies, finishing in the top half of his class for aircraft surveillance and operating radar. This made him proud of himself for the first time in his life. The highlight was his tour of duty at the Naval Air Facility at Atsugi in Japan, where some CIA U-2 spy planes were based. He also enjoyed the compulsory rifle training, quickly qualifying as a *sharpshooter*, though this later fell back to *marksman* level.

But his mental fragility still let him down from time to time. On one occasion he was court-martialled for accidentally shooting himself in the arm with a pistol, and on another for fighting with his sergeant. He spent a short term in prison and was demoted to private.

Joining the Marines had been one strand of his self-rehabilitation; the other had been to espouse Communism. The capitalist society of the United States had not been kind to him. In his early teens he had picked up a book about Communism and readily accepted that that kind of organised socialism would be infinitely preferable. Since then, including his time in the Marines, he had spoken openly about his preference and belief in Communism. He was an avid reader of the Communist Party of the USA's weekly newspaper *The Worker* (the *Daily Worker* prior to 1958).

He considered his prospects after being discharged from the Marine Corps on 11 September 1959. His future in the United States as a dedicated Communist with an insecure and problematic past would be bleak and unbearable. He decided, therefore, that the best course for him would be to live in the Soviet Union. He felt confident they would make a fuss of an American citizen who preferred to live in the Soviet Union;

an American citizen who would be used by the propaganda machine to show that even Americans preferred Communism to capitalism. He knew a lot about American military radar and a little about the astonishing U-2 spy planes. The Soviet authorities would want to know about these things.

His initial research showed that it was difficult and time-consuming to apply for and be granted a visa to enter and stay in the Soviet Union. His best course would be to travel to Helsinki in Finland and apply for a five-day Soviet visitor's visa there. This he did, and it worked well.

Oswald arrived in Moscow on 16 October 1959, just two days before his twentieth birthday. He stayed at the Hotel Berlin. Within minutes of his arrival he told his Intourist guide/interpreter of his intentions and asked where he should go to start the process of applying for Soviet citizenship.[†] He applied to the Supreme Soviet. Such applications were dealt with by the secretariat of the Politburo and that body immediately passed Oswald's application to the KGB for consideration. The KGB (in the guise of OVIR, the Visa and Registration Department) called him in for an interview on 20 October. According to Colonel Oleg Nechiporenko – a retired KGB officer, writing thirty-three years after the event – the KGB were not interested in Oswald and suggested to the Politburo secretariat that his application for citizenship should be rejected. The KGB told Oswald as much the next day, adding that he would probably be told to return to the United States.[‡]

On 21 October, OVIR phoned the Hotel Berlin and left a message for Oswald, asking him to attend a meeting with them at three o'clock that afternoon. At 12 noon, the hotel informed Oswald of the three o'clock meeting and told him that a train

---

[†]   Intourist was the official state travel agency of the Soviet Union, responsible for foreigners' access to, and travel within, the Soviet Union. The guides and interpreters reported directly to the KGB.

[‡]   See Oleg Nechiporenko, 'Chapter 1', *Passport to Assassination* (Carol Publishing Group, 1993). Translated from Russian by Todd P. Bludeau.

ticket to Helsinki had already been ordered for him, so he was clearly being sent back to America. He said he would be down in the vestibule at 2.45 p.m.

When Oswald did not appear, his translator went up to his room and found it locked from the inside. He got the hotel to open the door with a pass key and found Oswald lying unconscious in the bath. He had slashed his wrist, but his attempt at suicide – if, indeed, he had tried to kill himself – was unsuccessful.

Recovering in hospital, Oswald said he would again attempt to commit suicide if his application to stay in the Soviet Union were rejected.

Intourist had a responsibility for the safety of all foreign tourists, and that included Oswald. They were worried about him, not least because they had no idea how to deal with his breakdown, and Soviet psychiatry was more a pseudo-scientific rationale for declaring dissidents schizophrenic than any kind of medicine. Then, on 22 October, the head of Intourist wrote similar letters to the KGB, the Ministry of Foreign Affairs and the Central Committee of the Communist Party asking each of them to accept responsibility for Oswald.

Oswald had made no attempt to contact the American Embassy since his arrival in Moscow, which was unusual to say the least. However, Intourist, or the hospital, or a mysterious American in the same ward as Oswald informed the embassy of his presence in the Soviet Union and the consular section of the embassy contacted him, suggesting that he pay them a visit.

On 28 October, he left hospital and went to stay at the Metropol Hotel. The next day, he had a meeting with the head of OVIR and once again asked to remain in the Soviet Union and become a Soviet citizen. The head of OVIR told him no conclusion had yet been reached and that he could stay in Moscow pending a decision.

On 31 October he went to the American Consulate, determined to burn his bridges with the United States, thereby making it more difficult for the Soviets to expel him. He handed in his passport and said he wished to renounce his United States citizenship. The Consul agreed to take his passport but said he could not accept a formal renunciation of US citizenship until he had proof from the Soviet authorities that he would be granted Soviet citizenship. The Consulate could not, he explained, leave him stateless.

Oswald spent most of the following two weeks in his hotel room, largely to avoid Western reporters who had heard about him from the American Consul. He passed his time by studying Russian.

On 12 November, the head of Intourist, alarmed at the thought of what the Western media might publish about Oswald's treatment, wrote directly to Anastas Mikoyan, the Deputy Chairman of the Council of Ministers. Mikoyan consulted the Ministry of Foreign Affairs and the KGB and, between them, they came up with a proposal that they put to the party's Central Committee. The Central Committee approved the following resolution:

> In regard to the petition by the American citizen Lee Harvey Oswald for Soviet citizenship, let it hereby be resolved:
>
> To agree with the proposal of the Ministry of Foreign Affairs and the KGB to grant US citizen Lee Harvey Oswald temporary resident status for one year and to resolve the questions of his permanent residency in the USSR and Soviet citizenship during this period.
>
> To oblige the Belorussian National Economic Council to place Oswald in a job in electronics, and the Minsk City Council of Workers' Deputies to assign him his own small apartment.
>
> To instruct the executive committee of the Societies of the Red Cross and the Red Crescent to assign five thousand roubles for equipping the apartment for Oswald and to issue him an allowance of seven hundred roubles a month over the course of one year.[†]

---

†   See Oleg Nechiporenko, 'Chapter 1', *Passport to Assassination* (Carol Publishing Group, 1993). Translated from Russian by Todd P. Bludeau.

Was this a question of 'get him out of Moscow and away from the limelight and let's hope he'll want to return to the United States', or was it a solution that would enable the KGB to take a more considered view of Oswald's potential usefulness and perhaps groom him to work on their behalf?

17

MIAMI 1960

The introduction of Marxist–Leninist social and political reform was bringing about major changes in Cuba just a year after Fidel Castro came to power. The new government was becoming well established and the changes were accepted by the mass of the population in the hope – as they had been promised – of better things to come.

Castro had not wanted to be reliant upon the Soviet Union but economic sanctions imposed by the United States forced his hand, particularly with regard to importing oil from, and exporting sugar to, America. The Soviet Union readily stepped in to supply oil and to accept a quota of sugar. When the established oil companies in Cuba, such as Esso, Shell and Texaco, refused to refine Soviet oil, they were nationalised. The banks, the telephone company and virtually all of the tobacco industry, including the prestigious cigar companies, also became corporate wards of the state. Militant opposition was dealt with severely, with many opponents of the regime executed and others hunted down and imprisoned.

Many individuals, however, were convinced that Communism would not bring peace and prosperity. Those in the professions, along with other middle-class and upper-class Cubans left the island in their tens of thousands to settle mainly in Florida, but with a diaspora spreading out across the United States.

In Florida there was soon a ground-swell of feeling among the exiles that they should take action to overthrow the Castro government. They did not want the return of Batista, but rather a new democratic capitalist government without the corruption that had been endemic to Batista's regime.

In the early months of 1960, with the help of the CIA, Cuban expatriates flew missions over Cuba, dropping incendiary bombs onto sugar-cane fields and storage buildings and perpetuating other acts of sabotage. Several of the planes were shot down, or crashed due to mechanical failure. The dead pilot of one of the crashed planes was found to be an American.

It was in this climate, with the additional worry of the Soviet Union's increasing influence over Cuba, that in March 1960 America's President Eisenhower approved 'a programme of covert action against the Castro regime'.

The first objective of the programme was to bring about the replacement of the Castro regime with one more devoted – in the eyes of America – to the true interests of the Cuban people and more acceptable to the United States. It was to be planned and executed in such a way that the United States government would be able to deny any participation in it. '*Plausible deniability*' was the popular terminology in the CIA and other secret government circles. The programme confirmed the economic sanctions regarding sugar and oil exports, and authorised a budget for an extensive propaganda campaign. It included help for the Cuban exiles to organise a paramilitary force to launch an invasion, and provision to create a covert intelligence and subversive organisation within Cuba.

President Eisenhower passed political responsibility for the programme to his deputy, Richard Nixon. The CIA was responsible for implementation and its director, Allen Dulles, created a special unit for this purpose. Individual projects under the programme were executed by a group called *Operation 40*, which comprised forty experienced agents, soldiers of fortune and exiled Cuban soldiers. *Operation 40* was also known as the Cuban Task Force, and was described by one of its more celebrated members, Frank Sturgis, as an assassination squad. Bill Harvey and Ted Shackley (both Berlin tunnel veterans) had senior administrative roles in *Operation 40*.

There is still conjecture about the status of *Operation 40*. Was it a properly established, government authorised and funded operation, or was it a right-wing anti-Castro organisation funded by businessmen who had lost out in Cuba and wanted to see it returned to capitalism? Richard Nixon represented the government in it, but many claim that it was mainly funded by oil businessmen George Bush (Sr) and Jack Crichton, and that Bush was the driving force behind it.[†]

Within two months *Radio Swan* had been created to broadcast anti-Castro propaganda to Cuba. This station was one of the more successful ventures under the plan, though some of the propaganda broadcast over it was of the naive scaremongering variety usually associated with Communist hyperbole. Those in Cuba who listened to *Radio Swan* were warned, for example, that their children would be taken away from them and educated in state-run educational institutions where they would be indoctrinated with Communist ideas. Many feared for their children's future and sent them, unaccompanied, to Florida where individuals, churches and other charities found them foster families. This mass emigration – some might say evacuation – reached a total of nearly 15,000 children and has become known as Operation *Pedro Pan* (*Peter Pan*). Operation *Pedro Pan* was underpinned by the CIA.

The CIA agency also sought to bring some measure of coherence to the hundreds of anti-Castro Cuban exile groups, based mainly in Miami, aiming to coordinate their activities and, where feasible, to merge them in advance of organising a force to invade Cuba. By the end of June 1960, five of the main groups formed the *Frente Revlucionario Democrático* (Revolutionary Democratic Front), or FRD, which had direct links with the CIA.

With the help of the CIA, the FRD organised sporadic small

[†]   George H. W. Bush later became President of the USA (1989–93).

incursions into Cuba, most of which ended in failure, sometimes with disastrous results. In late September, for example, four boat-loads of exiles and anti-Castro Americans left from Miami with the intention of landing in Cuba and causing chaos through acts of sabotage. Only one of the boats managed to reach Cuba and the entire crew was captured. Three of them were executed.

‡

Although the gathering and transmission of intelligence was kept secret, the exiles' plans to retake Cuba soon became public knowledge, with reports of preparations for an invasion appear-ing in the press.

Perhaps surprisingly, diplomatic relations still existed between Cuba and the United States. In December 1960 the American Ambassador in Havana reported that popular support for Castro had started to drop rapidly, but this only served to increase the determination of the Cuban government to suppress opposition and build up the strength of its forces. Conventional armaments were arriving from the Soviet Union and other East European Bloc countries. 'Hispano-Soviets' (Spanish veteran officers of WWII and the Spanish Civil War who had lived in the Soviet Union since the end of those wars) had arrived to give military training. In these circumstances it was likely, advised the American Ambassador, that any invasion would lead to considerable bloodshed.

Contrary to the opinion of the American Ambassador, British intelligence indicated that Cubans were predominantly behind Castro and that there was no likelihood of mass defections or insurrections following an invasion. This intelligence was passed to the CIA.

‡

Another important project of *Operation 40* was to devise a plot to assassinate Fidel Castro. Richard Bissell, the CIA's Deputy

Director of Plans, obtained clearance from Director Allen Dulles to approach the Mafia for their assistance in organising a gangland-style hit. Castro, after all, had closed down the Mafia's lucrative gambling businesses in Cuba, making denial of the Eisenhower administration's participation perfectly plausible.

On advice from another section of the CIA, Bissell asked Robert A. Maheu to arrange a meeting with someone from the Mafia concerning 'getting rid of Castro'.[†] Maheu arranged the meeting with Johnny Roselli, one of the top Chicago mobsters who also helped to control Hollywood and the rapidly expanding Las Vegas.

During the meeting, Maheu claimed he represented a number of clients who used to have business interests in Cuba. These clients believed that if Castro could be removed, his whole government would fall and normal commercial ventures would be resumed. He put it to Roselli that many of his own friends would understand and sympathise with his position.

The suave and expensively dressed Roselli wanted this in plain English, and insisted on knowing exactly who the clients were. Maheu said he needed to take instructions from his clients, so another meeting was arranged.

At the next meeting, Roselli was accompanied by two others, who were introduced as 'Sam Gold', and 'Joe'. Maheu had been authorised to admit that his client was the CIA, but only if it were absolutely essential in order to get the Mafia's agreement, and then only with confirmation that this information would be held on a strict need-to-know basis. The offer was US$150,000 for the removal of Fidel Castro with the stipulation that, whether

---

[†] Maheu and William Harvey had been together in the FBI before both joined the CIA. Maheu soon left the CIA as a career employee to set up his own business and later worked in a senior position for the recluse industrialist Howard Hughes. Throughout this time he continued to do undercover work for the CIA. He was a friend and confidant of both John F. and Robert F. Kennedy.

successful or unsuccessful, there must be not the slightest whiff of US government or CIA involvement.

The three men agreed, laying down some of their own ground rules: they were good patriots and did not want the $150,000; the CIA would supply any goods they might need, and, the tax authorities and police would stop harassing the Mafia.

When Maheu reported back to the CIA he was shown photographs from which he identified Sam Gold as Sam Giancana, the boss of the Chicago outfit, and Joe as Santo Trafficante.

The Mafia leaders' favoured method of assassination was to poison Castro, so they asked the CIA for six poison pills which would be introduced into Castro's food by Juan Orta, Castro's personal secretary. Manuel Antonio de Varona, an associate of Santo Trafficante and now one of the leaders of the Cuban exiles in Miami, knew Orta and arranged to deliver the pills to him. However, Orta lost his nerve and fled. Another attempt to poison Castro was orchestrated by Frank Sturgis but this, too, failed.

Roselli, Giancana and Trafficante met regularly to discuss and organise various plans to kill Castro. The pills had been Giancana's idea, but most of the future ideas came from Trafficante, who was able to pass detailed warnings back to Castro.

‡

The United States Presidential election took place on 8 November 1960. Thanks to an amazing number of votes delivered suspiciously late by Mayor Richard J. Daley of Chicago, the young Democrat candidate, Senator John F. Kennedy, scraped through by the narrowest of margins over the Republican Richard Nixon. It has been widely alleged that the election was stolen by ballot-stuffing in the state of Illinois – undertaken by Mafia operatives at Daley's behest.

18

MOSCOW 1960

The New Year did not start well for Penkovsky. He was just about ready to leave for New Delhi, having completed his pre-posting training and briefing when, on 5 January 1960, the Deputy Chief of GRU Personnel, Major-General A. A. Shumsky, called him in to say his posting had been cancelled.

Shumsky told him the KGB had discovered that his father had fought for the Tsar as a 1st Lieutenant in the White Guards, and had been killed in fighting near Rostov in 1919. His grandfather had been a nobleman: a judge in Stavropol. People with such anti-revolutionary family backgrounds had an automatic question mark against their names when it came to permission to travel overseas. Shumsky acknowledged that none of this was Penkovsky's fault, but the real problem was that this information did not tally with what Penkovsky had originally said about his father, namely, that he was an engineer who had died of typhus in 1919.

When Penkovsky protested that he only recorded what his mother had told him, Shumsky suggested that he should ask his mother to provide a written statement about his father, and this she did: she wrote two pages recounting how, when she was eighteen, she met Vladimir Florianovich Penkovsky. They soon married and she became pregnant. Vladimir often disappeared for days at a time. He was called up for military service and, when Oleg was just four months old, Vladimir went away and never returned.

His mother's letter was placed in Penkovsky's file, but it was of little help. One small consolation was that the KGB had placed a note on top of the record of all of this saying 'We trust Colonel Penkovsky'. Nevertheless, the cancellation of his posting to India was final. Penkovsky was furious and this incident removed any lingering doubts he may have harboured about passing secrets to the West.

He spent nearly two months on the GRU reserve list, doing virtually nothing. Then, on 29 February, he was assigned to a senior position on the operational side.

Part of his duties was to take charge of military training, including the weekly 'Commander Day'. He conducted seminars and set examinations on new field service regulations. He also had to take his turn as duty desk officer, which entailed looking at telegrams and dealing with any emergencies that arose out of normal office hours.

He was the duty desk officer on the night of 1 May when the news arrived that an American pilot (later identified as Gary Powers) was in custody after his U-2 spy plane had been shot down. Powers was being taken to Moscow by plane and Penkovsky was asked to stand by to interrogate him as he was the only officer available who could speak English.

He immediately reported the incident to several generals who would need to know about it. Unhappily, from Penkovsky's point of view, the KGB suddenly found their own English interpreter and took Powers under KGB control. This upset Penkovsky, not only because he had narrowly failed to be the first person to interview Powers, but because the U-2 was a military plane that had been shot down by Soviet anti-aircraft weapons and the whole issue should therefore have been handled by the military GRU rather than the KGB.

Penkovsky was at first mystified that the U-2 had been brought down at all. It must have been operating at 65,000 feet and no Soviet weapons – either plane or rocket – had ever succeeded in hitting a target at that height. However, he quickly learned the true story and was later able to discuss it at his weekly 'Commander Day' class.

There had been a number of U-2 spy flights in recent months and the Soviet defence forces were expecting another anytime from 28 April onwards, because Penkovsky's successor in Ankara reported that on 26 and 27 April a U-2, a C-124 fuel transporter and a C-130 transporter had left the American Base at Incirlik in Turkey, and were seen landing at the American Base at Peshawar in Pakistan. The Soviets assumed it would fly right across the Soviet Union, taking in the missile sites on a route across the Aral Sea, Sverdlovsk and Plesetsk, before landing in Norway.[†] All of the Air Defence Units along that route were on Red Alert. The Lieutenant-General of the Air Force, Yevgeny Savitsky, was in charge of the operation. Over the previous three months he had had several Su-9s stripped of their armaments and modified so that they could fly much higher than their standard maximum of 55,000 feet, and he gave the pilots an order to ram the U-2 if they could get near it. (Penkovsky must have smiled to himself when he heard this part for he knew it would have been a futile exercise.)

The U-2 was detected on 1 May, soon after it crossed the Soviet border with Pakistan but the route it took kept it out of range of most surface-to-air missile sites. Four MiG-19s followed it all the way but there was nothing much they could do because the U-2 flew far above the maximum altitude the MiGs could reach. The spy plane reached Sverdlovsk before a battery of V-75 ground-to-air missiles launched. One of them headed for the U-2, exploding just before it reached the plane. However, the shock wave caught the U-2, causing sufficient damage to the tail and wing assembly to disable it. Powers was concussed but managed to eject. He blacked out several times on the way down.

On hearing the report from the KGB (not exactly the true report described above), Khrushchev decided to keep quiet

---

† Sverdlovsk was renamed Yekaterinburg in 1991.

about the incident and allow the Americans to confess their own violation of international law, or attempt a cover-up.

On 4 May – three days after the incident – the Americans announced that a *NASA* weather research aircraft had gone missing over northern Turkey. They said it had reported difficulties with the pilot's oxygen supply.

Khrushchev was then able to launch one of his most successful propaganda coups by condemning the American lies and announcing that the U-2 had been shot down by a Soviet surface-to-air missile. He did not say anything about the pilot.

The Americans naturally assumed that the pilot had been killed – as he most certainly would have been had the missile exploded into the aircraft – so they came up with the fanciful story that the plane may have strayed accidentally into Soviet air space if the pilot had passed out and the plane continued on automatic pilot.

On 7 May, a week after the spy plane had been brought down, Khrushchev announced that he had deliberately refrained from divulging that the pilot was alive and well. He joyfully said: 'Now, just look how many silly things the Americans have said.'

Not only was the pilot, Gary Powers, still alive but his plane was also largely intact. The Soviets recovered the surveillance camera and even developed some of the photographs. The incident resulted in great humiliation for Eisenhower's administration, caught in a lie.

While Khrushchev had a convincing propaganda victory in this U-2 incident, he was still disturbed by the fact that U-2s could fly over Soviet territory with virtual impunity. This may have triggered his dangerous reaction when another US Air Force plane was brought down just two months later.

On 1 July 1960 an American RB-47 electronic reconnaissance aircraft was following its planned route parallel to the Kola Peninsula in the Barents Sea when it was shot down by Soviet fighter planes. Only two of the six-man crew survived, having been picked up by Soviet fishing vessels. Penkovsky later confirmed to the Americans and British that the Soviets knew the American plane was in international air space, but Khrushchev nevertheless congratulated the Soviet Air Force, saying: 'Well done, boys, keep them from even flying close.'

✝

Shortly after the U-2 incident there was a programme of staff reductions within the GRU. Penkovsky managed to hold onto his job for another three months before being transferred to the Staff College of the Soviet Army in Senior Instructor grade. This college was more commonly known within the GRU as the Military-Diplomatic Academy (MDA). It was a joint GRU–KGB establishment under the administrative control of the GRU. Its foundation course was a three-year programme leading to a doctorate-level diploma in intelligence gathering and there were short mid-career, refresher and other specialised courses. The classes were run specifically for GRU, KGB, Ministry of Foreign Affairs and other staff headed for foreign assignments.

Penkovsky was disappointed at not being appointed the head of a course, which would have brought promotion to the rank of general. Initially, he was in the Mandate Commission, responsible for vetting applications and selecting the best sixty from the 150 or so applicants for each class. The process included lengthy interviews with the candidates by Penkovsky, and in this capacity he got to know an immense amount of personal and career information about the brightest officers in all of the services. He laboriously copied most of these records for his own further use.

Penkovsky was now determined to make his move. He wrote a letter to the American authorities giving full personal information, stating the kind of intelligence he could offer to the West and describing two ways for the American authorities to contact him: one, by chalk marks on a lamppost indicating that a message had been left in a specified dead-letter drop, and the other, as a last resort, by telephone. He put the letter in an envelope together with a photograph of himself alongside the American Colonel Peeke in Turkey as further evidence of his bona fides. In another envelope he placed copies of some secret documents as a sample of the quality of intelligence to which he had access. He kept both envelopes with him always, on the off-chance of meeting an American who could deliver them to the embassy.

Penkovsky was extremely popular with the staff and students and was well thought of by General Khlopov, the head of the academy. At the end of July, after the new academic year students had been selected, Khlopov encouraged Penkovsky to take some leave. He went to Odessa with his wife and daughter.

On the return journey, on 10 August, they were in the same compartment as a small group of American Russian language students, two of whom were older than the others: perhaps teachers rather than students. The teachers were called Eldon and Henry. (He later learned that their full names were Eldon Cox and Henry Cobb.) Penkovsky would like to have approached Cox and Cobb about delivering a message to the American Embassy in Moscow but he could not do so in front of his wife and daughter. In any case, the group was accompanied by a KGB agent in the guise of an official guide, as was standard practice in the Soviet Union at that time.

Back in Moscow, he started to spend some time near the American Embassy watching out for Cox and Cobb, or anyone else he might entrust with his envelopes. Across from the embassy was an alley with seats. He sat there for a long time, smoking and watching embassy cars come and go, but no suitable pedestrians passed by. He knew this was a risky tactic as there were always two Soviet militiamen guarding the embassy, on the lookout for possible defectors.

Having no luck there, he went to the American House; a large building that housed many junior members of the embassy staff, with recreational facilities for movies and bingo along with a well-stocked bar. Again, he was vulnerable to the watchful eyes of Soviet militia near the entrance, and, once more no opportunity arose to pass on his precious envelopes.

His luck changed the next day, 12 August, when he spotted Cox and Cobb walking through the rain from Red Square towards the river. He approached them and, with a smile, introduced himself as the man who, with his wife and daughter, had been in the same train compartment as them a few days earlier.

He explained that he could not have a conversation with them on the train because of the 'guide' who accompanied the Americans. Cox and Cobb acknowledged this and listened with some mistrust and even fear as Penkovsky explained that he wanted to help the West and would be eternally grateful if the students could deliver two envelopes that he produced from his pockets to the American Embassy.

Penkovsky had become aware of two militiamen a short distance along the road. One was talking to a woman and the other was walking along slowly in their direction. He quickly thrust the envelopes into Cox's hands. Cox looked at them with a dazed expression, but he, too, had noticed the militiamen and started to walk away quickly, still looking at the envelopes. Cobb went with him. Penkovsky had never felt so afraid in all his life, including his wartime ventures. He had intended to complete the exercise by telling them what they should do and say when they handed the envelopes over at the American Embassy, and by asking them to leave a mark with a ballpoint pen on the corner of a particular wall to report the safe delivery of the envelopes. As he watched, he saw Cox put one of the envelopes in his pocket. 'Please put the other one away, too,' he pleaded silently.

After Penkovsky had gone, Cobb – still fearing that it might be a trap – returned to his hotel, but Cox was more positive and decided to take the envelopes to the embassy right away. He arrived there just after midnight and nervously satisfied the Soviet militiaman standing guard outside the embassy that he was an American citizen. The Marine on security phoned through to John Abidian, the officer on duty that night. Cox explained what had happened and handed the envelopes to Abidian, asking him to pass them on to the Deputy Head of Mission.

After Cox had left the embassy, Abidian called in Edward Freers, the Deputy Head of Mission, who studied the contents of the envelopes. He came to the conclusion that Penkovsky was an *agent provocateur*, but he also consulted Ambassador Llewellyn (Tommy) Thompson. Thompson, a career diplomat, felt that CIA activities at overseas missions usually interfered with the normal process of improving diplomatic relations.[†] It was no surprise, therefore, that he strongly supported Freers's line. Freers sent a telegram to the CIA, describing what had happened and advising them of the embassy's conclusion that Penkovsky was an *agent provocateur*. The envelopes and their contents were dispatched to the CIA by diplomatic bag.

It seems strange that this action within the embassy was apparently taken by *bona fide* diplomatic staff. However, given the conditions in Moscow in those days it was exceedingly difficult for embassy-based members of the security services to function effectively. There was therefore no CIA station at the American Embassy, though there may have been a 'singleton' working quietly under cover of a diplomatic appointment, unbeknown to most members of staff and possibly even to the ambassador.[‡]

Penkovsky never saw Cox and Cobb again – they left Moscow on 15 August – so he did not know until several months later what had happened to the envelopes.

Washington

The cable and the envelopes arrived on the desk of Jack Maury, the head of the Soviet Division in the CIA's Directorate of Plans. Maury read the embassy's negative report and the content of

---

[†] The majority of American ambassadors were political appointees, particularly at larger, more important, embassies. The appointment of a career diplomat at such a large mission was unusual.

[‡] The first head of CIA station in Moscow was Paul Garbler, who did not arrive there until 30 November 1961.

the envelopes, but his reaction was positive, typifying the gulf between diplomatic and intelligence service perspectives. First, however, he would need verification of the American Embassy's report on Penkovsky passing the envelopes to Cox and Cobb, and to familiarise himself with the CIA's files on Penkovsky. He delegated these investigations to Joseph Bulik, the head of the CIA's Internal Soviet section.

Bulik, whose parents came from Slovakia, was a tall, handsomely rugged man in his mid-forties. He had studied animal husbandry at Wyoming University and held a degree in agriculture from Minnesota University. Towards the end of the war he was appointed as the agricultural attaché at the American Embassy in Moscow, holding that position from 1944 until 1948, after which he joined the CIA. He knew Moscow and understood the plight of the Soviet people, sympathising with their suffering during and after the war, and sensed the probable futility of their attempts to find economic, social and military solutions through Communism.

He was meticulous, methodical and careful. He tracked down first Cobb and then Cox, who had gone their separate ways after their travels. They each confirmed their parts in the story and identified Penkovsky from an 'identity parade' of photographs Bulik produced. He found confirmation of Penkovsky's service in Ankara in CIA files, but he considered it would not be appropriate, on security grounds, to contact Colonel Peeke. In the event that Penkovsky's offer was genuine, it would be essential to keep his name and identity absolutely secret.

The large envelope contained, among other things, Penkovsky's detailed notes on the Gary Powers U-2 incident. The Americans could not understand what had happened to the U-2 because their only sources of information were Khrushchev's announcements and the public exhibits. Penkovsky's notes gave them all the answers: now it made sense. On top of that, the notes belittled the Soviet inability to shoot down the U-2 with effective hits from missiles. The Soviets simply did not admit fault like this, even to give credence to an *agent provocateur*. Bulik's judgement, and that of other CIA experts he consulted without identifying Penkovsky, was that Penkovsky's offer was genuine and they should follow up on it.

Maury endorsed Bulik's recommendation and somehow got it past James Angleton, chief of the CIA's counterintelligence staff, who could never bring himself to accept that a Soviet defector could be genuine.

As noted above, one of the two letters in Penkovsky's smaller envelope outlined two methods to contact him. One was a dead-letter drop, with detailed information about its exact location and the placing of chalk marks to indicate that the drop had been made. The other was a phone call, to be made on a Sunday at exactly 10 a.m.: two rings and hang up, followed by a proper call.

The problem now was that the CIA had no one in place at the Moscow embassy to make the dead drop or the phone call, and Ambassador Thompson would not permit any of his staff to become involved in such activity. In fact, Ambassador Thompson would not even make any residential or office accommodation available for a senior CIA agent to be flown out to Moscow to engage with Penkovsky.

In the end, the CIA had to settle for sending a junior and relatively inexperienced officer who would be described as a janitor on the embassy staff list. His code name was COMPASS. The short, balding bachelor spoke very little Russian, but he was enthusiastic and committed.

Moscow

COMPASS turned out to be something of a disaster. After his arrival in Moscow he became paranoid about being followed by the KGB. He saw agents, imaginary and otherwise, everywhere. In the end, his paranoia advanced to the point where he was incapable of leaving the embassy. He began to drink too much. He decided that the best dead drop would be for Penkovsky to throw his material over the wall of embassy residential accommodation, even though the Soviet militia constantly watched that area.

Crucially, he was incapable of placing a message in the dead drop specified by Penkovsky in his letter. One Sunday morning he tried to make the phone call, but he phoned at 11 a.m. – an hour later than specified by Penkovsky – did not hang up after two rings and call back, as specified in Penkovsky's letter, and when he finally succeeded in making contact, managed only to spout a few words of incomprehensible gibberish.

COMPASS was sent home and that line of possible communication with Penkovsky was in ruins.

For the next three months Penkovsky lived in hope and fear: hope that his letters had reached the CIA and that he would be contacted by them; fear – increasing by the day – that the letters had fallen into the hands of the KGB or some other Soviet authority. He clutched at straws, seeing an apparently increasing number of Western diplomatic cars pass by his apartment, their drivers or passengers looking up as if searching for him. There had been one phone call, an hour after the appointed time, by some drunk who spoke unintelligible Russian and English.

At the worst, he hoped Cox had destroyed his letters rather than let them fall into the hands of the Soviet authorities. With this in mind, he prepared a new package of sample intelligence material and a covering letter which he could give to someone else to deliver to the American Embassy. He addressed it to 'President Dwight D. Eisenhower, President of the United States of America'.

‡

On returning to work after his holiday, Penkovsky was called in by Khlopov. After some pleasantries about his holiday, Khlopov told him they had been reorganising courses and were going to give him a senior instructor job, teaching tactics. This change had been approved by General Salodovnikov, the head of the

Faculty of Tactics, who was, said Khlopov, looking forward to Penkovsky joining his team.

Penkovsky refused the job which, he told Khlopov, was for 60- or 65-year-old officers, not for people like himself who were still young and had further to go in their careers.

He again went to General Shumsky, who immediately passed him on to the head of the directorate, General Smolikov. Penkovsky detested Smolikov: a heavy-drinking philanderer, he had a tasteless, eclectic collection of furniture in his apartment, at least one item of which (the refrigerator) he had won playing cards.

Speaking firmly to his superior officer, Penkovsky asked him what was going on. Was this – he asked – because his father had fought on the Tsar's side? Was this the end of his career?

Smolikov offered his sympathy but confirmed that it seemed that the noble blood in his veins was proving to be a serious liability in the eyes of the KGB's personnel security department. The party's Central Committee now knew his family history and were unlikely to approve any submission for him to work overseas.

Penkovsky still refused to accept the instructor appointment and was again placed in the reserves. He resorted to seeking assistance from his friend, Marshal Varentsov, who spoke to Serov.

Soon, on 15 November, Penkovsky was appointed to the State Committee for the Coordination of Scientific Research Work (GKKNIR), which came under the aegis of the Department of Foreign Relations.[†] This organisation was run jointly by the KGB and GRU with the purpose of gathering intelligence about scientific and technical developments in foreign countries. It operated

---

† He was actually appointed to the GNTK (State Committee for Science and Technology), which was reorganised in 1961 to become the GKKNIR. For ease of reference and continuity 'GKKNIR' is used throughout to cover Penkovsky's appointment to this body.

largely through overt trade mission visits, sending delegates to international trade fares. Penkovsky was initially put in charge of the Canadian section but within a month the Australian section was added. Then there was a staff shortage and they asked him to make arrangements for a forthcoming trade delegation from the United Kingdom, led by British businessman Greville Wynne.

Wynne, with his expensive suit, strongly coloured tie, pencil moustache and greased hair, tried to adopt the looks and disposition of a serious businessman but succeeded only in looking the part of a stereotypical used car salesman. He had served in the Army Intelligence Corps during the war, but was an engineer by profession and now represented about a dozen companies exporting machine tools, electrical and electronic equipment to East European countries and the Soviet Republics. He regularly attended trade fairs and exhibitions and visited the relevant ministries on behalf of his clients, but this was the first time he had organised a trade mission for eight of his largest companies.

It had become routine for someone from MI6 to debrief Wynne on his return to the UK after each visit to Eastern Europe or the Soviet Union. He would give information about the contacts he had made. He was an occasional agent for MI6 but not an employee.

In November 1960, MI6 officer Dick Franks invited Wynne to lunch and asked him not just to report back after his forthcoming trip to the Soviet Union, but to seek an appointment with the GKKNIR and make personal contact with some of its staff.

He went to Moscow on 1 December to discuss plans for his trade mission and arranged a meeting with several members of the GKKNIR. Around the table, one well-dressed and neatly groomed man stood out. It was Penkovsky.

Penkovsky let his work on Canadian projects drop so that he could concentrate on servicing the British delegation of twelve people representing eight companies, which was due to arrive on 8 December. He had to prepare presentations, get together a panel of specialist electrical engineering experts for each presentation, arrange receptions, and invite Soviet officials with an interest in the proceedings. There were many phone calls to make and schedules to be drawn up.

He met the members of the delegation when they arrived on 8 December. They spent the next three days in and around Moscow, and on 12 December he accompanied them to Leningrad. That night, Penkovsky found himself in a relatively private situation with two of the delegates: Arthur Merriman and John McBride. It was Penkovsky's nature to be impressed by military and scientific qualifications so he addressed himself to Merriman rather than McBride. McBride went to bed, leaving Penkovsky and Merriman alone.

Penkovsky explained that he had an important task for him. He had a package that needed to reach the American Embassy. Without hesitation, Merriman replied in his best 'old boy' voice that he most certainly could not do that.

Still sprightly and alert at sixty-eight, Dr Arthur Merriman GC, DFC, OBE, MA, MEd, DSc, CIMechE, FRSE had been an officer in the Royal Engineers during the war and afterwards became a government scientist. He was Britain's top metallurgist, and the Soviet Union was desperate for the most up-to-date information about metals, particularly those used in the design and production of military weapons and vehicles.

With hindsight, Penkovsky realised that his approach to Merriman had been too sudden and too blatant.

After returning to Moscow from Leningrad, Penkovsky saw Wynne as a potentially useful contact and tried to curry favour with him. But he refrained, at that time, from asking his assistance with the packet.

Penkovsky went to the airport to see off the members of the trade mission. He caught Merriman alone for a few moments and this time asked him simply to inform the Americans that they should phone him at home on any Sunday at 10 a.m., repeating what he had written in the covering letter that Cox had – hopefully – delivered to the American Embassy some months earlier.

Merriman, like Wynne, had debriefing sessions with MI6 after his trips to Eastern Europe. When he returned on this occasion, he reported his two encounters with Penkovsky. MI6, in turn, arranged for him to talk to a CIA representative at the American Embassy.

✝

In the summer of 1960 Ruari and Janet Chisholm returned early from an overseas posting in Singapore. Janet was expecting their third child and the doctor thought it would be safest for her to deliver in the UK. Chisholm was assigned to the East European and Soviet Section at MI6 headquarters on a temporary basis pending another overseas posting. He was then transferred to Moscow in the autumn of 1960 as head of the MI6 station, with cover as the chief of the visa section.

He and Janet, now with three children, were allocated a large apartment in one of the diplomatic blocks along Tsvetnoy Boulevard. Ruari's office was on the third floor of the east wing of the British Embassy building, from where he was able to look directly across the Moscow River to the Kremlin.

✝

On 4 January 1960, OVIR, the KGB-controlled Soviet Visa and Registration Department, summoned Lee Harvey Oswald and gave him the details of his new life under Communism. He arrived in Minsk on 6 January and, a week later, began work at an electronics factory.

Oswald's factory pay was supplemented by an equal amount from the Soviet Red Cross, which made him as affluent as the factory's most senior supervisors. He lived in an excellent apartment overlooking the river; again, well above the standard of

Soviet-born shop-floor workers. He was a good 'catch' for factory and other local girls and was far from shy in taking advantage of this. He was, however, disappointed with the technical level of work he was given: cutting metal on a lathe.

He worked hard at first but in the course of time his fundamental instability manifested, leading to arguments, and even fights, with his fellow workers. The KGB saw this and were far from impressed. He was not suitable material for a professional KGB agent, but his temper and limited intellectual capacity did not rule him out for single operations.

He did not communicate with his family members or anyone else in the United States during this period. All attempts to find him by his mother, Marguerite, and by the State Department and the US Embassy in Moscow, failed.

When Oswald had left the Marine Corps he automatically became a member of the US Marine Corps Reserves, which carried an obligation to serve again if called upon. The USMC Reserves' administration office, having heard of Oswald's attempted renunciation of US citizenship and his application for Soviet citizenship, gave him an 'undesirable discharge' on 17 August 1960. The official notification of this was sent to Marguerite.

Towards the end of 1960 Oswald started to tire of the lifestyle in the Soviet Union. The apartment, the wages and the girls were fine, but then there was the Communist Party regimentation, lectures and propaganda. He had to attend mass physical exercise sessions, and travel with his factory colleagues to a collective farm to help with the potato harvest.

In December, he wrote to the American Embassy telling them he wished to return to the United States and asking what action was required. The KGB intercepted the letter and it was never delivered.

19

LONDON 1960

Blake returned from Berlin in April 1959. His wife, Gillian, was pregnant and Blake took up a temporary London posting. Throughout this home posting he continued to pass high-level intelligence to his contact at the Soviet Embassy.

In September 1960, he was sent to MECAS to study Arabic.[†] The Middle East was becoming increasingly important for Britain and the West and MI6 needed men of Blake's calibre out there, speaking the language. The standard length of the MECAS Arabic course was eighteen months, so Gillian and their two sons accompanied Blake. He fell quickly into stride, having had a fair grounding in the language as a boy with his uncle and cousin in Cairo.

✝
✝

[†] MECAS – the Middle East Centre for Arabic Studies – was a language centre in the Christian village of Shemlan in the Lebanon. It was opened by the British government in 1947 and soon became famous throughout the world as possibly the best place to learn Arabic. Lord Hurd of Westwell (former British Foreign Secretary) wrote: 'To the Israelis MECAS was the place where Britain trained its brilliant young men to be sentimental about the Arabs and hostile to Zionism. To many Arabs it was simply the "School for Spies", the heart of Britain's post-war strategy of dominating the Middle East through its intelligence agencies.' MECAS was closed in 1978 due to civil war in the Lebanon.

In April 1959 – just as Blake was leaving Berlin – the CIA started to receive secret information from an unidentified informant in the Polish Military Intelligence (the UB). There were two particular items of intelligence that required further investigation: someone in the British Royal Navy was spying for the Soviet Union; the informant had seen secret documents originating from a Soviet agent inside MI6. Details were limited, and the identity of those involved unknown.

Towards the end of 1960, the KGB learned that the United States had a double agent in the UB. They attempted to warn the UB, but by good fortune the person who received this KGB message was the double agent himself. His name was Colonel Michael Goleniewski and he was the head of the UB station in East Berlin.

Goleniewski was able to escape before anyone else saw the message. He fled to West Berlin, contacted the CIA, and was then flown to Washington for debriefing. The information he gave was now much more detailed. He told the Americans that the Royal Navy informant was passing technical secrets about the Navy's latest underwater weaponry being developed and tested at the Admiralty Underwater Weapons Establishment at Portland. Goleniewski believed this spy had been recruited several years earlier and may actually have served in Poland, presumably in the British Embassy.

With regard to the Soviet agent inside MI6, Goleniewski said he had received copies of documents originating from that source. These often contained the names of MI6 field agents and targets.

The CIA informed MI6 and offered to send Goleniewski to London for further debriefing, which resulted in the positive identification of Harry Houghton as the Royal Navy spy. He had been a clerk in the Naval Attaché's Office in the British Embassy in Warsaw from 1951 to 1953.

Houghton was arrested on 7 January 1961, together with four other members of the Portland spy ring: Konon Molody (alias

Gordon Lonsdale), Ethel Gee, Peter Kroger and Helen Kroger. The Krogers were later identified as Morris and Lona Cohen.

Houghton and Gee were each sentenced to fifteen years in prison, the Krogers (Cohens) to twenty years each and Lonsdale (Molody) to twenty-five.[†]

Some of the officers involved in the investigation and arrests became suspicious that Lonsdale, and possibly also the Krogers, had been warned in advance that they were under intense official scrutiny. Evidence from cross-examinations at the trial lent some support to these suspicions.

[†] Lonsdale (Molody) was exchanged for Greville Wynne in 1964.

20

MOSCOW 1961 (PART 1)

When Oswald's one-year Soviet residence permit expired on 4 January 1961, the OVIR office in Minsk called him in to ask if he still wished to apply for Soviet citizenship. He said he had changed his mind about becoming a Soviet citizen, but he would like to have his residence permit extended for another twelve months.

Having received no response from the American Embassy in Moscow to the letter he had written in December (the KGB had intercepted it, as noted above), Oswald wrote to them again on 5 February, castigating them for not responding to his first letter and asking for his passport to be returned to him. He also asked if any legal proceedings against him would be dropped. (He must have assumed he might be charged with espionage.)

The embassy responded to the effect that he would have to visit them in Moscow to be interviewed about the possibility of returning his passport. Exchanges of correspondence continued through April. Oswald wanted to know why they could not just send him a questionnaire, protesting that it would be difficult for him to get to Moscow. The embassy insisted he attend in person, and they could not confirm or promise anything relating to possible criminal charges.

In February the Red Cross stopped paying him the handsome supplement he had received throughout his stay in Minsk.

Back in June 1960 Oswald had fallen in love with an attractive co-worker called Ella German. They danced together; he visited her at her parents' home – including over Christmas 1960 – and she was a frequent guest in his apartment. However, Ella always parried his sexual advances and eventually rejected his proposal of marriage.

In early March 1961, very much on the rebound from Ella, he began to date Marina Prusakova, a pharmacist he met at a dance. It was a whirlwind romance: they became engaged on 15 April and married on 30 April. Oswald wrote in his diary that this expedited union was at first a spiteful act of revenge against Ella, but that he soon grew to love Marina deeply.

When they had first met, Marina thought Oswald was from one of the Baltic States, but she did not mind that he was American, and nor did her family. He told her it was his intention to stay in the Soviet Union, so there was no question of her marrying him just to acquire US residency and eventual citizenship. He reported his marriage to the embassy in Moscow, saying that Marina would return with him to America, and again asked them to confirm that he would not be prosecuted.

The beginning of the flurry of correspondence with the embassy in December 1960 coincided with determined action by Oswald's mother, Marguerite, to find him. Marguerite at first corresponded with the State Department and when this appeared not to stir them into action she went to Washington to confront them in person. At this point, the CIA and FBI started to take a renewed interest in Oswald. Where, exactly, was he in the Soviet Union? What was he doing there? Why had he not kept in touch with his mother and brother? Had he been secretly corresponding with someone else in America? Could the CIA somehow make use of his presence there? Had someone in the deepest depths of the CIA sent him there on a top-secret mission?

As the correspondence progressed into 1961 and his whereabouts and circumstances became known, the questions changed. Was he being trained by the KGB? Would he return to the United States to spy for the Soviet Union? The files thickened but provided no definite answers.

Suddenly, on Saturday 8 July, Oswald turned up at the United States Embassy in Moscow. The consular section was closed so he made an appointment to meet Consul Richard Snyder on the following Monday. (It is remarkable how often Oswald turned up at embassies and consulates – in Moscow and in Mexico City – on a Saturday, when they were closed.)

Unlike his quarrelsome interview with Snyder on 31 October 1959, Oswald was now submissive and anxious to comply with all necessary requirements to secure the return of his passport and obtain a United States visa for his wife, Marina.

It took ten months for the ham-fisted American and Soviet bureaucracies to finalise the processes required to issue all of the requisite passports and visas for Lee, Marina and their baby daughter June Lee, who was born on 15 February. They left Moscow by train on 2 June 1962 bound for Amsterdam, and thence by sea to New York.

‡

After Penkovsky's failure to get Merriman, the British metallurgist, to take his package of secret documents to the American Embassy, he approached the Canadians. As part of his job, he had to meet Dr J. M. Harrison, the director of the Canadian Geological Survey, at the airport and liaise with him throughout his visit. At one stage, on 9 January 1961, he asked Harrison to arrange for him to meet William Van Vliet, the commercial counsellor at the Canadian Embassy. When they met, Penkovsky gave Van Vliet a package of secret papers and asked him to deliver it to the American Embassy. They met again the next day, but to Penkovsky's disappointment Van Vliet said he would not deliver the package and returned it to him.

Van Vliet reported this incident in detail to the Canadian Ambassador, who in turn informed his superiors in Ottawa.

‡

Unbeknown to Penkovsky, COMPASS was in Moscow, failing miserably to contact him either through the dead drop or the 10 a.m. Sunday phone call. This failure was in part occasioned by Ambassador Thompson's stubborn refusal to help, but mostly reflected COMPASS's ineptitude.

Eventually, on Sunday 5 February 1961, COMPASS attempted to make the phone call, which turned out to be a disaster. He phoned at 11 a.m. instead of 10 a.m., and spoke in English as well as Russian. Penkovsky could not understand what he was trying to say in either language and eventually hung up, not knowing who had called and assuming it was a wrong number.

Washington

In spite of the continuing mistrust of MI6 by the CIA, Dick Helms, the CIA's Deputy Director of Plans, decided they would have to bring in the British to help them to make contact with Penkovsky.

Harold Shergold, one of MI6's top agent handlers, paid a routine visit to CIA headquarters in January 1961. He brought up the subject of Penkovsky with Joe Bulik on 27 January. Up to this point MI6 had not been captivated by the prospects of approaching Penkovsky, whom they thought was probably an *agent provocateur*. However, when Bulik – reluctantly – informed him of Penkovsky's first letter and the material in the package that Cox had handed in to the American Embassy, Shergold changed his mind.[†]

Shergold was converted. He returned to London and persuaded

---

†   Bulik was under instruction from Dick Helms to tell Shergold about Penkovsky's two envelopes and to try to persuade the British to cooperate with them in contacting Penkovsky. He later said that the big lesson on the Penkovsky case was never to enter into a joint operation with another service.

Dick White not only to work with the Americans on Penkovsky, but to make much of the running because of the major problems the CIA faced when trying to operate in Moscow.

Moscow

Penkovsky encountered difficulties with organising the Soviet trade mission visit to the United Kingdom and the original date of March 1961 could not be met. Instead, the date was set for arrival in London on 20 April.

Wynne went to Moscow early in April to discuss the causes of the delay and to agree as much of the programme as possible, including which Soviet delegates would visit which British companies. The two men worked well together and soon developed a friendship, at least to the extent that they could talk frankly to each other, which was not common between Soviets and Westerners in those days.

Wynne was concerned about the kind of people proposed as members of the Soviet delegation: they were all academics or technical experts rather than managers who would know how to discuss a commercial agreement. He reaffirmed to Penkovsky that the purpose of the mission was to look for import and export opportunities, not to spy on the latest British technology and manufacturing processes.

Penkovsky agreed, but asked Wynne to understand that he – Penkovsky – had no power to change the delegates. He had already put Wynne's point to the relevant people in the ministries, but they were unmoved by his protestations. He begged Wynne to accept the list and allow the mission to proceed. He then suggested to him that they take a breath of fresh air and discuss the matter further.

Wynne sensed that Penkovsky was becoming agitated and judged, correctly, that the room could well be bugged. Penkovsky clearly wanted to say something without being overheard.

Penkovsky continued from where he had left off as soon as they were safely outside. He told Wynne it was essential for him to get to England and the mission would have to go ahead no matter what the composition of the team. A lot of things to which he objected were happening in the Soviet Union. He expressed his dislike for the way the Soviet Union was being governed; his concern for the country's economy and – most importantly – about his fears for the ultimate outcome of the military policies being pursued by Khrushchev. Khrushchev was making grossly exaggerated claims about the strength of the military and its nuclear capability and this was bound to result in disaster unless the West knew the truth. He had to get to England to tell them the truth.

He pleaded for Wynne's trust and help.

Following Shergold's visit to the CIA, Wynne had been briefed to take Penkovsky seriously and to cooperate with him to the extent he thought reasonably safe. He should do nothing to compromise his own position as a legitimate businessman trying to attract Soviet business for the companies he represented. Above all, he should not allow himself to listen to, or look at, any secret intelligence from Penkovsky.

Wynne was an excellent judge of character. More than most, he was aware of the possibility of meeting an *agent provocateur* in his dealings with Eastern Bloc countries, but Penkovsky was different. The words he had just heard took him by surprise but he felt they were sincere. Now he had to be careful not to let Penkovsky know of his involvement with the security services.

He agreed to accept Penkovsky's list of delegates. He insisted, however, that he was an import–export businessman earning an honest crust by representing a few British companies and could not, therefore, become involved in Penkovsky's cloak-and-dagger schemes.

During the evening of 6 April, in Wynne's hotel room, Penkovsky moved to the bathroom, signalling that Wynne should follow him. With the water taps turned on to prevent any hidden microphone from picking up what they said, Penkovsky handed

Wynne a heavily taped thick package and asked him to deliver it to the English Embassy.[†] Wynne did so that same evening.

Several days later, on 10 April, Penkovsky was relieved to hear that Wynne had delivered the package safely to the embassy, but he now asked him to take another thick envelope back with him to London and deliver it to the Foreign Office or the American Embassy. This time Wynne refused. It was one thing to deliver a package across Moscow to the British Embassy. To carry papers on his person, travelling through Soviet passport, customs and KGB checks would have constituted a far greater risk.

Penkovsky accompanied Wynne to the airport the next morning. Shortly before he was due to board the aircraft, he again tried to thrust the package on Wynne, who again refused to take it, saying he was bound to be questioned about the contents of such a thick package. Penkovsky, with some difficulty, then opened the package and extracted a single letter he had written on Christmas Day 1960. 'Well, this is not too thick,' he said. Wynne agreed to carry it.

It was a letter addressed to President Dwight D. Eisenhower, lamenting the lack of response to the package handed in by Cox, again offering his services, and suggesting means of arranging a clandestine meeting.

---

† Penkovsky always referred to Britain or the United Kingdom as 'England' and used the adjective 'English'. No one, it seems, ever tried to correct him. In fairness, virtually all Russians use the word 'Angliski' (English) when they really mean 'Britanski' (British).

21

LONDON 1961

Colonel Goleniewski's debriefing in London at the end of 1960, which enabled the security services to identify the Portland spy ring, also led to the identification of George Blake as the KGB's agent within MI6.

Sir Dick White, the head of MI6, was incensed. He was determined to show no mercy in Blake's case, despite a then recent tendency not to prosecute if the offender turned Queen's evidence (i.e. told everything he knew about Soviet strategies and about his Soviet contacts). Prime Minister Harold Macmillan was informed. He wanted the whole thing to be hushed up because of the embarrassment it would cause, particularly with the Americans. White, however, stood firm and insisted upon prosecution.

MI6's embarrassment increased when they looked again at Blake's personal file. As with Philby, hindsight showed that he should probably not have been allowed to work for MI6 or, at least, should not have been allowed to continue after his return from Korea.† His father was only a naturalised British subject; his mother was not British; and he had spent his formative years in Egypt, close to an uncle and cousins who were declared Communists.

---

† Kim Philby spoke openly in support of Communism when he was in Vienna and he married an Austrian woman who was an avowed Communist; yet he was never challenged about these conflicts with his MI6 work.

While none of this in itself precluded Blake from being invited to join MI6 then, surely, his experience in Korea should have raised a warning flag. The North Koreans had kept him prisoner for close to three years, and they had acquired a strong reputation, in part fictitious, for ideological re-education, brainwashing and even mind control.

It was perhaps incongruous that Philby, who had been put out to pasture owing to the continuing rumours about his loyalty, was at that time in Beirut in the guise of a correspondent for *The Economist*. Beirut was close to MECAS and he would probably have visited the organisation from time to time. Neither Blake nor Philby knew that the other was also a Soviet spy, though Blake would have reached his own conclusions about Philby in the light of the press reports and, no doubt, internal office gossip.

There was, as yet, little hard evidence of Blake's espionage activities. He was in a foreign country and still had a few months of his Arabic course to complete, so it would be difficult to recall him to the UK immediately without raising some misgivings. Sir Dick decided simply to send a message to him through Nicholas Elliott, the head of the MI6 station in Beirut, saying that he was required in London for consultations. No dates were given, so there appeared to be no hurry. Blake told his wife and colleagues it was either for news of his next posting, word of a promotion, or both.

He returned to the UK by air on 3 April 1961, which was Easter Monday – a national holiday – so he was able to stay with his mother prior to reporting to MI6's Broadway headquarters the next day.

He was taken straight up to the chief's office where White and two interrogators – Terence Lecky and Harold Shergold – were waiting for him.

Throughout the morning Blake denied their accusations of treason and espionage. At lunchtime he left the building by himself, took a circuitous route to a red public telephone booth, pulled the heavily sprung door open, and hesitated for a long moment before finally deciding not to dial the emergency number he had been given by his Soviet master.

Back in White's office after lunch he continued to deny the charges until Shergold asked him why he had not called his Soviet contact during the lunch break. This seemed to unnerve Blake, who had not realised he was under surveillance through-out the lunch break. Slowly, he allowed himself to acknowledge that he had spied and then, bit by bit, he confessed to everything. Between the confessions he put up a textbook defence of his support for Communism as the only way for world society to progress towards peace and equality.

He had given extensive thought to the consequences of being found guilty of espionage. It was peacetime, so the maximum sentence would be fourteen years: he had made certain of that on several occasions. He was now thirty-eight. With time off for good behaviour he could be out of prison before he was fifty, hopefully with many years still ahead of him.

The Americans were deeply troubled when they learned of Blake's treachery. Bill Harvey probably did not know whether to laugh or cry. He had always suspected that knowledge of 'his' Berlin tunnel had been leaked by the British, but to think that the Soviets had been aware of the plans prior to the breaking of ground for the tunnel's construction was a far more serious matter. It was another staggering blow for the relationship between the CIA and MI6, just at a time when Allen Dulles and Sir Dick White had mended some of the fences previously knocked down by Burgess and Maclean, and by the still mistrusted Philby.

It did not help the Americans' humour when, a week after Blake's confession, the Soviet Union beat the United States in the race to put a man into space.[†]

George Blake went on trial at the Old Bailey exactly a month after he had happily returned from his MECAS course in the Lebanon expecting a new posting and/or promotion. He was

---

† Yuri Gagarin became the first man in space on 12 April 1961.

charged with five counts of offences under the Official Secrets Act, each relating to a specific period of time. He pleaded guilty on all counts. In his written statement Blake freely admitted that he had passed every official document of any significance he could access to his Soviet contacts.

The judge, the Lord Chief Justice of England, Lord Parker, sentenced Blake to the maximum of fourteen years on each of the five charges, the first three counts to run consecutively and the last two concurrently, making for a total prison sentence of forty-two years. At that time it was the longest sentence ever handed out by a British court. Blake, expecting no more than the maximum of fourteen years, was devastated.[†]

‡

On his return to London on 12 April, after his meetings with Penkovsky, Wynne contacted Dick Franks at MI6 Headquarters and arranged to meet him. He gave him Penkovsky's letter and explained the circumstances that had led him to accept it. Wynne described the events of his visit to Moscow in detail, telling Franks he had a good feeling about Penkovsky and was sure of his sincerity.

Franks reported this to White and gave him Penkovsky's letter. White called Wynne in for a thorough debriefing with Shergold, after which MI6 agreed to run Penkovsky in a joint operation with the CIA.

It was only a week until 20 April, the day on which the Soviet Trade Mission would arrive in London. The CIA and MI6 exchanged many telegrams, mostly between Shergold and Bulik, agreeing the ground rules for the joint management of Penkovsky and making arrangements for his debriefing in the UK.

[†] Five years later, on 22 October 1966, Blake was helped to escape from prison. He made his way to Moscow where he still lives at the time of writing (August 2012).

In essence, MI6 would control Penkovsky in Moscow, at least until such time that the CIA could put someone in place to share the responsibility. Debriefing Penkovsky in London would be a joint operation run by two case officers on each team. MI6's team was led by Harold Shergold, who was assisted by Michael Stokes, a Russian speaker. Shergold had greatly enhanced his already high reputation by extracting George Blake's confession just two weeks earlier.

Joe Bulik led the CIA team, assisted by George Kisevalter. Kisevalter was born in St Petersburg, Russia. During WWI the Tsar sent his father to America to buy ammunition. He had his family – including young George, then seven years old – with him when the Russian Revolution started in 1917. The family remained in the United States, taking on US citizenship. George became one of the CIA's most experienced case officers, having worked on such high-profile cases as Germany's WWII intelligence chief Major-General Reinhard Gehlen and the GRU's Major Pyotr Popov, before becoming involved in the Penkovsky case.

Kisevalter's fluency in Russian and his outgoing personality made him the natural choice to take the leading role in debriefing Penkovsky.

22

PENKOVSKY DEBRIEFING (PART 1)

United Kingdom, April–May 1961

The first three weeks of April 1961 had been incredibly fraught for the intelligence organisations of Britain, the Soviet Union and America. George Blake was arrested on 4 April and confessed his treachery as a Soviet mole inside MI6. On 12 April the Soviet Union launched Yuri Gagarin into space. On 17 April, a small army of Cuban exiles supported and part-funded by the CIA landed at the Bay of Pigs in a dismally unsuccessful attempt to invade Castro's Cuba. On 20 April, a Soviet Trade Mission led by Oleg Penkovsky was due to arrive in London.

The two-man American team arrived in London on 19 April, giving them just enough time to finalise arrangements for debriefing Penkovsky and to discuss their modus operandi with the British team.

For obvious security reasons the four men used aliases, though with their actual first names: George McAdam [Kisevalter], Joseph Welk [Bulik], Harold Hazlewood [Shergold] and Michael Fairfield [Stokes].

Penkovsky and the other five members of the Soviet Trade Mission were greeted at the airport by Greville Wynne, who saw them safely into their hotel, the Mount Royal. They all met late in the afternoon for a final briefing about their itinerary and other administrative arrangements. An early dinner was followed by drinks and they were then encouraged to have an early night.

Wynne had warned Penkovsky that certain people wished to

see him at nine o'clock in the evening, or soon thereafter. After the drinks session Wynne and Penkovsky left together 'to tie up some loose ends', and soon arrived at Room 712 which was registered in the name of Harold Hazlewood [Shergold]. Shergold and Bulik were waiting there for them. Wynne left immediately, his task having been completed. After introductions, they took Penkovsky to Room 360 which was larger and more appropriate for the debriefing, particularly as it had no windows. Stokes and Kisevalter were already there and, after further introductions, they all sat round a small circular serving table.

Kisevalter: Would you prefer to speak in Russian or English?
Penkovsky: I would much rather speak Russian because I can express myself better in Russian.

Thereafter, for this and for all future meetings, the debriefing was carried out in Russian with Kisevalter taking the lead role. There were occasional switches to English when any of the other three wished to ask a question or seek clarification, and when Penkovsky himself decided that English would better illustrate his point.

Penkovsky had been preparing himself for this moment for years. He had studiously collected an incredible amount of secret information and could barely wait to get it off his chest. The debriefing team had decided beforehand that they would initially allow Penkovsky to speak freely, at his own pace, and only rein him in if he started to wander off track.

At the outset Penkovsky drew blood from the CIA team.

Penkovsky: Well, gentlemen, let's get to work. We have a great deal of important work to do. I have thought about this for a long time and I have attempted to make this contact taking a very devious path about which I feel I must report to you in full.
Kisevalter: You must know that we are in receipt of your original letter?

Penkovsky: You mean the one I gave to the two teachers? If you knew how many grey hairs I have acquired since that time; if you had only marked the signal so that I would have known the message got into the proper hands. I was worried so much about this.

To reassure him, Bulik pulled out the original copy of Penkovsky's first letter, including the photograph of Colonel Peeke in Ankara.

Kisevalter: This is to reassure you as to why we did not respond immediately. We deliberately delayed signalling you until a secure manner for receipt of the materials you wanted to pass could be devised. This was done exclusively in consideration of your security.
Penkovsky: And, between friends, admit that you did not trust me. That is the most unpleasant and painful thing to me.
Kisevalter: No, it is quite the opposite.

Penkovsky then launched into his life story, incorporating much detail about GRU and military people, training and deployment. He had an incredible memory for names, faces and the minutiae of people's lives. He was equally well versed in the disposition of Soviet forces and the technical specification and capability of their armaments. He spoke quickly and continuously and preferred his own idea of continuity to that of the debriefing team.

Kisevalter: Could you tell us about...?
Penkovsky: Yes, I'll come to that in a minute, but first I want to tell you about [something else].

Penkovsky: I'll remember the name of the Captain and tell you later.
Penkovsky: [About twenty minutes later, in the middle of talking about something completely different] The Captain I mentioned a while ago: he is Captain Yakovlev.

Penkovsky interposed his own thoughts and wishes with his intelligence reporting. They were sometimes surprisingly naive.

> Penkovsky: Mr Harold [Shergold], what is the status of my request to formally meet a government representative? I want to present myself officially. It doesn't have to be a specific lord, and I don't expect to meet the Queen.
> Kisevalter: [Not bothering to refer this to Shergold] Be assured; this is being taken care of.
> Penkovsky: Also, I need some more money.

On another occasion he spoke about his commitment to the West.

> Penkovsky: What I would like to do is to swear an oath of allegiance to you, to give you a signed statement and to swear an oath in order to formalise our relationship.

He gave his proposals for working for the Americans and British.

> Penkovsky: But please give me your opinion of a Strategic Intelligence officer, now your soldier, your worker ready to fulfil any missions you may assign to me now and in the future. All I ask is for you to protect my life, and I only have three persons close to me: my wife, my mother and my daughter. I would be happy now to live in England or America myself, but I cannot leave them behind. It would drive me insane in time thinking about this should I leave them behind. I have to prepare a basis for my future existence and I believe that I can serve you most usefully in place for at least a year or two, particularly if I were to work under a specific directive set by you to fulfil missions which would be within my capability to accomplish.

He continued, then, to discuss financial arrangements, which included funding to help him to purchase a dacha (country house) near Moscow, and regular payments into a Western bank account to provide him with ready funds when the day of defection came.

He said he thought the West did not react strongly enough to Khrushchev's aggressive statements, actions and threats.

> Penkovsky: With Cuba, for example, I simply cannot understand why Khrushchev should not be sharply rebuked. I do not know what answer Mr Kennedy will give him, but he certainly should be accused of arming Cuba with Soviet tanks and guns, right under the gates of America. Kennedy should be firm. Khrushchev is not going to fire any rockets. He is not ready for any war. I, certainly, in Kennedy's place, would be firm. This is my opinion and the opinion of many of our officers. The day we arrived in London – the 20th – I read in the newspapers the next day that Castro claimed victory at the Bay of Pigs. I do not understand what that was about but it seems he is claiming victory over the Americans. Tell me, Gentlemen, that this is not true. You are too soft in the West.

And, later:

> Penkovsky: Khrushchev will rant and rave and even send arms here and there just as he did to Cuba, and possibly even send small calibre rockets there. In fact there was talk about this with Castro, and possibly a few rockets are already there. But I read in that same newspaper, maybe it was the day before – that is, the day we arrived – that Khrushchev assured Kennedy that the Soviet Union has no bases or designs for bases in Cuba but warned him of the danger of any future invasions of the island by American forces, threatening renewed global war. Khrushchev is a liar and a warmonger.
>
> It is necessary to call together all the leaders of the Free World and to arrange first their coordination, secondly their unity, and thirdly the material sacrifices which they must make in the name of common victory. If this is not done there will

be a great disaster. Khrushchev and the General Staff can leave you behind. He is throwing together these rockets and he can do terrible damage with them. But in my estimation, and according to powerful people in the leadership, he will need two or three more years. But not longer, Gentlemen, not longer, believe me.

At one point Penkovsky said he had a plan to blow up all of the main military establishments in Moscow by placing small nuclear sabotage weapons in dustbins. He offered to plant the bombs himself and gave technical details about the timing devices (in the manner of later al Qaeda terrorists, he was intent upon simultaneous detonation) and the type of explosive that should be used.

Marshal Varentsov featured regularly in Penkovsky's comments, either in the context of a story about a particular meeting or, more often, as the source of secret information.

The debriefing team protected Wynne.

> Penkovsky: Tell me: do you think Wynne did the right thing by not taking all my material when I offered it to him?
> Kisevalter: Remember, he is a simple mortal, and not an intelligence man.
> Penkovsky: Don't tell him anything about this.

There were sixteen meetings with the debriefing team during this visit by the Soviet Trade Mission (20 April to 6 May 1961), most of them in London, but some in Leeds and Birmingham. Nearly all these meetings were held in the evening, after Penkovsky had put in a full day's work shepherding the Soviet delegates and dining with them. It was tiring but he thrived on it, being prepared to continue with the debriefing for as long as the team wished. It was often after midnight before they finished. Penkovsky, of course, also had specific assignments to perform for his GRU masters.

Kisevalter: Tell us about your mission here.

Penkovsky: I have to cultivate the acquaintance of people I meet, to get on good terms with them.

Kisevalter: What sort of man were they looking for: a businessman?

Penkovsky: Yes, but it doesn't matter because every Englishman or American has, in our opinion, some possibility or other as an agent. Even if we don't use them directly we can get in touch with other people through them, select those who are of interest to us, and give them money. We don't give much.

Kisevalter: In other words, a contact or a spotter.

Penkovsky: I give you my word that I got into no agent relationship with any member of Wynne's delegation. Quite the opposite, since I approached Merriman and McBride with my own problem; with my own life. Anyway, I have to find somebody, get to know them better, to work with them, estimate their value as agents, and if they have any value, to report to our *Rezident* in London about their possibilities. The *Rezident* would then assign an operational officer; probably Colonel Pavlov or Shapovalov. I would arrange a meeting with him and we might have a drink and so on. Then a further meeting would be arranged at which the Englishman's weaknesses would be explored; perhaps he might be in debt or something. It might be possible to take advantages of these weaknesses, compromise him, and eventually get him into a compromising position for recruitment. Today the *Rezident* said to me that I should look out for new acquaintances at the Exhibition of Industrial Engineering and report on them to him not later than three days before we are due to leave.

Shergold arranged for MI6 to brief Arthur Merriman, the 68-year-old metallurgist who had refused to take Penkovsky's envelope in Moscow, to be Penkovsky's potential agent. The *Rezident* assigned Shapovalov as his operational officer but soon changed this to Viktor Generalov. Shapovalov and Generalov met Merriman and were delighted with Penkovsky's 'find'. They later told Penkovsky that he was too old to be recruited as a full agent but that they would use him as a trusted informant.

A month later there was a hiccup in the GRU–Merriman relationship when Generalov claimed to have phoned Merriman to make an appointment to see him and Merriman refused. However, Merriman claimed that he had never had a phone call from Generalov. Penkovsky shrugged this off by saying that they should never deal with the elderly. This incident caused Penkovsky some loss of face, but inflicted no lasting damage on his excellent GRU record and reputation.

Another of Penkovsky's personal tasks was to purchase an incredible number of gifts for family, friends and colleagues back in Moscow. He had a notebook listing the items he wanted, including actual outlines of feet so that he could buy shoes. He explained that some of these gifts were extremely important as they enabled him to remain on the best of terms with people who could help him. MI6 gave him enough money to buy some of the gifts himself, so that he could join with other members of the delegation in this necessary part of any Soviet official's trip to the West, but most of the gifts were purchased by the four young case officers who supported the debriefing team. Two of the gifts, both of them for Marshal Varentsov, were particularly noteworthy: a silver rocket-shaped cigar and cigarette holder with a built-in lighter, and a rare bottle of sixty-year-old Napoleon cognac for Varentsov's sixtieth birthday party. The latter caused a problem because they could not find a sixty-year-old vintage. However, MI6's in-house document forger did an excellent job on the label of a fifty-year-old bottle. No one – not even Penkovsky – noticed.

At one of the meetings they instructed him in the use of a specially adapted Minox: a miniature camera for photographing documents. In all, they gave him three of these cameras because of the prolific number of documents he was in a position to copy. The photographs he later sent back were of such high quality that they suspected they were the work of GRU or KGB specialists, suggesting that their double agent may have been a Soviet plant.

At a meeting some months later the debriefing team surprised Penkovsky with an attempt to ascertain the extent of his own skill as a photographer: 'We're giving you an extra camera but we haven't tested it yet. Would you mind copying this document for us, Oleg, and we'll develop the cassette negatives overnight to see that they're OK?' The photographs he took were of superb quality.

The room telephone rang during one of the London meetings. Michael Stokes, the quiet one of the British pair, lifted the receiver.

Stokes: Michael Fairfield here. [He listened for a few seconds.] Good. I'll come down and fetch her. [He replaced the receiver.] Ann has arrived. Perhaps you could explain whilst I fetch her, Harold.

Shergold: Ann is the lady we told you about, Oleg. She's the wife of one of the diplomats in our Moscow Embassy. She has three young children. Do you remember what we agreed? She will be on one of the public bench seats in the park area opposite the Moscow Circus building on Tsvetnoy Boulevard. You will be walking casually by and notice the children – particularly the one in the pram – and stop to say hello to them, in Russian. Then do what you think seems natural so that you are 'coo-coo-ing' the child in the pram. At that point give the mother – that's Ann – the packet of sweets with all your film cassettes and messages in it; either give it to Ann or put it in the pram. Put your hand into the pram to touch the baby's face, but then reach gently under the pillow to see if there's anything for you to take away. There'll usually be more blank film cassettes to replace the ones you've used.

Penkovsky: Yes, I remember all that. Please don't talk to me as if I'm a child. I'm an experienced and successful secret intelligence officer. You must give me the essential basics and allow me to do the rest in a style that suits me and fits the circumstances.

Stokes: [Returns to the room with Janet Chisholm.] Oleg, this is Ann. She's flown here from Moscow just to meet you. We thought it would be important for you to meet her here so that you'll recognise each other in Moscow.

Penkovsky: [Standing up and shaking hands with Janet.] I'm delighted to meet you. I shall certainly not forget such an attractive lady.

Janet Chisholm: Nor I, you. I look forward to meeting you again in Moscow, and I shall try to be as casual as I can.

In the course of the April/May debriefing sessions the joint team showed Penkovsky approximately 7,000 photographs – many of them with groups of people – from the files of the CIA, MI6 and the British Security Service (MI5). He was able to identify about 10 per cent of the people in them. In all, he identified and described the positions and duties of more than 1,000 GRU officers and nearly 300 KGB officers.

23

MOSCOW 1961 (PART 2)

Less than a month after she had met Penkovsky at the debriefing meeting in London, Janet Chisholm took her three children out for a walk. She stopped to rest on one of the seats in the grassy area opposite the Moscow Circus building on Tsvetnoy Boulevard, allowing her two daughters, aged six and four, to play on the grass while she gently rocked her 14-month-old son in his pram. In her anxiety to see the handover succeed, she had arrived fifteen minutes ahead of the thirty-minute window that had been set for the operation. This was something of a mistake because the two older children had already tired of playing at that spot and wanted to move on.

Janet carefully positioned the pram so that it would have been difficult for anyone else to sit on the bench, though other nearby seats were occupied, and on this pleasant early summer morning there were lots of people about, some of them stopping to admire the beautifully dressed blond-haired youngsters. Janet was pleased about this because one more person doing the same thing would not seem suspicious.

She spotted Penkovsky when he was still some distance away and for the first time in years her heart started to pound with nervous excitement. She looked casually away, not daring to follow his progress in case someone should notice her eyes trailing after him. It seemed an eternity before the man helped the two older children to retrieve their ball and, smiling, started to praise the children's beauty in Russian. He talked of how much Russians loved children and mentioned his own teenage daughter.

Janet spoke passable 'school' Russian, having learned it at Queen Anne's School, Caversham, and her first six months in Moscow had provided an opportunity to brush up her grasp of the language.

Smiling, Penkovsky leaned over and put his hand into the pram as if to touch the baby, but deftly removed the package containing ten tiny film cartridges for his Minox cameras. He put his hand in his pocket, depositing the package and brought out a box of Russian sweets which he handed to Janet. She took the sweets and thanked him. The box contained exposed film cassettes of top-secret military documents.

'Ann' was pleased with the results of the exchange. She wanted to tell Ruari about it when he came home for lunch but knew she dare not say a word because all members of the embassy staff had to work on the assumption that the diplomatic flats and houses were bugged by the KGB. Besides, Martina Browne, their young children's nanny, who had come out from England with them, was ever-present and could not be allowed to share any knowledge of espionage activities. Ruari was simply the head of the British Embassy's visa section.

After George Blake's confession, Chisholm would have had to work in the knowledge that he had been exposed as an MI6 officer. This became abundantly obvious when he received more attention from the KGB than any other member of the British Embassy staff. All staff were followed and watched to some degree; Chisholm was followed and watched closely virtually all the time. As an expert in surveillance, he was able to spot two and sometimes three watchers in cars, on motorcycles or on foot, virtually every time he moved.

He sometimes tried to attract such attention. One of his tricks when driving was to increase speed and then swerve into a side street, stop suddenly, jump out and casually install himself on a nearby bench. His pursuers would then turn the corner to find their target at rest, perhaps smiling slightly at their consternation.

Attracting attention to himself was intended to remove suspicion from others, including Janet.

Unlike the American Embassy, the British Embassy housed a properly functioning MI6 station. Jeremy Wolfenden, using cover as the *Daily Telegraph* correspondent in Moscow, was a professional MI6 agent. Academically and intellectually gifted, he had been described as 'the cleverest boy in England' while at Eton, and he sailed through his Oxford degree with eight alphas, the highest possible marks. But he was an overt homosexual and a heavy drinker, which made him something of a liability in Moscow.

John Vassall, the homosexual clerk in the Naval Attaché's Office in Moscow during 1952–5 had been compromised by the KGB and spied for the Soviet Union for a number of years before being caught. There were at least three instances of Western diplomats being compromised during the first six months of 1962. Two British Embassy staff members were caught with their pants down in the company of attractive Soviet women controlled by the KGB. One of them was spotted by another member of staff, who reported the incident. The other reported himself as soon as the KGB attempted to blackmail him. Both were quickly sent back to the United Kingdom and kept out of harm's way. The Air Attaché at the French Embassy, Colonel Louis Guiband, shot himself after being shown compromising photographs of himself with his Russian girlfriend. The KGB's practices and procedures – as laid down by Serov before he transferred to the GRU – were still being vigorously applied in spite of Khrushchev's orders to the new KGB chief, Alexander Shelepin, to give the KGB a softer image.

Wolfenden knew Penkovsky, but was not directly involved in managing any aspect of his espionage activities, in all likelihood because of the risk of compromising his cover.[†]

[†]   When Wolfenden was posted 'by the *Daily Telegraph*' from Moscow to Washington he surprised everyone by marrying Martina Browne, the nanny of the Chisholms' children in Moscow. He drank himself to death in Washington at the still young age of thirty-one.

Several members of the embassy staff were subordinate to Chisholm, and some senior (non-intelligence) members were also used occasionally to facilitate the exchange of Penkovsky's Minox camera film cassettes.

It is possible that Chisholm, as head of the MI6 station, orchestrated and conducted the activities of these and other people, but it would not make sense for someone who was already known to the KGB through Blake to carry such responsibility.

Howard Smith was an extraordinarily good Head of Chancery.[†] He was a career diplomat, though he had spent five years with MI6 at Bletchley Park during and immediately after the war, working energetically and successfully on the Enigma code-breaking project. In 1978, after thirty-two years as a career diplomat, Smith (by then Sir Howard Smith) was appointed the 9th Director General of the British Security Service (MI5), a post he held until 1981. If Smith were the deep-cover head of the MI6 station in Moscow, with control over Chisholm, it was the embassy's best-kept secret.

‡

The CIA officers involved in the Penkovsky case resented MI6 for running Penkovsky; not simply because they thought the work should be more evenly shared, but because they still viewed MI6 as a dangerously leaky organisation following the Burgess, Maclean, Philby debacle and, more recently, Blake's exposure. However, in spite of its best efforts, the CIA remained incapable of placing reliable agents in Moscow. Ambassador Llewellyn Thompson was proving to be an obstacle.

The CIA were seriously worried about the security

[†] In essence, the Head of Chancery is the head of the political section of the embassy but he or she also has overall responsibility for staff management, morale and welfare, and is generally the coordinator of the work of all sections on behalf of the Ambassador.

consequences of so many meetings between Penkovsky and Janet Chisholm. They brought this up at a debriefing session and Penkovsky suggested he should be invited to official cocktail parties where he could pass over film cassettes and other material and receive new supplies of cassettes. His handlers agreed. Dr David Senior, the scientific attaché at the British Embassy, had met Penkovsky in the context of visiting trade delegations. It would be natural for him to invite Penkovsky to a reception at his house, but the purpose would be twofold: to enable Penkovsky to meet the Chisholms casually and in public so that they would be able to greet each other openly in future, and to facilitate the exchange of films. For the latter exercise, Penkovsky would ask Dr Senior the way to the lavatory. Senior would direct him to a toilet that had been prepared for the exchange. Penkovsky would recover a package of new film cassettes from the underside of the cistern cover and replace it with his package of exposed film, which would then be retrieved by a third party.

A similar event would be arranged at a later date in the house of the commercial minister, Mr Hilary King.

In spite of these occasional alternative arrangements, Penkovsky continued to meet Janet Chisholm virtually every week during the final three months of 1961, passing her twenty-seven rolls of exposed film, each capable of holding thirty-six exposures: a total of almost 1,000 pages of secret documentation in just three months. On top of that, he was taking ever greater risks. On one occasion he was briefly left alone in General Buzinov's office and, spotting a secret document on the desk, proceeded to photograph its pages, hoping to complete the task before anyone entered the room.[†]

Penkovsky was advised, for the third time, to stop taking unnecessary risks and to reduce the frequency of his meetings with Janet. But he paid no more than lip service to this. In Moscow, Penkovsky was his own master. He knew the city; he had his own

---

† General Buzinov was Chief Marshal Varentsov's aide.

network of contacts, both social and professional. He knew how the KGB operated and knew what the militia could and could not do. A professional; he understood the risks and could calculate them accurately. In Moscow *he* knew best and was careful in his own way, which did not necessarily mean observing the London and Langley-based protocols of MI6 or the CIA.

24

PENKOVSKY DEBRIEFING (PART 2)

United Kingdom, July 1961

Penkovsky arrived for his second visit to London on 18 July 1961, ahead of the other delegates who were to attend the Soviet Exhibition at Earls Court. Penkovsky was the leader of the delegation and his visit was to last three weeks.

It had been a traumatic fortnight prior to his departure from Moscow. The original authorisation by the Soviet Council of Ministers for a visit to the Soviet Exhibition in London by forty to fifty delegates was reversed a week later by Khrushchev. Penkovsky's authorisation was reinstated because of the work he had to do for the GRU, and then seven others (a group of metallurgy specialists) also received approval. More delegates were in the pipeline at the time of Penkovsky's departure.

Ivan Serov's wife, Valya, and his daughter, Svetlana, were going to London as tourists on the same flight as Penkovsky. It was a flight specially chartered for the Kirov Ballet Company, going to London as part of the Soviet Exhibition programme.

Serov was at the airport to see his wife and daughter off. It was six o'clock in the morning and there was a chill in the July air. In an unprecedented show of friendship he put one arm round Penkovsky's shoulder and asked him to look after Valya and Svetlana; to see that they had a car at their disposal; that someone helped them with their shopping; and that, in general, they had a good time. Serov always showed genuine love and affection for his family: it was one of the few ways in which he differed markedly from Stalin.

This was a perfect opportunity for Penkovsky to cultivate a close friendship with his boss, the head of the GRU.

The Soviet Embassy failed to meet the Serovs when they arrived at Heathrow Airport. Penkovsky arranged transport for them and said he would contact them again that evening.

Because of other appointments, it was 8.30 p.m. before Penkovsky called to invite them out. It had been a long day and they were already relaxing in their pyjamas and preparing to go to bed. Penkovsky told them boisterously that they were in London and could not afford to waste time in bed.

He took them to his hotel restaurant and paid for an excellent meal, for which he would be reimbursed by MI6. Over dinner, Penkovsky asked them about their shopping plans. Valya said her husband had given her the equivalent of about £20 in US dollars to buy a settee-swing for their dacha garden. Penkovsky told her that was not enough, but not to worry because he would get the swing for them. She thanked him profusely, promising to repay the difference and to invite him to their dacha.

Valya and Svetlana found Penkovsky charming. After the meal, they went on a nocturnal sight-seeing tour of the West End by taxi. The 22-year-old Svetlana – a little tipsy after the generous amounts of excellent wine consumed at dinner – squeezed up close to him. She looked into his eyes and told him she would like 'to dance the rock-and-roll' with him.

‡

Penkovsky reported the courtesies he had extended to the Serovs, and much more, during the debriefing meetings. There was more time than during the April/May visit, and the meetings were more structured now that Penkovsky was working as a proper agent for MI6 and CIA.

They discussed how to make the meetings with Janet Chisholm in Moscow more secure, and how to widen their contact base in Moscow, for example, by the British Embassy's Commercial Minister Hilary King inviting Penkovsky and other Soviet trade officials to a reception at his house. They firmed up arrangements for using Greville Wynne as a contact and considered suggestions as to where Penkovsky could hide his growing volume of espionage materials and equipment. They discussed possible methods of escape to the West in the event that his clandestine activities were discovered.

Above all, they went into astonishing detail about Soviet military armaments, especially rockets and nuclear warheads; their military strategies and intentions; the careers and private lives of senior military, KGB and GRU personnel and their pay and pension levels. Again, Penkovsky emphasised his view of Khrushchev's belligerent attitude.

Kisevalter: What new developments do you know about the Soviet position on the Berlin question? For example: what is the present Soviet position, what action have they taken, and what is their plan?

Penkovsky: The Soviet position is as follows: first of all, if it were possible, an advance by a huge army on a wide front using only conventional weapons and no rockets with atomic or hydrogen warheads. There would probably be mass defections to our (the West) side. I mention this as a preamble to the situation.

Kisevalter: Is this *your* view or do Varentsov and others share this view?

Penkovsky: This is a general view because our situation at home is rotten. They don't trust Khrushchev, they don't trust the Soviet government, and the people remain half-hungry as before. The people are very displeased with Khrushchev's militant speeches; Kennedy, Macmillan and De Gaulle have been forced to increase their armament programmes by two or three times. If Stalin were alive he would do everything quietly, but this fool is blurting out his threats and intentions and is forcing our potential enemies to increase their military strength. They dislike him and say that he is hurting his own cause and that he talks too much about Soviet military accomplishments in his effort to frighten the Western leaders.

We (the West) should react with firmness if he blocks the access roads to Berlin. Those blocking forces should be smashed, without striking with atomic weapons, at industrial centres or rear areas. Should he attempt to do this then he should be repaid in kind and the whole world told that the West is protecting its vital interests which Khrushchev has trampled upon in violation of the Potsdam Agreement signed after World War II. If he expands the conflict to some degree then he should be answered with corresponding counterblows. Actually, Khrushchev and the Soviet Army at this time are unprepared for this.

25

PENKOVSKY DEBRIEFING (PART 3)

France, September–October 1961

A Soviet Trade Fair in Paris in September 1961 created the next opportunity for Penkovsky to meet the same CIA/MI6 debriefing team. He arrived in Paris on 20 September and, at the first meeting, resumed his discourse about Khrushchev's belligerency.

> Penkovsky: This old man is striving to accomplish some fantastic coup during his lifetime. Khrushchev is stirring up all of the trouble that there is. He is the instigator of everything. He is the formulator and executor of all this dirty business and adventurism. If he died or was killed it would relieve and change the situation considerably to our (the West's) advantage. It seems that he knows he has not many years to live and he wants to do something like a maniac, which stems from his senility.

By this time, Penkovsky was able to report on Soviet plans for future actions. One of the most important of these concerned Soviet military manoeuvres scheduled to coincide with the 22nd Party Congress, due to start in Moscow on 17 October.

President Kennedy first met Khrushchev three months earlier, at the Vienna Summit on 4 and 5 June 1961. The agenda was wide-ranging but the most important outcome was their disagreement over Berlin.

Militarily, West Berlin was extremely vulnerable to any Soviet or East German move to compromise its status. Western forces within West Berlin were limited and certainly no match for Soviet forces in East Germany and neighbouring satellite countries. The Allied access corridor – a 100-mile-long autobahn running across East Germany – could not be defended. The Soviets and East Germans could now make it much more difficult to sustain an airlift similar to that of the blockade of 1948–9.

Khrushchev's threat at the Vienna Summit to sign a separate peace treaty with East Germany if the West did not enter into negotiations to settle the Berlin problem would give East Germany responsibility for the corridor. This contravened the post-war agreement for Allied control of Berlin and it could result in Allied forces and other officials having to deal directly with the East German authorities. This would constitute a major problem because the West did not recognise East Germany as a sovereign state.

On his return to the United States from the Vienna Summit, Kennedy was horrified to discover that American military plans to defend West Berlin in the event of Soviet aggression were to send tanks across East Germany. Should they meet with unassailable opposition, the battle would escalate rapidly into nuclear warfare.

A few weeks later Kennedy announced plans for a massive increase in the strength of American conventional forces to ensure continued Allied access to Berlin. This move was used by the Soviet and East German authorities as an excuse for finally closing the border between East and West Berlin on 13 August with the erection of the Berlin Wall.

More than ever, Berlin was now a strategic chess piece in the delicate and complex battle of wills between Khrushchev and Kennedy.

Khrushchev announced that the Soviet Union would sign the threatened peace treaty with East Germany at the end of the 22nd Party Congress in October. Penkovsky put it to the debriefing team like this:

Penkovsky: Since I left you in England I have had the opportunity of speaking with Varentsov, Zasorin, Buzinov and many others. This is what I must relate to you at once.

In the beginning of October this year there will begin extensive general strategic manoeuvres. There were never such manoeuvres in the history of the Soviet Army. This is because all headquarters of all military districts will participate and also all headquarters of groups of forces. Even all rear services in the military districts will participate in these manoeuvres. In other words, every Army formation will execute its assigned mission in these manoeuvres just as they would be called upon to do in case there was a war. In addition, all headquarters of all countries of People's Democracies will also take part in the manoeuvres. These strategic manoeuvres will begin in early October and will take place throughout the entire USSR and throughout all of the countries of People's Democracies, all based on combating a hypothetical enemy in the direction of Germany …

I will now try to explain to you in detail why these manoeuvres will take place and what their objective is … These manoeuvres will continue for a period of up to a month. The objective is to examine everything as a whole and to determine what units have specific capabilities. They will examine who can best fulfil offensive missions, shock action, defensive operations and to examine the state of training and combat readiness of all units, as well as their joint action. Through these manoeuvres deficiencies in training can be corrected and experience in joint operations gained.

But this is only one purpose: the second purpose is to have these huge forces in a state of combat readiness exactly at the time that the Peace Treaty with East Germany will be signed, so that if any difficulties occur immediately after the signing of this Treaty, which will be signed right after the Congress, they would be in a position to strike a heavy blow. In other words, what Khrushchev wants to do is to backdrop his signing of the Peace Treaty with East Germany with actual large-scale military preparations camouflaged as manoeuvres.

Khrushchev considers that if NATO swallows this second pill

(he considers that the first pill – the closing of the borders of East and West Berlin last month, on 13 August – has already been swallowed) ... and say 'very well, since you have signed a Treaty with East Germany we will deal with East Germany', then the strain will be relieved and the manoeuvres will terminate and the result of these will still serve as a valuable training exercise for joint operations. If not, the powder is still dry and military action can be employed. This is the dual purpose for which these manoeuvres are planned for the early days of October.

One cannot overestimate the value of this graphic statement of the Soviet Union's plans for a build-up of military strength in East Germany. Khrushchev's announced intention of signing a peace treaty with East Germany was an immediate threat to West Berlin. Now, with the intelligence provided by Penkovsky, the West could mobilise their forces to match the Soviet military build-up, and thus continue to threaten military action should either the Soviet or East German authorities try to block Allied access to West Berlin. There was the implied threat that nuclear devices could be used.

In the event, the Soviet Union did not sign a peace treaty with East Germany, the Allied corridor to West Berlin was not closed, and the threat of war was averted: a war that could have become nuclear, destroying much of Europe and killing millions of people.

This example of Penkovsky's value to the West is often over-shadowed by the emphasis placed on his contribution to the resolution of the Cuban Missile Crisis.

Penkovsky could also have warned the West about the plans to close the East/West Berlin border, except that the procedure for him to contact his handlers in an emergency was confined to only one day a week.

Penkovsky: Incidentally, I knew about this closing [of the East/West Berlin Border] four days before the fact and I wanted to pass this on to you but had no means for doing so, since the phone call arrangement was only good for Monday and this took place on a different day.

He reported details of Varentsov's sixtieth birthday party.

Penkovsky: Varentsov's birthday party was celebrated not on 15 September but on Saturday 16th in order to permit more time. On the 15th at 0900 hours I met Varentsov at Leningrad Railway Station where he had just arrived from Leningrad. I had given him his electric battery razor as soon as I got back after the last time I saw you, but on the 15th at the railway station I brought him a package containing the cognac, about which I shall tell you in a moment, and it is not without interest for you, as well as the rocket-shaped lighter and the cigarette box with the inscriptions thereon. He kissed me as he greeted me at the station. He was also met there by Lieutenant General Voznesensky and Lieutenant General Nikolayev.

We all got together at 1600 hours on 16 September at Varentsov's dacha. When I arrived with my family Ryabchikov, the Professor of Chemistry, was already there. Then Lieutenant General Semenov came, then General Fomin, then the Minister [of Defence] Malinovsky came with his wife. There were others.

The presents we brought were the best and most sensible of the lot. Malinovsky brought a magnum of Champagne and also a big cake shaped like the Horn of Plenty. Churayev brought a large wooden eagle on a stand. Varentsov said that 'my boy' (me) had really tried to do everything from his heart. I wanted to tell him that there were *five* boys doing this.

The only one in uniform was the Minister and when I was presented to him he asked if I didn't have a relative in the Far East, to which I replied that I had a distant relative of sorts. Varentsov said to Malinovsky that I was one of Serov's boys.

When we sat down Varentsov told me to do the honours so I opened our Cognac. It turned out to be out of this world (sixty years old). The Minister wanted to drink only that Cognac. I made

LEFT A stern image of Ivan Serov, taken in 1955 when he was Chairman of the KGB. His short stature is demonstrated by his feet being off the ground. © Corbis

BOTTOM A smiling Ivan Serov with his homely wife, Valya, speaking to Edmund Stevens, the veteran Moscow correspondent for several Western newspapers and magazines. © Getty Images

TOP LEFT The CIA and MI6 jointly built a tunnel under the Soviet Sector of Berlin to tap strategically important communications cables. The tap chamber (at the bottom of the photo) was just inches below the road surface. The tunnel was 'discovered' by the Soviets on 22 April 1956, but they had known about it from the early planning stages from information supplied by George Blake, the Soviet mole inside MI6. © Bundesarchiv

TOP RIGHT George Blake, an MI6 officer, arriving back in the United Kingdom on 1 April 1953 after being held captive for three years by the Communist North Koreans. The Communists had 'turned' him and he immediately started to spy for the Soviet KGB. © Corbis

LEFT Janet and Ruari Chisholm. During their posting to Moscow Ruari was head of the MI6 station but it was Janet who made regular contact with Penkovsky, the Soviet military intelligence officer who passed an incredible amount of high-quality military and other intelligence to MI6 and the CIA.

TOP Revolutionaries in Budapest burn a picture of Stalin during the Hungarian uprising in the autumn of 1956. This would have infuriated Serov, who was in Budapest largely controlling the Soviet political and military response.
© Corbis

LEFT Stalinist hard-liner Yuri Andropov was the Soviet Ambassador in Budapest during the uprising and gave strong support to Serov.
© Corbis

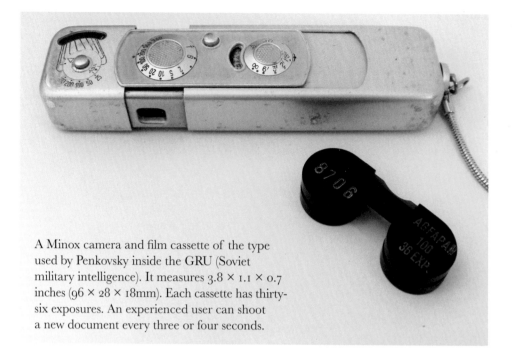

A Minox camera and film cassette of the type used by Penkovsky inside the GRU (Soviet military intelligence). It measures 3.8 × 1.1 × 0.7 inches (96 × 28 × 18mm). Each cassette has thirty-six exposures. An experienced user can shoot a new document every three or four seconds.

LEFT British Prime Minister Harold Macmillan talking to Soviet Premier Nikita Khrushchev at the British Embassy in Paris on 15 May 1960. © Corbis

RIGHT Greville Wynne (top, speaking into microphone) and Oleg Penkovsky (bottom) on trial in Moscow in May 1963 on charges of spying for the West. Penkovsky was sentenced to death and Wynne to eight years in prison. © Corbis

The Berlin Wall, April 1962. A young woman, accompanied by her boyfriend, stands –
precariously – near the top of the Wall to talk to her mother in East Berlin. © Corbis

Khrushchev embracing
Cuban President Fidel
Castro at the Soviet
Legislation Building in
New York, 23 September
1960. © Corbis

President John F. Kennedy meeting with Soviet Foreign Minister Andrei Gromyko
in the White House, 18 October 1962. Gromyko insisted Soviet arms in Cuba were
purely defensive but Kennedy already knew there were offensive weapons there.
© US National Security Archive

Crates holding Komar guided-missile patrol boats on the deck of a ship bound for Cuba, September 1962.
© US National Security Archive

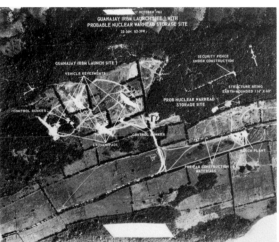

A U-2 photograph of the first IRBM site found under construction in Cuba. It was taken on 17 October 1962.
© US National Security Archive

Lee Harvey Oswald distributing 'Hands off Cuba' leaflets in New Orleans. © Corbis

President John F. Kennedy in the limousine on Main Street, Dallas, minutes before he was assassinated.

MIDDLE LEFT The view Oswald would have had, looking out from the sixth floor of the School Book Depository building to Elm Street, from where he shot President Kennedy. © Getty Images

MIDDLE RIGHT Jack Ruby shooting Lee Harvey Oswald on 24 November 1963. © Getty Images

LEFT Nightclub owner Jack Ruby: very much his own man. He shot Oswald for killing the President of the United States. © Corbis it go round for everyone three times; however I gave full glasses only to the Minister, Varentsov, Churayev and myself. They began to feel tipsy after the first round because the Minister made a toast to Varentsov and everyone drank bottoms-up. The Cognac was so good and everyone was so delighted with it that they talked about it for half-an-hour out of the six hours that the party lasted.

After that there were toasts by Varentsov and Semenov and finally it came to me. I remembered that no one mentioned the fact that Varentsov had just been presented with the Order of Lenin, so I said that I proposed to drink a toast of congratulations to Sergei Sergeievich for his having been the recipient of the highest governmental award, the Order of Lenin. As they began to applaud I thought I would pull a fast one on the Minister, so I continued by saying that this award represents the high esteem for Sergei Sergeievich by the Party, the government and personally by the Minister of Defence. After that he beamed and I could talk to him as a Comrade. He continued to drink Cognac and vodka and frankly the other cognac was junk. Churayev, about whom I shall give you details later, drank a lot and was getting tipsy. After this the men went into the next room to smoke and I kept my eyes and ears open as you would expect an intelligence officer to do.

Kisevalter: Was Khrushchev criticised by anyone at the party?

Penkovsky: No; they drank a toast to him. They are all people placed in their positions by Khrushchev.

Much of the information Penkovsky had reported about the military manoeuvres and nuclear warhead testing was from tongues loosened by the 'sixty'-year-old Cognac at that party.

Janet Chisholm appeared for a while at the meeting held in Paris on 27 September, when they discussed the schedule for Penkovsky's future meetings with her in Moscow:

After Janet [they now called her Janet rather than Ann, as heretofore] had described her normal pattern of movements on

Mondays and Fridays to the Arbat area, the following schedule was established to cover the rest of the month of October and the months of November and December. The October schedule would begin on Friday 20 October, which would be a personal meet at the Commission store on the Arbat at 1300 hours. For every Friday, beginning 20 October and running through until the end of November, this site and time would be considered as the basic meeting. Every Monday following the Fridays would be considered to be the alternative meeting for the preceding Friday. The place would be the left-hand store on the second floor of the Praga Restaurant and the time would also be at 1300 hours. Only in the event that no meeting took place on the Friday would Janet appear on the following Monday. For December, the basic meeting would still be on Fridays and it would take place on 1 December, but the site would now be in the park at 1600 hours. The alternative meeting would still be on Mondays at 1300 hours at the store above the Praga. There would be no alternative meeting on Christmas Day, which would be a Monday.

The final meeting in Paris, on 14 October – the forty-second meeting of the series that had started in London on 20 April – ended emotionally. After recording all of the business that had been transacted during the course of the meeting, the report concludes:

Now there was much photography done of the individual case officers with Penkovsky and of group photographs, and champagne toasts were drunk. There was a modest spread of canapés and, after the traditional and somewhat emotional farewell on the part of Penkovsky during which he kissed and hugged each case officer in turn, all sat down for a moment of silence in the traditional Russian style. Penkovsky left at 2245 hours to be deposited by Mike [Stokes] and Joseph [Bulik] in the neighbourhood of the Caravelle Bar where he was to be met by Wynne to finish his last evening in Paris prior to his rising at 0500 hours the next morning to be accompanied by Wynne for his scheduled flight to Prague.

At the London, Birmingham, Leeds and Paris debriefing meetings with Penkovsky, when the full extent of his ability to provide high-grade intelligence became increasingly apparent, there was a growing awareness of the need for increased security in passing the information. Towards the end of 1961 and into 1962, the team regularly suggested to Penkovsky that he should reduce his espionage activities in the interests of his own security, or even stop them altogether for a few months.

Kisevalter: We're concerned that the frequency of your meetings with Janet is too high. Weekly meetings make it a huge risk that you'll get caught. We'd much rather have less intelligence than see you getting caught. Your safety is paramount to us, as it should be to you.

Penkovsky: I'm an experienced intelligence officer. I'll take precautions.

Shergold: Well let's use other means then; start to use dead letter drops more often. There are other ways.

Penkovsky: No. I don't like dead letter drops; they're too dangerous and should be used only in emergencies. Besides, I like personal contact. Wynne is coming to Moscow in January or February, and he's also going to Belgrade and maybe Bucharest. There's talk of me organising and accompanying the Soviet delegation to the Seattle World Fair in May. I can use those opportunities, safely, to pass films and other intelligence to you, and that would reduce the number of times I meet Janet.

Kisevalter: Yes, but there are still big gaps. You have to be careful; this is not a game, you know.

Penkovsky: You'll have to arrange for me to be invited in my official capacity to Embassy parties. First of all I have to meet Janet at such a party so that I know her officially and I then have a legend for talking to her if I happen to see her in the Arbat area or in the park. I have already met Hilary King [commercial minister at the British Embassy] and Doctor David Senior [scientific attaché at the British Embassy] at trade exhibitions in the course of my duties. I should be invited to their parties and I could pass my material to someone there and not just Janet. That could be done with excellent safety.

Kisevalter: Right. We'll see what we can do.

‡

Kisevalter, for all his excellence at leading the debriefings, appeared to have difficulty in accepting that it was Britain and not America that had landed Penkovsky. He seems to have been uncomfortable with MI6's overall responsibility for hosting, organising and controlling the activities surrounding the debriefings.

Commenting afterwards on problems the Americans had in Birmingham (England) with the recording equipment they brought over from America, he said:

> In Birmingham we had a technical flap with the British, but we managed to luck out. We took along two large cases with Mohawk battery operated recorders just in case we should need them. Unfortunately they are albatrosses because we had no place to leave them except at the US Embassy. Therefore, in the hotel room, someone had to be with those damn pieces of equipment. On travelling, we took them along. Well, when we hit Birmingham on a Sunday night, the Scotsmen came in with some very incongruous expressions which sounded like 'whir oh whir, we are in trouble'. We had hit the tail end of the world in England. This part of the town, the centre part, is still on direct current. I have no place to get a converter at midnight on Sunday and the tape recorder can't work.
>
> So we said, 'however, for three thousand miles we have carried those damned instruments of ours on battery. Let's see if they can pick up the slack.' So we ran eight reels and they all came out.

This was a strange criticism, calling the centre of the modern industrialised city of Birmingham 'the tail end of the world' and mocking the accents of Scottish engineers. Above all, Kisevalter appears to have got the wrong end of the stick: Birmingham was on alternating current – not direct current, as he claimed – and the problem is more likely to have been that the American's standard AC recorders were set for 110 volts and 60 cycles (Hertz), while in Britain and most of the rest of the world the electricity current is 220 volts and 50 cycles. They should have known this and brought the correct specification of equipment, or transformers.

Then there were the snide little remarks:

> ... We were brewing tea now. Every four o'clock is tea. We are in Britain, you know. We are taking time out for tea...

It hurt Kisevalter that Penkovsky's contact in Moscow was with the wife of a British diplomat rather than someone from the American Embassy:

> At this point of history the wife of an MI6 officer, Ann [Janet Chisholm], was brought into the act. She was stationed in Moscow. Ann came and was introduced to Penkovsky in London... We didn't like it in terms of frequency of meetings, outside of official functions... All right, you can do this once or twice, but beyond that you are gambling. The British say: 'and what do you have, American, besides a big mouth?' They just about were as nasty as that. We didn't have very much going at that moment, but on the road we had plenty in the pipeline. Our object was to get an appropriate man in the [American] Embassy under appropriate cover, which was a big headache.

Kisevalter had more to say about the British after the debriefing meetings in Paris in September 1961:

> In the meantime we had cased more safe houses and more meeting sites and everything else that we needed in Paris. There, unfortunately, the British have assets far and away above anything we could dream of in the way of safe houses, support

assets and everything you want in Paris. After all, they are close to the continent themselves; they have been there for many, many years and they know how to operate. So, [expletive] the British safe house, the British vehicle, a lot of them hired, a lot of them right-hand drive. Every day I went from Orly to Le Bourget and back, a beautiful distance of about forty or fifty miles through French traffic; we had a special driver, Roger King, who drove [expletive]. He was a race track driver.

Conversely, Kisevalter was well aware that Americans were not universally liked. Talking about Soviets who might consider defecting to the United States, he rounded off his comments with this philosophical thought (bearing in mind that Kisevalter was born in Russia):

There are in-betweeners for whom the timing is off. The concept is ripe but the timing is off: family situations, obligations which may change. He might say, like Penkovsky said, 'If you see Colonel Peeke, give him my greetings'. Maybe Peeke did a great deal without really knowing it himself; of putting some seeds of thought to cooperate with us in Penkovsky's mind. Someone else may get the credit in the future for the contact, but there is where the seed comes in. So don't pass up the shit if the guy doesn't want to play ball because he can't at this time. Of course, in the case of the fellow who never would [defect], you still have an asset to generate by creating respect for you. At the very outside, he who hates the United States might at least tell another Soviet 'You know, all Americans aren't sons of bitches. I met one who wasn't.'

After the final debriefing meeting, in Paris in October 1961, Kisevalter was withdrawn from the CIA team and replaced by a more junior case officer.

The British team had nothing but praise for the brilliance of Kisevalter's work in handling Penkovsky. It was not just his familiarity with the language that impressed them, but the way in which he managed to get into Penkovsky's psyche; to see him through rough patches, to give this headstrong man his head and yet deftly rein him in when that was necessary. No one could have done it better.

While Kisevalter bemoaned the fact that MI6 were largely responsible for managing the Penkovsky case, other senior CIA officers refused to acknowledge it. Astonishingly, CIA Director John McCone even went so far as to claim that the CIA recruited and controlled Penkovsky and kindly allowed MI6 to participate because Penkovsky had to be managed outside the United States. The minutes of a 1963 meeting of the President's Foreign Intelligence Advisory Board record that:

> Mr McCone then turned to the Board's question on implications of the Penkovsky case as they relate to British and US security. He said that Penkovsky provided us intelligence from August 1960 through August 1962, and gave us more than 8,000 pages of translated reporting, most of which constituted highly classified Soviet defence documents. He stated that the case did not have any security implications for Britain or the US as this was a controlled agent *recruited by CIA and shared with MI6 who we got into the circuit because the contact was outside the USSR and we used London on several occasions for meetings.*

He continued, at the same meeting, to claim that the British were responsible for Penkovsky getting caught: '*We think that the case was blown because of a penetration of the British government who saw Wynne and Penkovsky together.*'[†]

---

†   The CIA have never claimed publicly that they think the British were responsible for Penkovsky being caught. They state on their website that: 'To this day, it is unclear who or what implicated Penkovsky. Some believe that George Blake informed the KGB about Penkovsky's work for the United States and Great Britain. At that point, the KGB began to keep a close watch on Penkovsky. KGB officers were stationed in apartments above and across the river from Penkovsky's home.'

26

WASHINGTON AND MIAMI 1961

John F. Kennedy was inaugurated as the thirty-fifth President of the United States on 20 January 1961. Prior to his inauguration there had been growing opposition to the proposed invasion of Cuba in some government circles, but Kennedy had made it clear he supported the plan and the voices of caution were drowned out.

In April, as the time for the invasion approached, the President asked CIA Director Allen Dulles for a full briefing on the plan. Dulles recapped that President Eisenhower had given approval for a programme of covert action against the Castro regime. The CIA set up a unit called *Operation 40*, which was based in the CIA's covert Miami station (*JM/WAVE*). He explained the complexities of dealing with thousands of Cuban expatriates who were anxious to have Castro removed as soon as possible, but the CIA had to train them first, and at the same time try to ensure that the US administration had plausible deniability of all aspects of *Operation 40*.

Dulles continued to give background information so that the new President would fully understand the problems. The eighty CIA operatives at *JM/WAVE* had to deal with more than 2,000 Cuban exiles who were to be involved in the planned invasion. In effect, the exile invasion force – called Brigade 2506 – was an extension of *Operation 40*. The CIA supplied Brigade 2506 with aircraft, boats and weapons and gave them training, mostly in Guatemala and Nicaragua.

Eventually, Dulles started to brief the President on the plan itself. Preliminary action – the bombing of airports – was scheduled for 15 April, with the invasion slated for the 17th. The ground and air forces would all embark from Nicaragua.

The President asked questions. The 15th was just a couple of weeks away: would everyone be ready by then? Two thousand seemed a very small number for an invasion force: would they be strong enough to carry out a successful invasion?

Ideally, they would like more time and more men – answered Dulles – but CIA intelligence reports from Cuba indicated a rapid build-up of Soviet bloc weapons for Castro's forces, and there was also an influx of Spanish-speaking military trainers and advisers from the Soviet Union. The longer they delayed the invasion, the greater the opposition would be.

The order of battle was to send over two waves of planes, starting two days before the actual landing. They would bomb Cuba's airports and destroy or ground the Cuban Air Force, thus enabling US air and sea cover for Brigade 2506. Some US Navy vessels and aircraft would be on standby, outside Cuba's three-mile territorial water limit, to intimidate the Cuban forces and encourage Brigade 2506. They would not be brought into action unless that was thought desirable in the light of the situation on the ground. Dulles assured the President that this was the method they had used – successfully – in 1954 to overthrow Jacobo Arbenz in Guatemala.

With regard to numbers, 2,000 was really a decent-sized force for a landing in one location. As planned, 300 men would be parachuted in to secure the roads for the sea-borne force. CIA intelligence indicated that once they secured a foothold on land, most of the population and many in the armed forces throughout Cuba would give immediate support to the counter-revolution and it would not be necessary to fight all the way to Havana.

The CIA also supported a number of anti-Castro counter-revolutionary groups within Cuba. For reasons of secrecy they were not part of the invasion plan, but once Brigade 2506 had landed they would be expected to help stabilise the situation.

The President queried the support that would be given by US forces, saying that it transgressed the precept of plausible deniability. He was on record as supporting President Eisenhower's policy of removing Castro and Communism from Cuba, and he was also on record for criticising Eisenhower's apparently leisurely approach to the issue. Kennedy now found himself morally committed to allowing the plan to invade Cuba to go ahead. He asked for written details of the battle plans, which he would return to Dulles within forty-eight hours.

On 4 April President Kennedy approved the plan, having made only one major change to it. The original plan was for a daytime landing at the town of Trinidad on Cuba's southern coast but the President, who had commanded motor torpedo boats on night-time operations during his time in the US Navy, said he did not like the idea of landing in a heavily populated area where there were bound to be widespread civilian casualties. Instead, he suggested a night-time landing on the beaches in the Bahía de Cochinos (Bay of Pigs).

☦

The Bay of Pigs was a humiliating disaster for the Americans. There was only one air strike on Cuban airfields before the landing and it did not inflict sufficient damage to prevent Cuban Air Force fighters from attacking the invading Brigade 2506. President Kennedy vetoed further strikes because of promises made at the United Nations to the effect that the US would not take an active part in any attack on Cuba.

The landing craft approached three beaches just after midnight on the night of 16 April. As dawn arrived, Cuban Air Force fighters started to attack them. Brigade 2506 aircraft counterattacked, bringing some relief and a beach-head of sorts was made. However, the invading forces came under attack from increasing numbers of Cuban ground forces and the battle was lost by the middle of the third day (19 April).

Of the 1,700 Cuban exiles and sympathisers in Brigade 2506, 114 were killed in action and many more injured. Casualties in Castro's forces were heavier. More than 1,100 members of Brigade 2506 were taken captive.[†]

The acutely embarrassed Kennedy administration laid the blame fairly and squarely on the CIA. A report on the Bay of Pigs operation, issued in November 1961 by the CIA's Inspector-General, cited nine major deficiencies in its management and execution. They included insufficient employment of high-quality staff and failure to collect and analyse intelligence competently.

Responsibility within the CIA fell on Director Allen Dulles, Deputy Director Charles Cabell, and Deputy Director for Plans Richard Bissell. President Kennedy required all three of them to resign over a period of nine months following the catastrophe.

The effect within Cuba was to strengthen Castro's position, to increase the build-up of conventional arms and to improve the training of Cuban forces. On 1 May 1961 – Mayday – Castro declared Cuba a Socialist Republic.

In their defence, the CIA said that Kennedy's order not to send a second air strike prior to the landings had seriously reduced Brigade 2506's chances of success. Also, the CIA's planning had been based on support from US forces immediately after the landings in the event that Brigade 2506 failed to meet its objectives. After all – they argued – President Eisenhower had authorised this in the successful CIA-sponsored coup in Guatemala and virtually all of the planning for the Bay of Pigs operation had occurred under Eisenhower's presidency.

Kennedy's decisions not to allow the second wave of air attacks prior to the landing and to forbid the use of US forces in the

---

† In December 1962, Castro agreed to exchange 1,113 prisoners for US$53 million worth of food and medicines.

event of the landings meeting insurmountable opposition incited great resentment within the CIA and anti-Castro organisations. For some individuals, this resentment festered until Kennedy's assassination in November 1963.

✝

The chastened President Kennedy was now more than ever anxious to dispense with Castro. He was determined that the next attempt would be properly organised, funded and managed. Within a few days of the failed invasion he appointed General Maxwell Taylor, who had retired as Chief of Staff two years earlier, to lead a task force to investigate the Bay of Pigs shambles. The other members of the task force were Attorney-General Robert Kennedy, Admiral Arleigh Burke and CIA Director Allen Dulles. The inclusion of Dulles appears an odd choice: Kennedy first sacked him over the failure of the Bay of Pigs invasion and then appointed him to the task force charged with investigating that failure. Was this some kind of an apology, or was he rubbing salt into the wound?

Taylor presented the report of the task force's findings to the President in June. It analysed the many reasons for the failure of the invasion in detail and went on to state that developments in Cuba represented a real threat. It recommended a new programme of action employing the full range of political, military, economic and psychological tactics.

Based on this report, Kennedy gave his approval for a covert programme of sabotage and subversion against Cuba. He created a new team called Special Group Augmented (SGA) charged with delivering it. Attorney-General Robert Kennedy was chairman and the other members were Allen Dulles (soon to be replaced by John McCone as director of the CIA), Roswell Gilpatric (Defence Department), McGeorge Bundy (National Security adviser), Alexis Johnson (State Department), General Lyman Lemnitzer (Joint Chiefs of Staff) and General

Maxwell Taylor. Secretary of State Dean Rusk and Secretary of Defence Robert McNamara also attended meetings, though they were not official members of the SGA.

At their first meeting on 4 November 1961, they decided to call the operation *'Operation Mongoose'*. Robert Kennedy also decided that Major-General Edward Lansdale (staff member of the President's Committee on Military Assistance) should control liaison between the SGA and *Mongoose* operations.

Allen Dulles's forced resignation as director of the CIA was scheduled for 28 November. In a surprise move, President Kennedy appointed a businessman, John McCone, to replace him.

It was a busy and sad day for Dulles. He was the father of the new CIA headquarters building in Langley, Virginia. It was he who, when he took up office in 1953, had pressed for a new building to replace the many offices the CIA occupied around Washington. He decided what kind of building would offer the best security and attract the best staff, also selecting its location. He was consulted at every stage of the design and construction. He designed his own office, but said he would not move in until all other staff were installed in their offices. It was harsh enough that President Kennedy required him to resign after the Bay of Pigs fiasco, but discovering that the date of his resignation was also the day the President presided over the dedication of the new building added salt to the wound. There was, however, some consolation during the ceremony when the President presented him with the National Security Medal.

Later that same day Robert Kennedy suddenly called a meeting with Dulles, his successor John McCone, and Major-General Edward Lansdale to discuss the CIA's role in *Operation Mongoose*.

Among other things, they discussed who should be in charge of the CIA's side of the operation. As there had been no written agenda and no time to prepare for the discussions, the only name that came up was Jim Chritchfield, a quietly successful and much respected senior Foreign Intelligence officer in the CIA. He was suggested by Lansdale. Dulles said he thought

Chritchfield would serve America better by continuing with his recent appointment as head of the CIA's Near East Division and that he would like a day or two to come up with an alternative nominee.

Dulles consulted Bissell, who had been allowed to stay on as the CIA's Deputy Director for Plans for another three months before he, too, resigned. Bissell proposed Bill Harvey to lead the CIA's side of *Operation Mongoose*. Harvey was at that time the chief of Division D, which was one of the CIA's most secret divisions, dealing with political warfare.

Dulles was sceptical. He thought well of Harvey's work and was satisfied with his competence, but he feared what might happen if – or rather, when – Harvey disagreed with Robert Kennedy.

Lansdale agreed, however, to put Harvey's name forward and the Attorney-General accepted him after being reminded that it was Harvey who had masterminded the Berlin tunnel. The appointment was approved by the President.

Bissell called Harvey into his office and told him about *Operation Mongoose* and his (Harvey's) appointment as leader of CIA operations under *Mongoose*. He also said that the President wished to meet him in the Oval Office. (Some maintain that Harvey was carrying a firearm when he met the President.)

For the next two months Harvey went into planning mode. *Operation Mongoose* had precedence over virtually every other CIA operation and this enabled him to raid other divisions for their best staff.

He called his team '*Task Force W*' and its CIA component moved into the basement of the new headquarters at Langley, Virginia. *Task Force W* became operational, officially, on 1 February 1962.

27

CUBA 1961

Fidel Castro had been in power for two years and the harsh realities of trying to run a strict socialist political and economic programme so close to the United States had begun to take its toll. This only served to increase Castro's determination to build an egalitarian utopia. In doing so, he had to rely increasingly upon the help and goodwill of the Soviet Union and other Eastern Bloc countries.

On 2 January the victory anniversary parade included Soviet Bloc rocket launchers, tanks and heavy artillery. In his speech, Castro demanded that the United States clear the nest of spies out of their embassy in Havana and leave only eleven people: the same number as staffed the Cuban Embassy in Washington. In response, the United States broke off diplomatic relations with Cuba the next day.

Castro insisted that his regime was not Communist, but by February 1961 he had started to soften these protestations. He acknowledged that Cuba's Communist Party was 'the only Cuban party that has always clearly proclaimed the necessity for radical change of the island's social structure. It is also true,' he said,

> that at first the Communists distrusted me and us rebels. It was a justified distrust, an absolutely correct position, ideologically and politically. The Communists were right to be distrustful because we of the Sierra, leaders of the guerrillas, were still full

of petty-bourgeois prejudices and defects, despite Marxist reading. The ideas were not clear to us, though we wanted with all our strength to destroy tyranny and privileges. Then we came together, we understood each other, and began to collaborate. The Communists have given much blood, much heroism, to the Cuban cause. Now we continue to work together; loyally and fraternally.

Sporadic acts of sabotage and terrorism against Cuba ran in parallel with the arrest of spies, such as the CIA's Carlos Antonio Cabo, and leaders of anti-revolutionary groups still based in Cuba, some of whom were executed. The actions against Castro's regime culminated in the bombing of Cuban airfields on 15 April and the Bay of Pigs invasion on 17 April.

Two weeks later, chastened to some extent by the attempt to invade but emboldened by its failure, Castro gave a powerful May Day speech at the end of a long day of celebrations. He spoke about the success over imperialism and condemned President Kennedy's support for the invasion, saying:

Let us not talk about what would have happened if the imperialists had won. There is no sadder picture than a defeated revolution. That is why we were thinking that every smile today was like a tribute to those who made possible this hopeful day. The blood that was shed was the blood of workers and peasants, the blood of humble sons of the people, not blood of land-owners, millionaires, thieves, criminals, or exploiters...

Rights do not come from size. Right does not come from one country being bigger than another. That does not matter. We have only limited territory, a small nation, but our right is as respectable as that of any country, regardless of its size. It does not occur to us to tell the people of the United States what system of government they must have. Therefore it is absurd for Mr Kennedy to take it into his head to tell us what kind of government he wants us to have here. That is absurd.

He likened Kennedy to Hitler and Mussolini, and continued:

> We do not endanger the security of a single North American. We do not endanger the life or security of a single North American family. We, making cooperatives, agrarian reform, people's ranches, houses, schools, literacy campaigns, and sending thousands and thousands of teachers to the interior, building hospitals, sending doctors, giving scholarships, building factories, increasing the productive capacity of our country, creating public beaches, converting fortresses into schools, and give the people the right to a better future – we do not endanger a single US family or a single US citizen.

The revolutionary government continued to prosecute and severely punish those who participated in the Bay of Pigs invasion and other acts against Cuba. On 23 September, an American and five Cubans were executed by firing squad for their part in the Bay of Pigs.

Administratively, or perhaps simply organisationally, the economic and social reforms were successful, but they did not bring with them any degree of prosperity. More help was needed. Castro at last succumbed to the inevitable and, on 2 December 1961, declared himself a convert to the Marxist–Leninist cause.

28

WASHINGTON AND MIAMI 1962

William Harvey's indefatigable work on setting up *Task Force W* – the team that would implement *Operation Mongoose* – was more or less complete by the beginning of February 1962. *Task Force W* became officially operational on 1 February.

The operational element was based in Building 25 on the South Campus of the University of Miami. This CIA station, code named '*JM/WAVE*', became the largest CIA station in the world apart from its headquarters in the Virginia suburb of Langley, near Washington D.C. The abysmal Bay of Pigs invasion had been planned in this building but now, with Harvey in charge at Langley and Ted Shackley in charge at *JM/WAVE*, there was a revitalised team that at one stage numbered more than 300 full-time staff and agents, up to 100 of whom worked 'behind enemy lines' in Cuba.[†] In addition, *JM/WAVE* was giving financial and practical support to nearly 15,000 anti-Castro Cuban exiles in Florida.

The existence of the *JM/WAVE* station was supposed to be secret and to this end there were front companies based in Building 25. The main one was Zenith Technical Enterprises, famous for making what were generally acknowledged to be the best mass-produced portable short-wave radios in the world. (Penkovsky specified a Zenith model when he asked the MI6/CIA team to supply him with a short-wave radio.) This cover was

---

†   Ted Shackley had also worked under Harvey in Berlin.

of little avail as the size of the *JM/WAVE* work force and their big budget spend (US$50 million) created a localised miniature economic boom. It was also difficult to hide the commando, espionage and seamanship training provided to the Cuban exiles.

But acute frustration had started to set in within a couple of months. Harvey took stock of the difficult situation.

Operation Mongoose was being controlled by a committee: the Special Group Augmented. (He probably had a few choice words to say about that name.) The SGA was chaired by Attorney-General Robert Kennedy, whom Harvey considered to be a bit of an ass when it came to project management. Kennedy insisted that *Task Force W* had to take stronger, more decisive action, but without making any 'noise' or doing anything that could possibly be attributed to the government: a virtual impossibility in the present situation.

As Harvey was not a member of the SGA he had to put his ideas and proposals to General Edward Lansdale, who would present them to the group. He had no gripe about Lansdale, who was sensible and appeared to do his job quite well, but Harvey's proposals were usually rejected by the SGA or returned in a diluted form. Maybe the new CIA Director, John McCone, did not carry enough weight to defend Harvey's proposals.

McGeorge Bundy seemed to be the main stumbling block in the SGA. He wanted to leave Cuba alone as long as Castro did not do anything to threaten the United States, and he believed that Khrushchev would never put nuclear or any other offensive weapons in Cuba.

The latest assessment of the National Intelligence Board did nothing to lighten Harvey's mood. According to their assessment:

- The substantial increase in Soviet Bloc armaments and military training had given the Cubans greatly increased capability to suppress insurrection or repel invasion;
- The Castro regime retained the positive support of at least a quarter of the population;

- There was active resistance in Cuba, but it was limited, unco-ordinated, unsupported, and desperate;
- The Castro regime, with all the power of repression at its disposal, had shown that it could contain the present level of resistance activity;
- Cuba's apparatus for surveillance and repression should be able to cope with any popular tendency toward active resist-ance; and
- Any impulse toward widespread revolt was inhibited by the fear which the apparatus inspired, and by the lack of dynamic leadership and of any expectation of liberation within the foreseeable future.

Harvey had to accept that all of this was bad news for *Task Force W*. It meant that much of the work they had been doing to encourage and assist insurrection had been, and continued to be, ineffective. Some of it could be construed as direct criticism of *Task Force W*'s work and Robert Kennedy would not let that go by without a mention.

But there was one encouraging piece of news. The SGA had now set a target date of October to create some kind of an erup-tion in Cuba: any kind of flare-up would do as long as it moved Cuba significantly towards ending the Castro regime. It could take the form of a rebellion from within Cuba, an invasion, an economic meltdown fuelled by tighter trade sanctions and *effective* sabotage such as bombing Cuba's harbours and other strategic targets affecting the economy.

The other item weighing on Harvey's mind was the absence of a result on the 'executive action' against Castro. Harvey had been in touch with Roselli from time to time. Numerous plots were hatched; some, such as deploying explosive seashells in places where Castro was known to scuba dive, stretched the boundaries of possibility, but most of the ones they had tried used the more traditional method of poisoning. The CIA had given Roselli poison pills and even a box of cigars laced with lethal bacteria, but nothing, so far, had been successful. Roselli insisted the Mafia had the right contacts and that Trafficante was still enthusiastic and the right man to take the lead in this project. He was determined to kill Castro so that he could get back into Cuba and reopen his casinos. They were going to stick at it. Something was bound to get through to Castro sooner or later.

Harvey was frustrated by the lack of progress and by the shackles Attorney-General Robert Kennedy had put on *Task Force W*'s modus operandi, but he was not demoralised. It was not in his character to do anything other than fight on with determination and hard work.

He went down to Florida and had a meeting – a pep talk – with Shackley, David Morales (chief of operations), Gordon Campbell (chief of maritime operations) and George Joannides (chief of psychological warfare).

He sympathised with their frustration at the lack of action and progress and, no doubt using the kind of foul language that was his hallmark, he explained the problems facing them. They must not allow themselves to be disheartened by the difficulty of the operation, but use it as a spur to greater action. They still had a job to do and were more than capable of doing it, if only the SGA would let them.

For three days Harvey, Shackley, Morales, Campbell and Joannides brainstormed new ideas to fulfil the aims of *Operation Mongoose*, and prepared a list for Harvey to take back to General Lansdale. Some of the ideas even involved acts of sabotage and terrorism against American targets in Florida and among the Cuban exiles, for which Castro would get the blame, thus supplying cause for robust retaliation.

‡

Johnny Roselli called a meeting with Santo Trafficante, Carlos Marcello and Salvatore 'Sam' Giancana to discuss the failure of their attempts to assassinate Fidel Castro. Trafficante said he was mystified. He would trust his contacts in Havana with his life. They assured him the poison was getting as far as Castro's living quarters or his office, but never made it past his personal staff. Fabian Escalante, Castro's personal minder, seemed to be able to smell a rat from a mile off. Maybe there were straightforward house rules dictating that absolutely nothing was given to Castro – food or otherwise – unless its origins had been thoroughly checked and approved.

They considered other approaches. Why not kill Raúl Castro (the Minister of Defence and Fidel's brother) or Che Guevara (now in charge of the economy)? If they took either or both of them out it would destabilise Fidel and his government. After some consideration they decided such a course of action would only anger Fidel Castro and bolster his determination. Why did they not just kill him in the traditional Mafia style? No, they had already put that to Harvey and he was strongly opposed. The CIA and Kennedy administration would be blamed and it was no longer acceptable for officialdom in one country to assassinate a foreign head of state.

They would try to be patient, but time was running out. Harvey had intimated to them that the job had to be completed by October.

They discussed another problem: there had been something of a moratorium on law enforcement against Mafia tax evasion and gambling activities, but it seemed that Attorney-General Robert Kennedy had given the nod to the FBI and the Internal Revenue Service to start to hound some of the Mafia leaders again. Roselli may have promised to broach the subject with Harvey, and Harvey may, or may not, have brought it to Robert Kennedy's attention, but there is no doubt that this matter contributed to a worsening relationship between the Mafia and the Kennedys. Harvey, inevitably, was caught up in this.

For the next six months Harvey's team at *JM/WAVE* worked hard to destabilise Cuba but most of the ideas he felt *would* have made a real difference continued to be watered down or rejected outright by the SGA. There were a few courageous acts of sabotage but the relentless improvement in the Castro regime's policing and military capabilities made such acts more dangerous and many of them failed, with dire consequences for those involved. The actions that did succeed contributed little to the objective of destabilisation.

The training programme for anti-Castro exiles continued, so that there was now a more disciplined, more capable and better equipped force than the cadre that had been decimated in its painful attempt to establish a bridgehead at the Bay of Pigs, but there was no sign of the SGA authorising an attack supported by American forces.

The news from Harvey's agents within Cuba was soul-destroying, if not frightening. There was a relentless build-up of Eastern Bloc armaments – mostly defensive, but now with some reports of offensive weapons arriving. There were reports of sightings of Soviet SS-2 surface-to-air missile units, of Soviet MiG-21 fighter aircraft and even of Soviet IL-28 bomber aircraft.

In the middle of August, CIA Director John McCone received intelligence of substantial ship movements from the Black Sea and the Baltic to Cuba. He went out on a limb and expressed his suspicions in a memorandum to President Kennedy that medium-range ballistic missiles (MRBMs) were being sent to Cuba. The President's advisers – particularly McGeorge Bundy – ridiculed the suspicion, saying that Khrushchev would not dare to place MRBMs, or any other strategic attack weapons, in Cuba.

McCone repeated his suspicions at a meeting of the SGA, this time saying he had circumstantial evidence that the Soviet military were constructing offensive missile installations in Cuba; he was knocked down once again by Secretary of Defence Robert McNamara who maintained the installations were purely defensive.

A week later, Harvey again vented his frustrations on Lansdale who in turn spoke to General Maxwell Taylor, bypassing Attorney-General Robert Kennedy. Taylor sent a memorandum to President Kennedy saying the Castro regime could only be overthrown through direct United States military intervention. The President responded and Lansdale brought the news to Harvey. He reported that the President said he had been disappointed that *Operation Mongoose* had so far met with virtually no success. He authorised the CIA to develop 'with all possible speed' more aggressive plans to get rid of Castro. He still insisted, however, that there had to be no overt US military involvement in any of the plans.

How, wondered Harvey, could the CIA do any more without overt military action?

Harvey's frustrations on this score came to an end within a month because, in the light of the now very evident build-up of Soviet military hardware and personnel in Cuba, the United States Congress authorised the use of military force in Cuba if American interests were threatened.

‡

While Harvey and his *Task Force W* were concentrating on *Operation Mongoose,* other parts of the CIA, and the FBI, were dealing with what might be described as routine matters to guard against Communist subversion.

When Lee Harvey Oswald arrived in Fort Worth, Texas, on 13 June 1962, his file was passed to FBI agent John Fain whose duty it was to interview him. It was a difficult interrogation that only added greater confusion to Oswald's Communist history and his future intentions. Oswald was unpleasant and arrogant. He refused to answer many of the questions put to him or to submit to a polygraph test. He denied that he had collaborated with the Soviets and passed secrets to them. He started to shout, growing so belligerent that at one stage agent Fain thought Oswald was going to punch him.

A second interview, on 16 August, proved to be even less productive. Fain decided to waste no more energy on Oswald for the time being and moved the file to 'inactive' status. When Fain retired in October, Oswald's file was officially closed instead of being passed to agent Hosty.

✝

The Fair Play for Cuba Committee (FPCC), based in the United States, was established in the summer of 1960, overtly to support the right of Castro and his regime to govern Cuba without let or hindrance from the United States. Behind the scenes it had close connections with the American Communist Party, with the Communist-oriented Patrice Lumumba (the leader of the Congo), and of course with the Castro regime, which provided it with crucial financial support.[†] For these reasons the FBI took the FPCC seriously and appointed two of their best agents – James McCord and David Phillips – to monitor its activities and the people who supported it.

On 18 July 1962, the KGB's Vladimir Kryuchkov sent a telegram to Ramiro Valdés, the head of Cuban intelligence, suggesting that they contact Oswald with a view to using him.[‡]

On the surface this might appear to be quite unremarkable: one Communist national security organisation giving the nod to a fellow Communist state. That would have been normal practice had Oswald been in Cuba, but he was not. He was residing in the United States and one would have expected the KGB – thick on the ground in America –automatically to maintain communications with Oswald themselves. Were the KGB trying to lay

---

[†]   Lumumba and Castro were both CIA assassination targets.

[‡]   The same Vladimir Kryuchkov who had given much help to Serov during the Hungarian Revolution when he (Kryuchkov) had been the Third Secretary at the Soviet Embassy in Budapest.

a false trail, trying to place some distance between themselves and Oswald?

With the FBI monitoring the activities of the FPCC and its members, it was not long before they spotted Oswald and reopened his file. They discovered he was purchasing Communist books and periodicals, attending FPCC meetings and distributing leaflets.

29

MOSCOW 1962

The series of debriefings between Penkovsky and the MI6/CIA team came to an end in Paris in October 1961. Penkovsky, however, continued to pass a seemingly endless stream of high-value secret military intelligence to the West through a variety of channels: meetings in Moscow with Janet Chisholm; meetings with Wynne at trade missions and fairs in Moscow, Bucharest, Prague and Budapest; contacts at official receptions given by Dr David Senior and Hilary King at the British Embassy in Moscow.

His handlers in Moscow (Chisholm and possibly Howard Smith), London (Shergold and Stokes) and Washington (Kisevalter's replacement and Bulik) still found it difficult to penetrate the mind of this often naive and at other times highly complex character.

He loved his family, yet he was most certainly not averse to enjoying passing relationships with other women. He delighted in the attention paid to him by Serov's teenage daughter in London and, in Paris, he paid romantic attention to a particularly attractive receptionist at his hotel, even prevailing upon his MI6 team to organise his dates with her.

Penkovsky was a man who schemed and methodically took advantage of any and every opportunity to cultivate friendships with anyone who might be useful to him. He had the character and personality to raise these friendships to the level of close family relationships, as in the case of Chief Marshal Sergei

Varentsov. In London, late at night when he should have been taking a rare opportunity to rest, he insisted on showing Serov's wife and daughter a good time. He bought well-chosen presents for these and many other friends and colleagues during his trips to the West, knowing that such gestures were likely to reap great future rewards.

Above all this – or perhaps driving it – Penkovsky believed he had a mission in life to somehow save the world from the catastrophe that he saw as a consequence of the reckless military policies and posturing of Khrushchev.

Or was it his obsession with the Communist apparatus thwarting his clearly deserved (to him) promotion to general? Had he not worked hard and successfully for this, committing himself wholeheartedly to the Communist Party since the days of his youth?

Or was it his paradoxical need for material luxuries such as a dacha on the outskirts of Moscow? He had asked MI6/CIA to help him pay for such a house.

His family background had been of minor nobility and worthy professions. His father died honourably fighting for the Tsarists against the Bolsheviks. His mother still lived with him and she would, from time to time, talk with nostalgia about 'the good times' with plenty of room in their large house, and servants. Now she bemoaned the family's circumstances, living in a small apartment near the centre of Moscow. His wife, Vera, also had a proud family history and openly shared Oleg's frustrations concerning his lack of promotion and shared his desire for worldly goods.

Would he have offered his services to the West if he had been awarded promotion in the mid to late 1950s, giving him status and access to a dacha and other luxuries? Did he ever ask himself this question?

It did not matter. He was now firmly on this path. In a year's time, or thereabouts, he would be living with his family in England or America. He would have a house with four bedrooms, a beautiful garden and his own choice of car. He would have a pension that would enable him to live in comfort. His mother would probably not attempt to learn English but she would pick up enough to get by and would be happy in her final years.

Vera, Galina and the second child (due quite soon), would quickly learn to speak English: Vera already spoke quite good French and Galina had studied English at school. Galina and her little brother or sister would go to university, marry into prosperous families and give him (Penkovsky) three or four wonderful grandchildren who would grow up as British or American children.

It was with these dreams that he continued to work with great vigour and diligence, mostly gaining access to and photographing secret military documents, classified telephone lists and dossiers on senior military, political and GRU personnel. He also passed on gossip about military and political dispositions and intentions.

The virtually weekly meetings with Janet Chisholm from mid-October 1961 continued into the new year, until the meeting on 19 January when he gave her four film cassettes and told her he had to go to Leningrad, arranging a subsequent meeting for 2 February. During this short gap, Janet went to London for a medical check-up and returned with the news that she was pregnant. She would be able to carry on – but with some changes to the routine – until June or July, after which someone else would have to take over.

Plans were already in place for the Chisholms to be replaced by Gervase Cowell and his wife Pamela who, like Janet Chisholm, was a former MI6 secretary. The Cowells had three children, two of whom were a little too old to accompany their mother to her assignations with Penkovsky, but the third child was still an infant, conveniently confined to a pram.

Penkovsky did not appear for the scheduled meeting with Janet on 2 February, nor did he turn up on the alternative dates for more than a month.

He had accompanied a group of American tobacco business-men on his trip to Leningrad at the end of January. Some of

them would return to America via London and Penkovsky culti-
vated one of them, eventually asking him to deliver a message
to a certain person in London. He listened to what Penkovsky
had to say but, at the last moment, refused to become involved.
The CIA and MI6 were perplexed, agitated and worried over
Penkovsky's failure to meet Janet, so much so that MI6 went to
the extreme of tracking down the American tobacco business-
men in London, on 9 March, including the one whom Penkovsky
had tried to use as a courier. He told them as much as he could
remember which was, in essence, that Penkovsky had noticed
Janet being followed after their meeting on 19 January and he
did not wish to compromise her safety with further encounters.

Penkovsky had also told the businessman that he would probably be going to the Geneva International Motor Show from 15
to 25 March and the Seattle World Fair starting on 21 April.

The CIA case officer who replaced Kisevalter travelled to
London to further debrief the tobacco man. He also had a
meeting with Shergold. The two men disagreed about what
was happening – and what should happen – in Moscow. The
American was of the opinion that things had become too hot for
Penkovsky and all activity should cease for up to a year. Shergold
said that Penkovsky's report indicated that it was Janet who was
under surveillance and not himself. He would be devastated –
said Shergold – if the CIA/MI6 stopped using him. He would
take it as an insult and a sign of mistrust. They could change
the manner of contact with Penkovsky (no more meetings with
Janet) but they should still give him work to do.

Bulik and Shergold went to Geneva on 11 March, but
Penkovsky did not turn up at the Motor Show.

Dr Senior, the British Embassy's scientific attaché, invited
Penkovsky to a reception on 28 March, in honour of the British
Baking Industries Research Association. Ruari and Janet
Chisholm were there and, in the course of the evening, they
and Penkovsky engineered a highly professional and successful
pass. Penkovsky approached the Chisholms with another Soviet

official. Ruari struck up a conversation with the official and eased him away, leaving Penkovsky and Janet together. Janet was now visibly pregnant and Penkovsky suggested she might like to go to the host's bedroom to rest. Janet left the room. A few minutes later Penkovsky approached Mrs Senior and, as he usually did on these occasions, asked if she would show him round the beautiful apartment. When they entered the bedroom where Janet was resting, both he and Mrs Senior apologised for disturbing her. Penkovsky winked at Janet before turning round to leave. He swung one hand behind his back, exposing a Russian cigarette packet in the palm of his hand. Neither Mrs Senior, nor anyone else who may have been passing by the door, could have noticed either the packet or Janet deftly taking it from him. It contained eleven film cassettes and three written messages.

The procedure for all material passed over by Penkovsky was to send it, unopened, to MI6 in London for examination. Military and political intelligence was translated and sent to the British Joint Intelligence Committee for assessment, before being passed on to appropriate users, such as the Prime Minister, the Foreign Office and the armed forces Ministries.[†] It was a few days, therefore, before Ruari Chisholm received information back from his headquarters that the package handed to his wife at Dr Senior's party on 28 March contained a letter Penkovsky had written as far back as 26 January. In it he reported that he had noticed surveillance on Janet after their meetings on 5 and 19 January, but not on the 12th. He urged that street and park meetings with Janet should stop for a few months. There were also later letters in the package, dated 5 and 28 March (the day of the party). He recorded that his trip to Geneva had been cancelled, but he was still hopeful that he would get to Seattle on 19 April. If his trip to Seattle were to be cancelled, that would change everything. It would almost certainly mean that he would be transferred out of

---

†   The Admiralty, the War Office (relating mainly to the Army) and the Air Ministry did not merge into the Ministry of Defence until 1964.

the GKKNIR, and that he would have to retire in the autumn, having completed twenty-five years in the army.

The CIA made elaborate plans to receive Penkovsky in Seattle, but he did not turn up: none of the Soviet delegation did. The Central Committee decided not to send any representatives because they believed the Americans were planning some kind of provocation against them at the World Fair. As this decision did not single out Penkovsky, he could continue with his work on the Central Committee.

The GKKNIR, supported by the GRU, nominated him to lead a group to the Soviet Industrial Exhibit in Brazil. He had his visa, but two days before he was due to travel the KGB wrote to Serov advising him they had reason to believe the Americans had a particular interest in Penkovsky and may attempt to provoke an incident with him. Serov had little alternative but to withdraw him from the group.

†
†

Oswald, still working in Minsk, had been trying for more than a year to retrieve his American passport from the embassy in Moscow and return to America. He often met and sometimes socialised with Cuban intelligence service trainees attending a Soviet Ministry of Internal Affairs spy academy in Ulyanova Street in Minsk, just a block from where he worked. He developed a fondness for Cuba through these meetings and decided he would do something to support Castro's administration.

The academy was run by Colonel Ilya Prusakov whose niece, Marina Prusakova, was a pharmacist in Minsk. Oswald met Marina; they fell in love, and married on 30 April 1961.

After extensive correspondence with Moscow, and embassy consultations with the American nationality and immigration authorities, Oswald received clearance on 10 May 1962 to return to America with Marina and their three-month-old daughter, June Lee. They left Moscow by train on 2 June, travelling to

Holland where they boarded a ship sailing to New York, arriving there on 13 June 1962.

✝

On a beautiful day in late April 1962, Khrushchev lay sunbathing in the gardens of his holiday retreat in Yalta. Looking directly south, he pondered on the threat posed by American nuclear missiles based just across the Black Sea in Turkey and decided it was time he did something about it.

On his return to Moscow he called a secret meeting with Deputy Prime Minister Anastas Mikoyan, his close political ally and Secretary of the Central Committee Frol Kozlov, Defence Minister Rodion Malinovsky, Foreign Minister Andrei Gromyko and Commander-in-Chief of the Strategic Missile Force Marshal Sergei Biryuzov. He knew he would have to work harder to convince Mikoyan and Malinovsky than for the others. He also suspected that Mikoyan would acquiesce if he could win Malinovsky over to his idea.

This was an informal meeting – he assured them – to seek their advice on an idea that had come to him while on holiday, and he hoped they could reach agreement on whether or not to take it forward. Khrushchev's opening sounded innocuous enough but he followed up with a forceful presumption of their agreement to support his idea in principle, and pressed for their approval of the details.

He referred to intelligence reports that America had intentions to get rid of Castro's government in Cuba by October. The Soviet Union had to prevent such a coup and he thought the solution would be to install offensive nuclear weapons in Cuba as a deterrent to US intervention.

Those present argued at first that such a course of action could precipitate WWIII, but Khrushchev insisted the Americans would not go that far. He could see no alternative, because it would be logistically impossible for the Soviet Union to help Cuba to defend itself from an American invasion with conventional forces and weapons.

Perhaps it was Malinovsky who suggested they greatly increase the number of surface-to-air missiles (SAMs) and MiG-21 fighter aircraft provided to Cuba. The Americans would realise, in the face of such an armoury, that they would suffer great losses, not just of aircraft but also on the ground in Florida. They would be reluctant to sustain such losses, particularly with the mid-term elections approaching. Mikoyan and Gromyko would have supported this approach, but Khrushchev deemed it too risky. The Americans, he believed, would win such a battle because the distance from the Soviet Union to Cuba would make it impossible to bring in supplies and reinforcements as quickly as they would be needed.

Marshal Biryuzov allowed the politicians to have their say before weighing in with a military assessment. Logistically, he saw no great problem with deploying both defensive and offensive nuclear weapons in Cuba. The Soviet SS-4 medium range ground-to-ground missiles had a range of just over 2,000 kilometres which, from Cuba, would put Washington just within range. Their SS-5 intermediate range missiles could target virtually everywhere in the United States other than Alaska. Both of these weapons were capable of carry-ing nuclear warheads. Unfortunately, their rockets were huge and it would be difficult to hide their existence from the prying cameras of American U-2 aircraft. Biryuzov volunteered to go to Cuba to scout out the terrain and decide whether or not they could be hidden. Soviet SAMs could, of course, now shoot down American U-2 spy planes as soon as they reached Cuba, but the Americans would not allow that to happen more than once without taking retaliation that would be unacceptable to the Soviet forces. Nor, some argued, would the US just sit back and watch as the USSR constructed missile bases a mere ninety miles off the Florida coast.

Absolutely right, agreed Khrushchev, which was why the

whole exercise would be performed with a level of secrecy unprecedented even in the Soviet Union. The Americans would eventually discover the missiles once they were on site, but by then they would not dare to take military action from fear of outright nuclear war. Cuba would be saved from an American invasion by a policy of deterrence.

The high-powered group agreed to send a delegation to Cuba, seeking Castro's agreement to deploy strategic offensive nuclear weapons there.

†

One of a series of secret Soviet 'Military Thought' papers that Penkovsky had copied to the West was about 'maskirovka', the Russian term for denial and deception techniques in warfare. The Americans would have done well to pay more immediate attention to this paper as the Soviets were masters of maskirovka. They employed these techniques to great effect in dispatching an arsenal, including nuclear missiles and bomber and fighter planes to Cuba during the summer and autumn of 1962.

From the outset, only eight people knew about the exercise: Khrushchev, Deputy Prime Minister Anastas Mikoyan, and Defence Minister Marshal Malinovsky were on the political side, while the military side was led by General Semyon Ivanov (head of the Chief Operations Directorate), who was assisted by Marshal Sergei Biryuzov (commander of the Strategic Rocket Forces), two other generals, and Colonel Vladimir Udalov.

Consultation with Fidel Castro was masked in secrecy. A Soviet agricultural delegation led by Politburo member Sharaf Rashidov arrived in Havana on 29 May. Among the delegates were General Ivanov and several missile and other military specialists who would decide on the feasibility of deploying the missiles in complete secrecy. The Soviet Ambassador approached Defence Minister Raúl Castro and explained that one of the delegates, listed as an engineer called Petrov, was actually

Marshal Biryuzov and that he needed to meet Fidel Castro as soon as possible. The meeting took place within fifteen minutes and in due course the Castro brothers and Che Guevara gave their approval in principle, with different degrees of enthusiasm.

Back in Moscow, all records of meetings and agreements were initially handwritten by Colonel Udalov, an excellent penman, and passed by hand. Malinovsky approved the fully fledged plan, still handwritten, on 4 July and Khrushchev approved it on 7 July.

More people were made privy to parts of the plan on a strictly need-to-know basis in the implementation phase. All messages and instructions were carried by hand: never by ciphered telegraph.

The code name for the operation was '*Anadyr*', the name of a river and town in the extreme north-east of Russia. This was designed to mislead lower-level Soviet commanders and Western spies into thinking it was a military exercise in that region. Troops being mustered for the operation were told they were going to a cold region. Those involved with nuclear missiles were informed that they would be transporting the missiles to a site on the Arctic island of Novaya Zemlya, where nuclear weapons had been tested in the past. Many units were given winter clothing and equipment, including skis.

Even before the plan had been finally approved, the Soviet Union began to charter Western ships to carry general cargo from the Soviet Union to Cuba, reserving their own freighters for matériel.

Raúl Castro led a Cuban delegation to Moscow in early July to discuss Soviet military shipments, including nuclear missiles. He had two cordial meetings with Khrushchev and later, together with Marshal Malinovsky, the Soviet Defence Minister, initialled a draft treaty on the deployment of Soviet forces to Cuba. The Cubans agreed not to make the treaty public until Khrushchev arrived in Cuba on a visit planned for November.

Hundreds of Soviet military specialists started to arrive in Cuba by air under the guise of civilian technical and agricultural experts. One of these experts was General Issa Pliyev, who arrived on 10 July to take command of the Soviet forces in Cuba. With their total lack of expertise in adopted disciplines such as agriculture or urban planning, and their need to pay attention to their true purpose on the island, CIA agents soon became suspicious that something big was afoot.

Suspicions grew when, on 17 July, the Cubans announced a Civil Air Route Agreement for regular Moscow–Havana flights. The CIA suspected that these flights would be used mainly to convey Soviet military personnel and sensitive equipment to Cuba.

Che Guevara, at that time the Minister for Industry, led the next delegation to Moscow at the end of August, bringing with him Fidel Castro's proposed revisions to the draft treaty. Castro wanted the deployment of nuclear weapons in Cuba to be made public in order to forestall US overreaction when the missiles were eventually discovered. He argued that they were not contravening international law, and keeping it secret would only attract extra suspicion, but eventually he bowed to the Soviet Union's greater experience in these matters.

Forces personnel and immense amounts of equipment were transported across the Soviet Union by road and rail under incredible and successful measures of secrecy, destined for eight different ports: four in the Baltic and four in the Black Sea. The surface-to-surface missiles were loaded onto the ships under cover of darkness. Easily recognisable deck cargo was covered with planks as a means of camouflage. Crates containing missiles and launchers were lined with metal sheets to foil attempts at infrared photography. Common cars, trucks and farm machinery were carried as deck cargo to give the impression that the ship's hold contained only industrial products and materials.

Each ship's captain was given two envelopes just prior to departure from the Soviet port. The first, to be opened immediately, told him to sail to given coordinates in the Atlantic Ocean where the second envelope would be opened in the presence of the senior KGB representative on board. The second envelope revealed the final destination: a Cuban port.

Conditions on board were at times unbearable for the troops. They had to stay below deck or under tarpaulin sheets where they endured temperatures of up to 100° Fahrenheit (38°C). They were allowed fresh air only during the hours of darkness. Some of them were rendered unfit for duty in Cuba. On arrival in Cuba, the troops were allowed to disembark and move to their assigned positions only under cover of night.

As the ships docked, fully briefed Cuban officials assisted with yet more maskirovka techniques to hide the nature of the cargo as it was unloaded. No Cuban dock-workers were allowed in the area and in some cases local inhabitants were evacuated for several days until offloading and dispersal of the goods was complete.

Serov was informed of the huge increase in the numbers of Soviet military 'trainers and advisers' going to Cuba and increased the number of GRU personnel in Cuba in proportion. He was *not* informed – and neither was KGB Chairman Vladimir Semichastny – of the transportation of offensive nuclear weapons. The highest level of intelligence operations were not, accordingly, to a standard commensurate with the importance of the situation. Neither the GRU on the military side, nor the KGB on the political side, had any agents in place to probe the likely reactions of the top military brass and the White House to the presence of offensive nuclear weapons on their doorstep. Both of these organisations performed low-standard mundane operations which contributed nothing to a complex and volatile situation.

Serov was later to be severely reprimanded for this, but it was in the context of his disgrace on another matter – the revelation of Penkovsky as a spy – when the KGB and the party were looking for whatever mud they could find to stick on him. Semichastny, whose KGB's performance in Cuba had been worse than that of the GRU, was not criticised.

In the true maskirovka style of denial and disinformation, on 4 September the Soviet Ambassador, Anatoly Dobrynin, gave Attorney-General Robert Kennedy the assurances of

Khrushchev that the Soviet Union would not place any surface-to-surface or other offensive weapons in Cuba. Throughout the first half of September, Ambassador Dobrynin gave further similar assurances to Theodor Sorensen, the special counsel to President Kennedy and to Adlai Stevenson, former Governor of Illinois and two-time failed Presidential candidate, now serving as US Ambassador to the United Nations. These assurances were genuine on Dobrynin's part: he did not know about the delivery of offensive weapons. He conceded that the Soviet Union was supplying military equipment and training to Cuba but maintained that it was purely defensive and of no great significance or threat to the United States.

The first SS-4 intermediate-range ballistic missiles arrived in Cuba on 8 September. Their nuclear warheads arrived on a single ship, in a massive consignment of nearly one hundred, on 4 October.

In spite of some CIA suspicions, the strict application of maskirovka techniques was effective. The CIA failed to discover the true nature of the increase in Soviet shipping to Cuba until the logistics of operation *Anadyr* were virtually complete. By then, there were more than 40,000 Soviet troops on the island: four times as many as US Intelligence had estimated. Eighty-five shiploads of various military items, supplies and personnel had arrived and more ships were on their way.

With the virtual impossibility of keeping these movements secret for much longer, the Soviet and Cuban intelligence agents permitted the leaking of accurate details to Cuban exiles and exile groups in Miami. This was an inspired act of deception-by-honesty, as the CIA officers at *JM/WAVE* found the news too incredible to believe.

‡

The KGB's preoccupation with Penkovsky's father had again come to the fore. It seemed they now believed he could still be alive and living in another country, because they were unable to locate his grave and could not find a death certificate or any other documentation recording his death. It was unlikely that there would be any more proposals for Penkovsky to travel outside the Soviet Union, but he could continue to work for the GKKNIR for the time being.

Penkovsky was invited to the British Ambassador's reception, held on 31 May, to celebrate the Queen's birthday. There was again a successful pass with Janet Chisholm, this time in the cloakroom on the ground floor of the embassy's East Wing, which also housed Ruari Chisholm's office. The material passed to Janet included a three-page letter written by Penkovsky on 15 May in which he recorded the first signs of his frustration and even expressed despair at the increasing difficulty of fulfilling his personal commitment to the West. The KGB had evidence that the Americans knew he was a GRU officer and, if they granted him a visa it would be to trick or provoke him in some way. He was sick and tired of it all – he wrote – and was ready to come across. He asked which Soviet city he should go to, if he retired in September, to make it easier and safer for him to leave the Soviet Union. He wanted to know how much money was in his account. He even asked the team to send him a small pistol that he could carry about with him.

The letter ended on a happier note, announcing the birth of the Penkovskys' second daughter, Marina, on 6 February. Somewhat oddly, in the context of intelligence and counter-intelligence, he requested a package of baby clothes.

The alarm bells were ringing in London and Langley.

Greville Wynne was due to go to Moscow in early July to meet with the GKKNIR and the Ministry of Foreign Trade. He was instructed to tell Penkovsky not to attempt to pass any material at the American Ambassador's Fourth of July party. While the passes at Dr Senior's party and the British Ambassador's party had been successful, they were also exceedingly dangerous. It must be assumed that Penkovsky was now being watched by the KGB, so they could not take any further risks.

CIA case officer Rodney Carlson arrived in Moscow on 24 June to join the American Embassy's diplomatic staff complement. The CIA had fought hard to get this concession from Ambassador Thompson. Carlson's overt job included liaison with the GKKNIR, so he would be able to make official contact with Penkovsky.

Wynne arrived in Moscow on 2 July to discuss bringing his trade exhibition truck to the Soviet Union. On the way into Moscow from the airport Wynne surreptitiously gave Penkovsky 3,000 roubles, a letter, twenty film cassettes for his Minox camera and a parcel of clothes for little Marina.

In Wynne's hotel room, with the bathroom tap running, the two men started to talk. Penkovsky broke down and cried. He had had enough. He wanted out.

In the early evening, Wynne went to the British Embassy Club on the top floor of the East Wing to meet Ruari Chisholm, whose office stood directly below. Chisholm gave him a small package to be delivered to Penkovsky. Wynne then returned to his hotel room for his appointment with Penkovsky, who again broke down, but soon recovered his composure.

Wynne showed Penkovsky photographs of both Pamela Cowell (the wife of Gervase Cowell, Ruari Chisholm's successor) and of Rodney Carlson (the new CIA contact at the American Embassy). Pamela Cowell would take over the role of Janet Chisholm, but there would be a new method of exchanging material. Virtually all bathrooms of British Embassy staff had a tin of Harpic (a liquid lavatory detergent) sitting on the floor near the lavatory pedestal. At receptions where Pamela and Penkovsky were both present, Pamela would go to the bathroom and replace the tin of Harpic with a specially designed fake with a hollow base that contained material for Penkovsky. After a suitable interval Penkovsky would go into the bathroom and exchange the material in the base of the tin. Pamela would later return to replace the original tin, putting the special tin with its contents into her handbag. Wynne showed an example of the specially designed tin to Penkovsky, who practised opening and closing the special compartment.

They met again the following evening for dinner, after which they walked together in a park. Penkovsky repeated his request for a pistol. He said he would be able to carry on working at the GKKNIR until September, but still desired to go over to the West without his family. He could not explain how or why he had come round to that way of thinking; he just wanted to get out of the Soviet Union.

At the GKKNIR meeting the next day, 4 July, two members questioned Wynne at length about the companies, people and products he represented. He had not met either of them before. They insisted he should provide an inordinate amount of detail and printed matter in support of his request to bring his mobile exhibition to the Soviet Union. He was in no doubt these two were KGB officers checking on his bona fides as a pure business-man and nothing more.

That evening, Penkovsky attended the American Ambassador's reception. Early on, he spotted Rodney Carlson, recognising him from the photograph Wynne had shown him. As numbers thinned out after a couple of hours, he introduced himself to Carlson in the company of some of his colleagues from the Central Committee. At one point they were alone for a few seconds and both confirmed they had nothing to exchange. Penkovsky said, however, that he would have something at their next meeting.

The following afternoon Penkovsky went to Wynne's hotel room and gave him two cassettes of exposed film, a letter, a coded document and six passport photographs, all of which Wynne handed to Ruari Chisholm a few hours later at the American Embassy Club in America House: commonly called the *Yankee Dom*. Penkovsky and Wynne arranged to meet again at nine o'clock that evening outside the Peking Restaurant.

Wynne arrived first. Not seeing Penkovsky, he walked casually around the area and soon noticed he was being followed by two men. He spotted Penkovsky but avoided making contact with him until it appeared safe to do so. Penkovsky, too, had noticed that Wynne was being watched, told him to break contact immediately, and advised him to leave Moscow first thing next morning. Wynne went back to the *Yankee Dom* and was relieved to find Chisholm still there. He told him what had happened.

Penkovsky met Wynne at the airport in his GKKNIR capacity to see him off. He told him the KGB were suspicious of him (Wynne) and it was of the utmost importance that he produce everything that had been asked of him relating to his mobile exhibition and demonstrate his truck to people at the Soviet Embassy in London. He should follow that up by definitely coming to Moscow with his truck in September. Only by concentrating on his legitimate business could he hope to allay the KGB's suspicions.

Penkovsky was, for a while, alone and virtually helpless. There were emergency procedures for contacting the MI6/CIA team and there were three dead drop sites, but the circumstances were not right to use them. This cooling off period was enforced by circumstance rather than intentional, but it was probably a good thing just the same. Wynne was now back in England, Janet had returned to England to have her child, and there were no embassy receptions to which Penkovsky might be invited.

At last, he attended a reception at the apartment of the American agricultural attaché, to be held on 27 August. After some milling around, Penkovsky and Carlson met and chatted in the presence of others. Carlson excused himself and went to the bathroom where he taped some items for Penkovsky to the underside of the lid of the lavatory cistern. The exchange, however, did not go well. At one point both Carlson and Penkovsky were in the bathroom at the same time and Carlson locked the door. Penkovsky handed Carlson a package of seven exposed film cassettes and three messages. He appeared not to know the procedure because he then asked Carlson if he had anything in exchange. Carlson had to remove the cistern lid to give Penkovsky the items. The men left the bathroom separately and, fortunately, no one noticed either of them.

One of the three messages in Penkovsky's package was a letter he had written on 25 August. It conveyed a calmer disposition and a more measured approach to his work than of late. He accepted that he was now being watched by the KGB, which annoyed rather than frightened him. He had been commended for his work with the GKKNIR and expected to continue to work for them at least until the middle of September, at which time he might have taken leave until the end of October. If the Central Committee tried to dismiss him in September he would ask Malinovsky, Varentsov and Serov to plead on his behalf to be kept in the army.

He gave warnings about Wynne and the need for him to prove his worthiness as a businessman representing reputable British companies and industries.

He suggested that the money in his account in the West did not reflect the true value of the material he had passed to them and asked if it could be increased.

The other two messages from Penkovsky were devoted to answering the still continuous stream of requests from the team for information about current political and military matters, including the build-up of Soviet arms and personnel in Cuba and the possible installation of offensive nuclear weapons there.

Penkovsky appeared again at an American Embassy reception on 5 September, this time at the Ambassador's residence. Carlson was there, but his attempt to tape a package for Penkovsky to the underside of the cistern lid failed because the tape would not adhere properly to its surface. The pass was aborted.

Shergold and Bulik agreed the wording of a letter to Penkovsky, to be delivered to him in Moscow before the middle of September. It praised him for his past work and continued dedication. It reported an increase in the amount in his account from US$40,000 to US$250,000, with a promise to discuss this further the next time they met. It tried to set his mind at rest with regard to Wynne. It then carried out a detailed review of his recent work: the secret documents he had photographed and his messages about the current political and military situation, particularly in Berlin and Cuba.

The letter ended with warm greetings from Janet Chisholm, who had given birth to a son.

Gervase Cowell arrived in Moscow on 2 September to replace Ruari Chisholm. Penkovsky had been told there would be no operational procedure for meetings or exchanges of material with him. Cowell's wife, Pamela, with whom there *was* an operational procedure for exchanges using the Harpic tins, arrived ten days later, on 12 September.

A film show and reception at the British Embassy was arranged for 6 September. A few weeks earlier the British Ambassador – the diminutive Sir Frank Roberts – called Warrant Officer Peter Edmonds to his office and asked him to obtain a prestigious British film to show to 'some people from the Kremlin'. Edmonds, who worked in the Air Attaché's Office, was responsible for obtaining films from the Army Kinema Corporation on a weekly basis for staff welfare purposes. The BAFTA award-winning *A Taste of Honey*, starring Rita Tushingham, was selected. Of the seventy Soviet officials invited, only twenty-four turned up. Penkovsky was one of them, and he was able to meet Gervase Cowell, though it was no more than a brief double-take as they passed each other. Yevgeny Levin, the KGB station chief inside the GKKNIR, was also present, so Penkovsky had to be even more careful than usual. There were no exchanges of film cassettes or documents.

The Ambassador had personally asked Edmonds to obtain the film: not Ruari Chisholm, not Howard Smith, not even Edmonds' boss, the Air Attaché. The Ambassador told Edmonds the guests were 'some people from the Kremlin' and that it was they who had initiated a request to be shown a good British film. This kind of contact and innocuous disinformation represented

internal security of the highest order. Edmonds was not introduced to any of the guests. At the end of the film, however, the
Ambassador and 'a short, round, bald man in a light grey suit'
entered the tiny projection room and thanked him.[†]

A farewell party was held for Dr Senior on 13 September
to which Oleg and Vera Penkovsky were invited, as well as
Gervase and Pamela Cowell. Few of the invited Soviet officials
attended and the Penkovskys were among the absentees. The
MI6/CIA team were not unduly worried, partly because so few
Soviets were authorised to attend and partly because there was
another party two days later to which Penkovsky was invited and
he may have judged it best to attend only one of them.

The other party, given by the American acting economic
counsellor, was held on 15 September. Carlson was there and
had made full preparations for an exchange with Penkovsky.
Again, however, Penkovsky failed to attend.

By now there was great concern for Penkovsky's well-being.
He had said he would be going on holiday from mid-September
until the end of October, so the worst was not yet feared, but it
was troubling that, if indeed on vacation, he had not confirmed
his travel plans prior to departure.

---

†   In the dim light of the projection room, Edmonds was convinced this
    was Khrushchev. Ten months later, at the 4 July 1963 reception at the
    American Embassy, the same little man pushed through the crowd and
    beamed at Edmonds, saying 'A Taste of Honey'!

30

OCTOBER 1962 (PART 1) THE DEVELOPING CRISIS

Havana

Fidel Castro was pleased with the Soviet Union–Cuba agreement for the deployment of abundant quantities of weapons and equipment in Cuba, together with the tens of thousands of Soviet troops and advisers to manage them. There was the obvious advantage of discouraging a United States-backed invasion and it would bring Cuba the national and international status Castro wanted. He had no problem with Soviet army personnel commanding the missiles at first but hoped that Cubans could be trained to use at least the SS-2 surface-to-air missiles in time.

Castro's sense of enhanced prestige and security did not last long. The more Soviet matériel that arrived, the more the Soviets shrouded it in secrecy, refusing to allow Cuban troops to see it, let alone help to unpack and transport it. Some Soviet officers perceived their men as superior to their Cuban counterparts, and did not trust Castro's troops and officers to keep secrets.

Washington

October 1962 was a good month for John McCone in his capacity as director of the CIA. He emerged from the substantial shadow of his predecessor, Allen Dulles, to be his own man. He gained immense respect for the way in which he handled the Cuban crisis, in spite of having to deal with a family tragedy just as that crisis approached its climax.

As evidence of the build-up of Soviet personnel, military

equipment and weapons in Cuba poured in, McCone used Penkovsky's *Ironbark* and *Chickadee* material to inform his interpretation of events.[†] As early as 10 August, at a high-level meeting in Secretary of State Dean Rusk's office, McCone warned that the build-up would lead to the introduction of offensive strike weapons including medium- and intermediate-range ballistic missiles (MRBMs and IRBMs) in Cuba. No one believed him, and they continued to dismiss his claims right through to early October. Indeed, on 30 September, Rusk said on US television that the configuration of Cuban military forces in Cuba was 'defensive'.

There was a short-tempered meeting of the Special Group Augmented on 4 October to discuss progress on *Operation Mongoose*. Attorney-General Robert Kennedy was in the Chair:[‡]

Robert Kennedy: I've been discussing the Cuban situation with the President. We're both unhappy about lack of action with regard to sabotage. Nothing is moving forward: the situation in Cuba is developing fast, but nothing is moving forward under *Operation Mongoose*.

General Lansdale, trying to avoid confrontation, reviewed the operations that were in process and concluded:

All of these operations are proceeding in accordance with the plan, both in time and scale, as agreed by this Group.

McCone, possibly fearing the wrath of Bill Harvey as much as that of Robert Kennedy, dared to say:

[†] *Ironbark* was the CIA's code name for documentary intelligence from Oleg Penkovsky. *Chickadee* was their code name for the material from his debriefing sessions.

[‡] Author's interpretation based on McCone's 'Memorandum of MONGOOSE Meeting Held on Thursday, October 4, 1962', from CIA documents on the Cuban Missile Crisis.

Mr Chairman, we are still on phase one which was principally intelligence gathering, organizing and training. Only one act of sabotage has been considered – the one against a power station – but it was discouraged by this Group. I had a meeting with Bill Harvey and some others this morning to review matters. Our lack of forward motion – as you put it Mr Chairman – is due principally to hesitancy in government circles to engage in any activities that could be attributed to the United States government.

Robert Kennedy:

Damn it, John; how can you say that? To my knowledge, this Group has *not* withheld approval on any specified actions. On the contrary, it has urged and insisted upon action by your people.

The heated exchanges continued for a while, but the group left the argument unresolved and simply 'reaffirmed their determination to move forward'.

They agreed that the phase-two plan they had approved on 6 September was now out of date because the level of action that could be attributed solely to local Cubans, maintaining plausible deniability, would no longer be effective. Lansdale was instructed to consider new and more dynamic approaches. His orders were to bring forward some of the previously considered acts of sabotage and develop new ones such as mining harbours and capturing Cuban soldiers for interrogation.

McCone took advantage of this new mood for effective action, asking the group to reconsider their past caution about overflights and to authorise complete sweeps of Cuba by U-2 spy planes. This would provide incontrovertible evidence of the existence of SS-4 medium-range ground-to-ground missiles which were reportedly being installed on new sites. It was agreed that Colonel Ralph Steakley (US Air Force) would present recommendations for overflights to a special meeting of the group to be held on 9 October.

At Robert Kennedy's request, McCone and McGeorge Bundy

(President's special assistant for national security affairs) met on 5 October to try to resolve some of the issues that had caused the bickering at the meeting on the 4th. Bundy was the strongest critic of McCone's view about the likelihood of offensive nuclear weapons in Cuba. Far from resolving the issues, the two men were at loggerheads. The discussion went like this:[†]

> McCone: Look, Mac; I believe it's not just possible but *probable* that Soviet-Cuban operations will end up with an *offensive* capability in Cuba including MRBMs and IRBMs such as the SS-4 and the SS-5. I've been warning of this for the past two months, even in cables from France when I was on honeymoon.[‡]
>
> Bundy: But you're wrong, John; the Soviets wouldn't go that far. I'm satisfied that no offensive capability would be installed in Cuba because of its world-wide effects. It's not only me: the President is satisfied about this and so are the Attorney General, your own CIA Board of National Estimates and most of the rest of the American intelligence community. You're out on a limb with your assertions. The reason you can't produce hard information on this is simply because there isn't any.
>
> McCone: We haven't hard evidence because our hands are tied behind our backs. The Attorney General was totally wrong when he said the SGA hadn't put unacceptable restrictions on the kind of action that could be taken under *Mongoose*; and you know it. You're the main protagonist for weak non-attributable action, but let me tell you this, Mac: the United States cannot afford to take a risk on there *not* being MRBMs.
>
> Bundy: Look at it this way, John. Our policy on Cuba isn't clear. We don't have any objectives so our efforts aren't productive. On this basis I'm not criticising the *Mongoose* operations, nor am I

---

†   Author's interpretation based on McCone's 'Memorandum of Discussion with Mr. McGeorge Bundy, Friday. October 5. 1962, 5:15p.m' from CIA documents on the Cuban Missile Crisis.

‡   McCone had been on honeymoon in France from 23 August to 23 September.

criticising Edward Lansdale's operations. I'm not in favour of a more active role because I don't think any of the operations Bill Harvey's team are likely to come up with would bring Castro down; and equally, they would be detrimental to America's position of world leadership.

McCone: I'm not sure where you're going with this, Mac. Maybe you're admitting you don't support the more dynamic action we agreed at the SGA meeting; but look, the President and the Attorney General both agree that the whole government policy with reference to Cuba must be resolved promptly. That's a necessity before we can take further action.

Bundy: That may well be, but I see it like this: we should either make a judgment that we would have to go in with the military, which to me is intolerable, or we would have to learn to live with Castro and his Cuba and adjust our policies accordingly.

This exchange illustrated the polarity of thought in Washington's top-level political, intelligence and defence circles in early October. A particularly telling point was Bundy's assertion that: 'Our policy on Cuba isn't clear. We don't have any objectives so our efforts aren't productive.'

This may have been on President Kennedy's mind when, with the US congressional election campaign in full swing and dominated by fears over the military threat from Cuba, he appealed in a television interview that Cuba should be left off the campaign agenda. He suggested that Castro was an irrelevance: 'We are all concerned about Cuba, and as you know, we are taking a lot of steps to try to isolate Castro, who we believe eventually is going to fall,' he said.

The President attended the SGA meeting on 9 October and approved the recommendation for a U-2 flight. However, poor visibility over Cuba caused the flight to be postponed until Sunday the 14th. The mission was successful and encountered no resistance.

On 15 October, McCone received news of the death of his stepson and immediately flew to the West Coast to be with his family.

The deputy director of the CIA, Lieutenant-General Marshall Carter, was left in charge at the CIA's Langley Headquarters.

That evening, Carter was informed that the photographs from the previous day's U-2 flight indicated the deployment of MRBMs. He immediately authorised the dissemination of this information on a strict need-to-know basis to US Intelligence Board members and their immediate commanders.

He gave the news to McGeorge Bundy at 8.30 p.m. but Bundy – the man who refused to believe the Soviets would place strategic offensive weapons in Cuba and was convinced that even if they did it would not justify attacking Cuba – decided *not* to notify the President until the next morning.

On hearing the news, the President called a meeting of the National Security Council at the White House. Carter, assisted by two experts on offensive missile weapons and photographic interpretation, made a preliminary briefing to the group.[†] In essence, the photographs showed three mobile medium-range ballistic missile sites.

Secretary of State Dean Rusk opened the discussion by saying how disturbed he was about this development but pointed out that CIA Director John McCone had predicted such a possibility back in mid-August.

Discussions, which lasted for several hours, centred on considering the following courses of action:

- A quick-strike surprise attack by air to destroy the bases;
- expanding this into a total invasion to take over the island;
- the US should not act without first informing their allies, at least in part;
- announcing the discovery of the MRBM sites, which would enable them to consider calling up the Reserves;
- getting in touch with Castro through a third party and warning

---

† Carter was still deputising for McCone, who returned from the West Coast later in the day.

him that he was jeopardising his government, people and Cuban Sovereignty by getting involved with Soviet missile bases;

- trying to create maximum confusion in Cuba by infiltration and sabotage efforts;
- reviewing US policy on a provisional government for Cuba and trying to get all the anti-Castro factions working together.

In the context of keeping their allies informed, Rusk warned that America's allies in Europe might not give their wholehearted support to aggressive action against Cuba. They could, justifiably, point out that they had been targeted by Soviet missiles for many years without firing so much as a warning salvo, so why was military action necessary, especially at such great risk, when America faced the same danger?

Many were anxious that any US attack on Cuba might have serious consequences for West Berlin which, notwithstanding the recent massive increase in NATO conventional forces in Europe, was still precariously vulnerable to sudden military attack and occupation, and to isolation by closure of the Allied rail and road corridors.

The only significant action taken at the meeting was the President's authorisation of unlimited U-2 flights over Cuba. Kennedy also selected a team of twenty-four advisers – including McCone – that would make meetings about the Cuban situation more manageable than gatherings of the entire National Security Council. It subsequently became known as 'ExComm', short for Executive Committee of the National Security Council.

One of the State Department representatives on ExComm was Llewellyn Thompson who, as Ambassador in Moscow, had obstructed local CIA management of Penkovsky. He was now 'Ambassador at Large' and had the ear of the President, who valued his knowledge of both the Soviet Union and of Khrushchev as a person. Both men shared the inclination to blame the CIA when things went wrong.

Havana

Oblivious of America's discovery of the offensive missile sites, tension began to build between Cuban and Soviet forces as an American attack or invasion became an increasing likelihood. Resentment and disillusionment among Cuban soldiers and civilians over their treatment by the Soviet visitors bubbled to the surface and word of it reached Fidel Castro through his brother Raúl.

Fidel was enormously upset. His vision of Communist brothers facing the common enemy with unity, equality and brotherhood was starting to tarnish in the face of Soviet arrogance. He was particularly perplexed because he had originally taken the view that they should be open about the deployment of Soviet military weapons and manpower in Cuba. It would be better for the Americans to know what was going on so that they could take measured, rational decisions to deal with it, and learn to accept the situation. Sudden discovery – which was bound to happen sooner or later – could precipitate a disastrous knee-jerk reaction. Castro was beginning to feel that Khrushchev was using Cuba to promote his own military agenda rather than cooperating with and assisting Castro.

Castro and Soviet Ambassador Aleksandr Alekseev had struck up a close friendship soon after Alekseev had arrived in Havana in October 1959. His appointment at that time had been as the KGB *Rezident* in Cuba, with cover as press attaché. He was 'promoted' and appointed ambassador in August 1962. Now their friendship was being tested.

Castro called Alekseev in on 17 October and poured out his feelings. Cubans were a proud people, he told Alekseev, rightly happy and excited about the Soviet presence in their homeland. It enhanced their international status and served as a powerful defence against American-backed aggression. But they were now wondering if they would be able to live comfortably together – Cubans and the multitude of Soviet visitors – because some Soviet army personnel were riding roughshod over Cubans as if they were all ignorant peasants or possible American agents.

Alekseev took a side-swipe at the GRU, blaming them for much of the problem.[†] He promised, nevertheless, to inform Khrushchev of Castro's complaint and felt sure that things would become more harmonious.

Moscow

Khrushchev had more than enough on his plate when, on 18 October, he received Alekseev's telegram about Castro's complaints. Alekseev would have emphasised that the problem was mainly caused by GRU officers, and it may have been this that later propelled the propaganda machine into condemning Serov and the GRU for 'the most corrupt and unproductive period in its history'.

Had Khrushchev found the time in the midst of this critical state of affairs to reprimand Serov, the latter would have protested the charges and defended his organisation's honour. The GRU had not been informed of the Soviet Union's true political and military intentions in Cuba. They did not know that strategic nuclear weapons had been installed on the island. They had not been consulted about the viability of hiding the launch sites from prying American eyes. The GRU had expertise in these matters and, had they been consulted, they would have either advised against attempts to conceal the weapons, or made a better job of it.

Washington

There were sixteen U-2 spy flights over Cuba from 15 to 22 October, most of them bringing in evidence of new missile sites or continuing preparations for the operational readiness of known sites. The final count was forty-eight MRBMs with a range of 1,100 miles (1,800 km), which would just about reach

---

[†]   During his early years in Cuba, Alekseev had resisted the appointment of any GRU personnel to Cuba: he wanted the ear of Castro solely for the KGB. However, in October 1961 the Chief of Staff of the Cuban Army, General Sergio del Valle, specifically requested the presence of GRU officers and Alekseev was forced to accept this.

Washington; thirty-two IRBMs with a range of 2,500 miles (4,000 km), which would take in most of the US, and twenty-three sites with operationally ready SA-4 surface-to-air missiles. There were also twenty-five MIG-21 advanced interceptor fighters and twenty Illusion-28 medium bombers.

At a meeting of members of ExComm on Wednesday 17 October, Ambassador Thompson strongly advocated a blockade of shipping to prevent any increase in Soviet offensive weapons in Cuba. He urged that there should be no military action unless Castro and Khrushchev refused to reverse their activities and remove the missiles already in place. It was important, he said, to communicate with Khrushchev. He also said that any action, whether a blockade or direct military intervention, should be preceded by a declaration of war.

On 18 October, Kennedy held talks in the White House with Soviet Foreign Minister Andrei Gromyko, ostensibly about a summit with Khrushchev proposed for later in the year and the continuing disputes over West Berlin, although it later emerged that Cuba had also been high on the agenda. Kennedy then left Washington for a campaign tour.

Each day's fresh intelligence generated more meetings, particularly of ExComm and the US Intelligence Board, but also of small groups of up to half a dozen people.

Most parties, including Kennedy and McCone, initially favoured direct and immediate military action to eliminate all missile sites. Some said this should be attempted only after a warning to the Soviets but others proposed a surprise attack. When political opinion gradually moved towards a blockade of shipping there were still those on the military side – particularly Robert McNamara (Secretary of Defence) and General Maxwell Taylor (Chairman of the Joint Chiefs of Staff) – who advocated an immediate attack, for which preparations had already been made.

The 18th Airborne Corps, including many of America's front-line forces, were put on standby on 16 October and a squadron of fighter aircraft flew to the Key West base just ninety miles from Cuba, in what the Pentagon described as a 'precautionary measure'. Some forty ships, including aircraft carriers, and 20,000 troops were holding an exercise in the area between the Florida Keys and Puerto Rico, although the Pentagon insisted it was a pre-planned exercise with no extraordinary significance.

Moscow

Oleg Penkovsky had warned the Americans about Khrushchev's warmongering inclinations, including the possibility of Soviet weaponry in Cuba, and he provided technical intelligence about the missiles themselves. One detail that was of immense importance as the situation rapidly moved towards crisis point was the protracted time required to fuel, arm and launch Soviet offensive missile rockets compared to their American equivalents.

The Soviets were still unaware that the Americans had discovered the missile sites, and they did not know of the frenetic meetings that were taking place in Washington.

It was therefore by a bizarre and cruel coincidence that the KGB decided to raid Penkovsky's apartment in Moscow on 20 October, discovering one of his Minox cameras. Penkovsky had not been in regular contact with MI6/CIA during this period, which caused some unease, but they had no inkling of the KGB raid.

Washington

On the weekend of 20 and 21 October, President Kennedy and Vice-President Lyndon Johnson pulled out of their campaign schedules to fly back to Washington, both saying they had 'a slight cold'. Secretary of State Dean Rusk stayed in Washington 'to cope with a backlog of work that had accumulated because of his long talks with Soviet Foreign Minister Gromyko on Thursday'. They, together with McNamara and a number of other officials, discussed the growing crisis and briefed key Congressional leaders.

An ExComm meeting on the 20th was devoted largely to detailed discussions of the two main options for action: a naval blockade or an air strike. Opinions, including the President's, were gradually swaying towards the former, though the military remained sworn advocates of the latter. There was agreement that the President should address the nation, but not about what he should say.

Records of ExComm meetings throughout this intense period show that the President was constantly concerned about the likely reaction of America's allies in Europe and Latin America to whatever action America finally took to resolve the Cuba problem. He wanted to show strong action without precipitating some kind of a disaster. He was also conscious of the diplomatic need to consult his allies.

He spoke to British Ambassador David Ormsby-Gore – a close and dear friend of many years standing – on 21 October, immediately before another ExComm meeting. Having now made up his mind about which option to pursue, he suggested to the Ambassador that a blockade was the better option and left the Ambassador with little opportunity to argue otherwise. This was not consultation in the true sense. Ormsby-Gore reported the discussion to Prime Minister Harold Macmillan.

The President then attended the ExComm meeting. Discussion was now focused on the wording of the President's speech. A blockade was now the consensual preference, though there was some debate about whether it should be called a blockade, which conjured up thoughts of the Berlin blockade, or a quarantine. This was a purely semantic choice with no legal bearing. The President opted for 'quarantine'.

They discussed plans for a military strike in the event that the quarantine failed to bring the stand-off to an end. Defence Secretary McNamara said that planning was based on an initial air strike followed seven days later with landings. Twenty-five thousand men would be put ashore the first day, and by the eighteenth day, 90,000 would be ashore. There was an alternative plan for the landing of 90,000 men in a 23-day period. The President asked that everything be done to reduce the length of time between a decision to invade and the landing of the first troops.

The President went on to say he believed that, as soon as he had finished his television speech, the Soviets would (a) speed up the development of their missile capability in Cuba, (b) announce that if the US attacked Cuba, the Soviet would launch offensive rockets, and (c) possibly act to eject Western forces from West Berlin.

The ExComm members agreed to emphasise international action through the Organisation of American States (OAS), rather than the United Nations. Failure to give prominence to the OAS could jeopardise that regional alliance, seen as crucial to limiting the spread of Communism in South and Central America.

After this meeting, Kennedy sent a telegram to Macmillan informing him of his intention to impose a blockade.

There was another ExComm meeting on the 22nd, which opened with the reading of Macmillan's response to the President's telegram of the night before. It registered reservations about imposing a blockade, which could be construed as an act of war. Macmillan reminded the President that Western Europe had been a target for Soviet nuclear weapons for some years with little difficulty, so he need not expect too much support from other European countries. More importantly, he warned Kennedy that a blockade would give the Soviets an excuse to impose a retaliatory blockade on West Berlin, opening up a serious rift between Western Europe and America.

Rusk thought Macmillan's reaction to the news of the proposed blockade 'was not bad'. Kennedy commented that the Prime Minister's message 'contained the best argument for taking no action'.

In the course of this meeting the President admitted he had finally come down in favour of a blockade rather than an air strike only the previous morning, just prior to his conversation with Ambassador Ormsby-Gore.

The meeting clarified some of the points to be included in the President's TV speech that evening and covered a wide range of 'what if?' scenarios. The President said there was risk in whatever action they decided to take. 'That risk should be carefully measured,' he said, 'and the chance taken; because it would be a mistake to do nothing.'

After the meeting had ended and before he addressed the nation, the President had a telephone conversation with Macmillan in the course of which he said: 'Some action is necessary. It could result in WWIII; we could lose Berlin.'

31

OCTOBER 1962 (PART 2) THE CRISIS DAYS

Washington

At 7 p.m. on the evening of Monday 22 October, President John F. Kennedy addressed the nation on television. The speech was read in a confident, business-like manner at a smart pace and with a minimum of emotion.[†]

Good evening, my fellow citizens.

Within the past week, unmistakable evidence has established the fact that a series of offensive missile sites is now in preparation on that imprisoned island [Cuba]. The purpose of these bases can be none other than to provide a nuclear strike capability against the Western Hemisphere. These new missile sites include medium-range ballistic missiles, capable of striking Washington DC. Additional sites appear to be designed for intermediate-range ballistic missiles capable of travelling more than twice as far. The size of this undertaking makes clear that it has been planned for some months. Yet, only last month, after I had made clear the distinction between any introduction of ground-to-ground missiles and the existence of defensive anti-aircraft missiles, the Soviet government publicly stated on September 11 that 'the armaments and military equipment sent to Cuba are designed exclusively for defensive purposes'. Only last Thursday, Soviet Foreign Minister Gromyko told me in my office that Soviet

---

†   See Appendix 1 for the full transcript.

assistance to Cuba 'pursued solely the purpose of contributing to the defence capabilities of Cuba,' that 'training by Soviet specialists of Cuban nationals in handling defensive armaments was by no means offensive, and if it were otherwise the Soviet government would never become involved in rendering such assistance'. That statement was false.

This secret, swift, extraordinary build-up of Communist missiles in an area well known to have a special and historical relationship to the United States, this sudden, clandestine decision to station strategic weapons for the first time outside of Soviet soil, is a deliberately provocative and unjustified change in the status quo which cannot be accepted by this country. This nation is opposed to war. We are also true to our word. Our unswerving objective, therefore, must be to prevent the use of these missiles against this or any other country, and to secure their withdrawal or elimination from the Western Hemisphere.

Our policy has been one of patience and restraint, as befits a peaceful and powerful nation which leads a worldwide alliance. But now further action is required, and it is under way. We will not prematurely or unnecessarily risk the costs of worldwide nuclear war in which even the fruits of victory would be ashes in our mouth; but neither will we shrink from that risk at any time it must be faced.

Kennedy said he had ordered a number of defensive measures:

- A complete blockade on any offensive military equipment being delivered to Cuba;
- Increased surveillance of Cuba and 'its military build-up';
- Preparations by the US Armed Forces for 'any eventualities' should the 'offensive military preparations' at the missile sites continue.

The President made it clear that the US would regard any nuclear missile launched from Cuba at any country in the world to be 'an attack by the Soviet Union on the United States, requiring a full retaliatory response upon the Soviet Union'. He ended his address to the nation by calling on Khrushchev to 'halt and eliminate this clandestine, reckless, and provocative threat to world peace and to stable relations between our two nations'.

> I call upon him further to abandon this course of world domination. We are prepared to discuss new proposals for the removal of tensions on both sides, including the possibilities of a genuinely independent Cuba, free to determine its own destiny. We have no wish to war with the Soviet Union. But it is difficult to settle or even discuss these problems in an atmosphere of intimidation. That is why this latest Soviet threat must and will be met with determination. Any hostile move anywhere in the world will be met by whatever action is needed.
>
> My fellow citizens, let no one doubt that this is a difficult and dangerous effort on which we have set out. No one can foresee precisely what course it will take or what costs or casualties will be incurred. The cost of freedom is always high, but Americans have always paid it. And one path we shall never choose, and that is the path of surrender or submission. Our goal is not the victory of might, but the vindication of right; not peace at the expense of freedom, but both peace and freedom, here in this hemisphere and, we hope, around the world. God willing, that goal will be achieved.
>
> Thank you and good night.

Until this point, only those who had been involved in the series of meetings, and a few other experts who had to be consulted individually, knew about the discovery of the missiles. Only those subordinates who *had* to know were put in the picture. The state of readiness of US armed forces had been raised from DEFCON 5 (the lowest state of readiness) to DEFCON 3 (increase in force readiness above that required for normal readiness), but no detailed explanation had been given for this.

Messages had gone out to the heads of most US diplomatic missions around the world asking them to inform the leaders of the governments to which they were accredited, in advance, of the general content of the President's public address. As predicted by Macmillan, the news had a 'mixed' (the diplomatic euphemism for poor) reception in the Western world.

United Kingdom and Western Europe

Initially most people in the Western world outside America had doubts that the published photographs actually proved the existence of missile sites – those shown on television and reproduced in newspapers could just as easily have displayed farms with large barns – and with that doubt came the possibility that the American government were playing some kind of mysterious and dangerous game.

There were anti-war demonstrations outside the American Embassies in London and in other Western capitals.

The mood in Britain was one of concern. The leader of Britain's opposition Labour Party, Hugh Gaitskell, gave voice to an opinion that was widely held by many throughout Western Europe.

> If it is indeed true that long-range missile bases have been set up in Cuba, then it is a provocative action that must be condemned. We must have some sympathy with the Americans in the position in which they have found themselves and we suggest that if there is any doubt about it, observers appointed by the UN should go in and see what is actually happening.
>
> At the same time we are worried about the US blockade; we are worried about its legality in international law, and of course it can have very serious consequences in the Caribbean and in other parts of the world. In particular, we regret that the US government didn't consult its allies before taking this decision, and didn't take it to the UN Security Council first.
>
> We believe that everything should be done to try to settle the

dispute. There should be the utmost constraint by all concerned to avoid actual conflict. Mr Macmillan should go to Washington to explore with the Americans, and indeed with the Russians if he can meet them, what should be done in this way. And also I think he should go there because we must have, now, very close consultations with the United States.

Moscow

On the day that President Kennedy spoke on television to the American people and an astonished world about the discovery of the missiles, the KGB arrested Oleg Penkovsky, charged him with espionage and began to interrogate him. He soon admitted his treachery and informed on Greville Wynne.

Many Soviet politicians, officials and citizens would call it poetic justice rather than a cruel coincidence.

Serov was informed of Penkovsky's arrest. His world was becoming the mother of all nightmares: first the unfounded accusations of GRU incompetence in Cuba, and then the arrest of his subordinate and personal friend, Oleg Penkovsky, for spying on behalf of the capitalist, imperialist West. Both of these would reflect badly on him, even though he was not responsible for either.

He may well have slept badly that night, awakening to the news of President Kennedy's announcement to the world that the Soviet Union had placed offensive intercontinental ballistic missiles in Cuba.

Brooding on this, Serov may have wondered briefly if he should have gone to Cuba himself, as he had done in Hungary. But he accepted that he would not have been able to exert the same degree of control because the circumstances were quite different: in Hungary the enemy was internal and finally outnumbered and outgunned by Soviet military might, while in Cuba the enemy was overseas and better armed than even the USSR.

His thoughts turned to Penkovsky. Surely it could not be true that Oleg Vladimirovich had been arrested for espionage. There must be some mistake. This man had looked after his (Serov's) wife and daughter in London and helped them to find wonderful presents for him. He worked exceptionally hard at his cover job, yet also managed to get good results in his GRU assignments. Yes, he had been sore about his lack of promotion and the KGB's obsession with his father's royalism, but that would not have turned him into a traitor.

Penkovsky had been a model member of the party since his early youth, with never a black mark against his name. And yet – thought Serov – there was something peculiar about it all. Why did the KGB stop his posting to India and then grant approval for a job that gave him trips to the West where he could not easily be supervised? Oleg loved his beautiful family and would not, surely, endanger them, though he did occasionally allow his eyes and maybe other parts of his anatomy to wander. He had been a close friend of the wily Comrade Marshal Sergei Varentsov for many years – and there was no way Oleg could pull the wool over Varentsov's eyes.

These and a hundred other thoughts and visions about Penkovsky would have gone through Serov's mind, over and over again.

His attention would momentarily return to Cuba as the television screen filled with a picture of Kennedy, a brash, self-assured young man who – in the eyes of Serov – used the imperialist might over which he ruled to confront Communism. It is easy to imagine Serov's fury with Kennedy. All the evidence suggests he was incandescent. Damn Kennedy for what he had done to Cuba. Damn him and his CIA for luring Oleg into spying for America. Damn him for ruining my career.

Serov had demonstrated over many years that he was not the kind of person to forgive or forget.

Havana

Castro called Ambassador Alekseev in again on 22 October after President Kennedy's television appearance. He was beside himself with anger.

He gave Alekseev an I-told-you-so lecture, reaffirming his own view that they should have been open about the defence pact. Now Kennedy was making it into a huge episode and Castro was sure that virtually all of the West would support strong American action. If ever Cuba was going to be invaded by America it would be now.

Castro wanted Alekseev to tell him how the Americans had been able to photograph the missile sites. From the photographs that the Americans had published it was clear that the Soviet military had made little effort to camouflage them. The Cuban Army – insisted Castro – would have made a better job of it.

He responded to the crisis by putting the Cuban armed forces on a war footing and reacting belligerently to the idea that independent UN observers might inspect the missile sites. 'We reject all attempts at inspection,' the Cuban leader said. 'We will never surrender our independence and sovereign right to let only whom we want into our territory.'

‡

Kennedy, Khrushchev and Castro all requested an emergency meeting of the United Nations Security Council which called upon acting UN Secretary-General U Thant to negotiate a solution. U Thant sent urgent appeals to Khrushchev to suspend arms shipments to Cuba, and to Kennedy to suspend the blockade, so that talks could take place.

But despite these public efforts to resolve the crisis, exchanges of letters between Kennedy and Khrushchev reveal just how close to the brink of nuclear war the world's two most powerful nations stood.

Kennedy sent Khrushchev the text of his address to the nation on 22 October, accompanying it with a letter which insisted that the missiles be removed, but it went on to warn of the threat of all-out nuclear war:[†]

---

†   See Appendix 2 for the full text of this letter and of the exchanges of letters that followed.

The one thing that has most concerned me has been the possibility that your Government would not correctly understand the will and determination of the United States in any given situation, since I have not assumed that you ... would, in this nuclear age, deliberately plunge the world into war which it is crystal clear no country could win and which could only result in catastrophic consequences to the whole world, including the aggressor.

Khrushchev's response, dated 23 October, accused the US of interfering in the internal affairs of both Cuba and the Soviet Union, avoiding any direct reference to war.

I must say frankly that measures indicated in your statement constitute a serious threat to peace and to the security of nations. The United States has openly taken the path of grossly violating the United Nations Charter ... We affirm that the armaments which are in Cuba, regardless of the classification to which they may belong, are intended solely for defensive purposes, in order to secure the Republic of Cuba against the attack of an aggressor.

I hope that the United States Government will display wisdom and renounce the actions pursued by you, which may lead to catastrophic consequences for world peace.

But in a letter to the veteran British peace campaigner Bertrand Russell, Khrushchev spelt out precisely what those catastrophic consequences would be:

We shall do everything in our power to prevent war from breaking out. We are fully aware of the fact that if this war is unleashed, from the very first hour it will become a thermo-nuclear and world war. This is perfectly obvious to us, but clearly is not to the Government of the United States which has caused this crisis.

United States
It was an anxious time for everyone in the United States. Although

the majority of Americans supported Kennedy's actions, three-fifths of the adult population expected war. At the peak of the crisis people's thoughts focused on the international situation in general and on atomic war and fall-out in particular, but the American public were not paralysed by events.

Nonetheless, someone who was twelve years old at the time recently recorded his memory of people wondering if there would be a tomorrow; or whether they would manage to return from work to see their families before they were all killed by a nuclear explosion. He remembers, at school, performing daily duck-and-take-cover drills. There was panic buying at food stores, and even gun sales soared in the preparation for a land invasion. They provisioned and checked their hastily built fall-out shelters. These things were happening everywhere, in every neighbourhood in the country.

In his response to Khrushchev's warning of thermo-nuclear war, Kennedy reiterated that it was the Soviet Union's decision to place long-range missiles in Cuba which had led to the crisis and urged 'prudence', calling on the Soviet leader to order the twenty-five Soviet ships reportedly on their way to Cuba to comply with the US blockade.

The following day, 24 October, Khrushchev responded with a long and emotional letter.

Just imagine, Mr President, that we had presented you with the conditions of an ultimatum which you have presented us by your action. How would you have reacted to this? I think that you would have been indignant at such a step on our part. And this would have been understandable to us.

In presenting us with these conditions, you, Mr President, have flung a challenge at us. Who asked you to do this? By what right did you do this?

You, Mr President, are not declaring a quarantine, but rather are setting forth an ultimatum and threatening that if we do not give in to your demands you will use force. Consider what you are saying! And you want to persuade me to agree to this! What would it mean to agree to these demands? It would mean guiding oneself in one's relations with other countries not by reason, but by submitting to arbitrariness. You are no longer appealing to reason, but wish to intimidate us.

No, Mr President, I cannot agree to this, and I think that in your own heart you recognize that I am correct. I am convinced that in my place you would act the same way.

Khrushchev accused Kennedy of acting not just out of hatred for the Cuban people and its government but also for electoral reasons.

What morality, what law can justify such an approach by the American Government to international affairs? No such morality or law can be found, because the actions of the United States with regard to Cuba constitute outright banditry or, if you like, the folly of degenerate imperialism. The Soviet Government considers that the violation of the freedom to use international waters and international air space is an act of aggression which pushes mankind toward the abyss of a world nuclear-missile war.

The Soviet Union, wrote Khrushchev, would not stand by while American ships carried out 'piratical acts on the high seas'. It would take whatever measures it felt necessary to protect itself and had everything it needed to do so.

Cuba

In the middle of this exchange of threats and counterthreats, the first of the Soviet ships still heading towards Cuba reached the quarantine line on 24 October. Despite Khrushchev's condemnation of the quarantine as illegal and piracy on the high seas, the Soviet ships, surprisingly, stopped just short of the American armada.

Washington

Nerves were on edge. There was every possibility of serious action – even war – against Cuba. Bill Harvey knew from his field agents about the rapidly increasing volume of Soviet military personnel and equipment in Cuba but he had not been aware of the discovery of MRBM and IRBM sites nor of the frantic series of meetings until shortly before the President's television announcement on 22 October.

He had mixed feelings about unfolding events. On the one hand he was pleased to hear that, at last, decisive action would be taken to resolve the Cuban problem. On the other hand he was hurt that the Special Group Augmented, and particularly its chairman, Robert Kennedy, had denied him the scope of action he felt he needed in order to do a proper job.

Harvey had organised nine teams, each of half-a-dozen men, to go to Cuba, gather intelligence and, if required, assist the military in the event of an invasion. These men – all Cuban exiles – would be landed off small submarines in the dead of night.

Typically, Harvey had told neither the Joint Chiefs of Staff nor the Special Group Augmented about the teams until the after-noon of Friday 26 October when there was a meeting composed mostly of SGA members in the JCS Operations Room.

It was an extraordinary meeting in which tempers flared.[†]

Harvey had just described the teams that would be going to Cuba in small submarines.

General Edward Lansdale: This is a bit of a surprise to me, Bill. As the overall head of *Mongoose* I should have been told you were preparing to send these teams into Cuba.

Bill Harvey: There was no need for you to know until now,

[†] Author's interpretation based on McCone's 'Memorandum of MONGOOSE Meeting in the JCS Operations Room, October 26, 1962, at 2:30p.m.', from CIA documents on the Cuban Missile Crisis.

General. I need to gather intelligence before taking any direct action approved by the SGA and I have your authority and the authority of the SGA to send agents to Cuba to gather that intelligence. This is part of that operation. At this critical time we need intelligence and I'm taking appropriate action to get it. I've consulted the military at operational level about specific targets but I didn't see any need to inform either the SGA or the JCS formally of these activities in advance.

General Maxwell Taylor (Chairman of the Joint Chiefs of Staff): Yea; General Johnson told me you offered these groups to help in the situation of an invasion. They could prove to be very useful.

General Edward Lansdale: Just a minute, here. Bill's working under me on *Mongoose* projects. Now, suddenly, he's working directly for the Joint Chiefs? Is this not getting a bit out of hand Mr Chairman?

Robert Kennedy: Ah; you've made a valid point there Edward.

John McCone (CIA Director) [addressing Lansdale, came to the Attorney-General's rescue]: As I understand it, the *Mongoose* goal is to encourage the Cuban people to take Cuba away from Castro and to set up a new government. Bill and his *Task Force W* have supported, and will continue to support you in this, Edward. You're the director of the operation. No doubt about it. But you have to recognise – we all have to recognise – that CIA operatives are obligated to support the military to the extent desired by the JCS in any combat theatre. Maybe you've misunderstood that bit of our commitment, Edward.

McCone [smiled, trying to ease the tension, before continuing]: I think most of us would agree that *Mongoose*, operating through authorisation by the SGA, is not the fastest way to achieve results. We've reached the point – have we not, Mr Chairman? – when we have to be prepared for direct and attributable action. *Mongoose* just isn't geared to that.

Robert Kennedy: Thank you, John; I couldn't have put it better myself. That OK Edward: you're in charge of *Mongoose* but not all clandestine activities in Cuba come under *Mongoose*?

[Lansdale gave a grudging nod and the Attorney-General continued speaking]: Mr Harvey: I'm asking you to be careful about the use of these teams. I can't give you the details but I can assure you that delicate talks and negotiations are going on at the present time and we don't need any incidents that could upset these proceedings.

[Harvey continued to slouch in his chair and simply stared at Kennedy with his bulbous eyes, which irritated him.] Do I make myself clear Mr Harvey?

Bill Harvey: You carry on with your negotiations, Mr Attorney General, and I'll continue to train and prepare my men. I know my job and I'll do it. I'll do it damned well, as I've always done.

The Attorney-General spoke to McCone after the meeting, asking him to get rid of Harvey, who he found to be obnoxious and dangerous. McCone, while agreeing that Harvey could be infuriating at times, defended him as a hard and efficient worker. That did not matter to Robert Kennedy: Harvey clearly did not like or respect him, so he had to go.

McCone did not relish the idea of removing Harvey from the leadership of *Operation Mongoose* and replacing him with someone else. He believed *Mongoose* had run its course and could, perhaps, along with *Task Force W*, now be killed off. He could then find Harvey a new job well away from the Attorney-General. The Attorney-General, however, thought it might be a bit premature to end *Mongoose* and suggested they wait for a few days to see how the present negotiations progressed.

‡

Kennedy's response to Khrushchev's letter of 24 October merely restated that the crisis had been sparked by the Soviet decision to place missiles on Cuba in spite of having denied any such intent. Khrushchev's response came on 26 October in the form of a remarkably long and rambling letter with an ending that seemed to develop in the course of dictation rather than having been carefully thought out beforehand:

> I see, Mr President, that you too are not devoid of a sense of anxiety for the fate of the world understanding, and of what war entails. What would a war give you? You are threatening us with war. But you well know that the very least which you would receive in reply would be that you would experience the same consequences as those which you sent us. And that must be clear to us, people invested with authority, trust, and responsibility. We must not succumb to intoxication and petty passions, regardless of whether elections are impending in this or that country, or not impending. These are all transient things, but if indeed war should break out, then it would not be in our power to stop it, for such is the logic of war. I have participated in two wars and know that war ends when it has rolled through cities and villages, everywhere sowing death and destruction.

Did Kennedy really believe that Cuba and the Soviet Union could attack America from Cuban soil? Stopping the Soviet ships would be piracy. If the Soviet Union attempted to do the same to US ships, the Americans would be just as indignant as the Soviets were at the US blockade. He had agreed to U Thant's proposal that the Soviet shipments should be suspended to allow negotiations to go ahead. If the US also agreed to suspend its blockade, it would 'give the peoples the possibility of breathing calmly'. If the Kennedy administration was ready to give an assurance that it would not attack Cuba and recall its ships 'this would immediately change everything' and the need for Soviet military specialists at the missile sites would disappear, Khrushchev said.

> Let us therefore show statesmanlike wisdom. Mr President, I appeal to you to weigh well what the aggressive, piratical actions, which you have declared the USA intends to carry out in

international waters, would lead to. You yourself know that any sensible man simply cannot agree with this, cannot recognize your right to such actions. There, Mr President, are my thoughts, which, if you agreed with them, could put an end to that tense situation which is disturbing all peoples. These thoughts are dictated by a sincere desire to relieve the situation, to remove the threat of war.

Respectfully yours,

N Khrushchev

Khrushchev must have reflected – or been told – that this letter of 26 October was too weak, because he sent another letter on the 27th pointing out that while the Americans complained about the presence of Soviet missiles ninety miles away from US territory, it had its own missiles based in Turkey, which had land borders with the Soviet Union. If America withdrew its missiles from Turkey, the Soviet Union would withdraw its missiles from Cuba.

This letter caused a major problem for Kennedy because the Turks were adamant that the NATO missiles should stay and, in any case, the United States could not unilaterally decide to remove the NATO missiles.

That day, 27 October 1962, saw the world move closest to an all-out nuclear war.

A trigger-happy Soviet commander gave an order to fire an SA-4 missile that made a direct hit on an American U-2 spy plane, killing the pilot. A recently approved US military standing order covering such an occurrence called for immediate retaliatory action with an air strike on the site used to fire the missile. When the President was informed of the incident, however, he gave an order *not* to retaliate because 'maybe someone just made a mistake'.

Three ExComm meetings were held that day. Those present were preoccupied for much of the time with the military response to the general situation in Cuba and to the downing of the U-2 in particular. The military representatives were clamouring for action: they wanted to destroy the SAM missile site that had been used to shoot down the U-2. At one point General Taylor summarised the conclusions of the Joint Chiefs: unless the missiles were defused immediately, the Chiefs recommended implementation the next day (28 October) of a major air strike, and implementation of the invasion plan a week later. This was *not* agreed by the committee.

The US plan for an airborne attack followed by invasion included three massive strikes a day until all missiles and other air capability were destroyed. The first day of operations alone included more than 1,000 bombing sorties.

Meanwhile, Kennedy had decided, on advice, to circumvent the Turkish issue by ignoring Khrushchev's letter of 27 October and responding instead to the previous one, dated the 26th. He agreed to a commitment not to invade Cuba so long as the Soviet Union withdrew its missiles.

Moscow

The final agreement reached in this fateful correspondence was that all MRBM and IRBM missiles and other offensive weapons and aircraft would be removed from Cuba in exchange for guarantees that the United States would not invade, nor encourage anyone else to invade, Cuba. On 28 October, Khrushchev gave orders to begin the removal of all offensive weapons. Kennedy confirmed that there would be no invasion of Cuba.

The world had stepped back just in time from what could have been a catastrophic nuclear war. The crisis was over as long as everyone on both sides abided by the spirit of the agreement.

32

OCTOBER 1962 (PART 3) THE AFTERMATH

Washington

That very same day, 27 October, even as Kennedy was giving the commitment not to invade Cuba, Harvey gave orders for three of the clandestine teams to set off for Cuba with instructions to support any United States military operation against Cuba through acts of sabotage.

He also decided to revitalise the 'executive action' against Castro because he now believed that its success would avert the need for military action in Cuba. He spoke again to Mafia godfather, Johnny Roselli, drawing his attention to the situation in Cuba as described by the President on television. He asked Roselli to consult with his friends and come up with new ideas to assassinate Castro. They had to redouble their efforts, because that was the best way to prevent outright war.

Roselli said they were doing their best, but they were surprised how difficult it was. He suggested that if they could somehow lure Fabian Escalante – Castro's personal bodyguard – away from Castro's camp they would have a better chance. Santo Trafficante was – said Roselli – already working on that.

Trafficante continued to back both sides, just as he had done in Cuba before Castro had come to power. If Castro were to be overthrown, he had many influential friends among the exile groups who would help him to re-establish the casinos under a new non-Communist government. Should Castro remain in power he would continue to spy on his behalf, thus – hopefully

– avoiding an unexpected and unwelcome visit from Cuban intelligence officers.

Havana

Castro was away from Havana when news of Khrushchev's 'capitulation' was announced. Again, he was furious; not with Khrushchev's agreement to remove the offensive weapons – he thought Khrushchev had made the correct decision on this under the circumstances – but because it had been a unilateral Soviet decision. The Soviet Union had broken the terms of the Soviet–Cuban defence pact by not consulting Castro before making the deal. Castro also thought Khrushchev could have made a better bargain by, for example, insisting that America give up their sovereignty over the Guantanamo Bay Naval Base in south-eastern Cuba. And Castro was, of course, also of the opinion that this situation would never have arisen if the existence of the Soviet-Cuban defence pact had been made public at the outset.

On 1 November the Hungarian Ambassador in Havana sent a long telegram to his country's Foreign Minister reporting that:

> ... since 20 October I have not once managed to talk to any Cuban leaders. Since then, no ambassadors of the friendly countries [Eastern Bloc countries] including Czechoslovakia have managed to contact any Cuban leaders. As for the Czechoslovak ambassador, who is the first representative of the socialist countries to Havana, he used to meet Foreign Minister Roa several times a day and often other leaders as well. In the United States, Cuban interests are represented by Czechoslovakia. In this period he has not been able to get in to see any Cuban leaders [the Castro brothers and Guevara]. Foreign Minister Roa, who had the closest and most confidential relationship with him, has behaved towards him coolly and has not been willing to say anything important to him.

Che Guevara, who, unlike Castro, had all along been a Marxist–Leninist, took stronger and more fundamental issue with Khrushchev's decision. He felt that Khrushchev had let world Communism down; that he could have advanced the cause of socialist liberation by firing the nuclear missiles that were in Cuba. Such an attack against global imperialist aggression would ultimately have been worth, in his eyes, the resulting devastation and deaths. He maintained that if the Cuban Army had controlled these weapons they would have fired them. This is a disturbing insight into the mind of someone who is generally romanticised as a heroic cavalier and revolutionary, rather than the murderous – and in this case, explicitly genocidal – anti-imperialist, anti-capitalist fanatic that he really was.

West Germany and Berlin

Throughout the crisis, President Kennedy was deeply concerned that the Cuban situation had the potential to spark Soviet retaliation. The West Germans – more frightened than most for their own security during the Cuban crisis – gave strong support to Kennedy's tough response. Perhaps it was perceived as a relief that 'at last they're doing something to put Khrushchev in his place'. At the same time, they were fearful of how the Soviets might respond in West Berlin.

Within West Berlin, the Wall – now more than a year old – offered a small, somewhat ironic sense of physical protection. Overall, however, the feeling was of courage and hope for a peaceful settlement, tinged with fear.

China

The Sino-Soviet relationship had been frosty before the Cuban Missile Crisis and the events of 1962 did nothing to improve it. China watched carefully as events unfolded, keeping their own counsel. When the crisis ended, China's leader Mao Zedong denounced Khrushchev for yielding to the Americans and offered strong support to Castro.

This was another nail in Khrushchev's political coffin. It would also have given Serov a sense of vindication.

Washington

On 30 October, three days after the three submarine teams had set sail for Cuba, the Attorney-General gave instructions for all *Mongoose* operational activities to cease, but it was too late to abort the mission because the teams – for security reasons – carried no communications equipment that could link them to the CIA or US military. However, the leader of one of the teams did manage to send a message to the Attorney-General asking if, in view of the apparent settlement of the crisis, there was still a need to carry out their assigned operation.

Robert Kennedy was incensed. He told McCone to reprimand Harvey and get rid of him without delay.

McCone pulled no punches. He asked Harvey what he thought he was doing. Did he have a vendetta against the Attorney-General and was he taking it out on him by defying his orders?

Harvey denied any vendetta or grudge: that was not how he operated. When he had sent those teams to Cuba there was a strong possibility that America would be invading or at least striking the island and the members of the team could have proved extremely useful.

McCone accepted Harvey's reasoning but told him that, nevertheless, the Attorney-General insisted on him being moved out of his sight. He told Harvey he was sending him to Rome as head of the CIA station.

Harvey was not interested in Rome. He had been head of station in Berlin ten years earlier, when there was a *real* job to do. A posting to Rome, he felt, was an insult to an agent of his standing. McCone told him it was not a matter for debate. If he did not accept the post in Rome, he would have to be retired from the CIA.

Harvey must have wondered what had become of his world. He had no time for either the President or Robert Kennedy. The President had been responsible for the failure of the Bay of Pigs landing. He had prevented the CIA from taking the level of action required to do the job and then blamed the CIA for the failure. Whatever had happened to 'the buck stops here'?

And now, for the past nine months, Robert Kennedy had acted in a similar manner by preventing Harvey and his team from taking decisive action to end the Castro regime, and he was blaming Harvey. A plague on both the Kennedys, he thought.

Harvey reluctantly accepted the posting to Rome.

London

MI6 were, and continue to be, extremely secretive about their agents and their work. In the 1960s, their chief – Sir Dick White – was known only as 'C'. Even within the organisation individual projects were ring-fenced and this was particularly so with the Penkovsky case.

In the early days of running Penkovsky, when the quality, quantity and value of the military intelligence he was able to produce became apparent, White had expanded MI6's Ministry of Defence liaison section and brought them into the ring. After initial assessment, the material had been sent to scientific and technical research experts – without reference to its source – for detailed analysis, interpretation and comment.

Anyone leaving the Penkovsky case ring on transfer to other duties was warned never to say anything about Penkovsky or the case, not even to their new bosses.

One of the drawbacks of this level of secrecy is that there can be no public praise, award or reward for their achievements. White was determined, nevertheless, to use the Penkovsky case to boost the morale of his troops and stress the importance and practical value of their work.

Shortly after the Cuban Missile Crisis, he took the possibly unprecedented step of assembling MI6 London staff in the headquarters cinema room and addressing them thus:[†]

[†]   See Anthony Verrier, *Through the Looking Glass: British Foreign Policy in an Age of Illusions* (London: Cape, 1983).

I have been asked by the CIA to let you know of the absolutely crucial value of the Penkovsky intelligence we have been passing to them. I am given to understand that this intelligence was largely instrumental in deciding that the United States should not make a pre-emptive nuclear strike against the Soviet Union, as a substantial body of important opinion in the States has been in favour of doing. In making known this appreciation of our contribution, I would stress to all of you that, if proof were needed, this operation has demonstrated beyond all doubt the prime importance of the human intelligence source, handled with professional skill and expertise.

It is irrelevant whether or not the CIA actually asked White to thank his staff. White was trying to draw a line under the disasters of the Burgess, Maclean and Philby, the Blake, and other cases that had been blighting the relationship between the CIA and MI6. MI6 were now in the ascendancy; they had done a grand job with Penkovsky and, using the lessons learned from it, should look forward with enthusiasm to a new and successful world of greater coordination and cooperation with the Foreign Office, the Ministry of Defence and the CIA.

On 10 November the British Ambassador in Havana, Herbert Marchant, sent his first post-Crisis dispatch to the Foreign Office. He analysed the critical events and the failure of the intelligence community to foresee them:

Most Cubans have now been waiting – some hopefully, some fearfully – for at least two years for 'something to happen'. All this time we have lived in an atmosphere of the wildest rumours, 90 per cent of them totally without foundation and many of them specifically about gigantic nuclear missiles. Intelligence agencies must therefore be excused if they tended to discount the hundreds of recent rocket stories from their usually unreliable sources. The arrival of much of the Russian equipment, the daily movement of technicians, of the sand and cement, all this was cheerfully accounted for by the generally accepted fact that the Russians were known to be busy building ground-to-air rocket sites all over the country. What we did not see anything of until too late was the vital equipment and the larger missiles which were almost certainly moved only at night.

My own early disbelief, shared by most of my colleagues, was based on the contention, which I still hold to be true, that Castro's first principle in all his thinking and doing has been to survive and 'defend the Revolution'. It was consequently our opinion, and we thought it was also Castro's opinion, that the installation of offensive missiles in Cuba was the one thing that would justify United States invasion. We therefore believed that neither Castro nor Khrushchev would consider such a move. Although we still do not know exactly where our reasoning went astray it seems probable that the fault lay in not realising how high the stakes were that Khrushchev was prepared to play for.

The Ambassador's final sentence strongly supports Penkovsky's regular warnings, during his debriefing sessions, about the danger of underestimating Khrushchev's military ambitions and determination.

✝
✝

The United States lifted the naval quarantine on 20 November 1962, in recognition of the progressive removal of Soviet armaments from Cuba.

33

MOSCOW 1963 (PART 1)

News of Penkovsky's arrest had been kept secret, so there was no obvious reason for Wynne not to attend a trade fair in Budapest at the beginning of November 1962. He was arrested there on 2 November. The Hungarians handed him over to the Soviet authorities and he was flown to Moscow to stand trial.

‡

Serov continued to lead the GRU until March 1963 when final preparations for the trials of Penkovsky and Wynne were under way, though he was not allowed to become involved in those proceedings. Frol Kozlov – the Second Secretary of the Communist Party, seen by some as Khrushchev's heir apparent – prevailed upon Khrushchev to get rid of Serov. On 12 March 1963 – nine years to the day after his appointment as chairman of the KGB – Serov was dismissed as head of the GRU and demoted from Field Marshal to Major-General. He was given the lowly appointment of Assistant Chief of Staff of the Volga Military District, though it seems he did not bother to take up this appointment.

By now it was clear that the intelligence Penkovsky had passed to the West had been an important factor in how Kennedy handled the Missile Crisis and this aggravated Serov's mental wounds. Serov – the ruthless, tightly focused workaholic who thrived on action at the highest level – would have been emotionally upset, perhaps for the first time in his life. He was considering what he might do to rehabilitate himself. It was too late to do anything further in Cuba: the Soviet offensive missiles had been dismantled and were already on their way back to the Soviet Union together with the mass of GRU personnel who had accompanied them to the Caribbean.

Serov's hatred of Kennedy – the figurehead of the ultimate enemy – became an obsession. In this state of mind, it seems likely that he would have sought solace in the company of his like-minded associates Yuri Andropov and Vladimir Kryuchkov, both of whom had been towers of strength in crushing Nagy's Hungarian Revolution. Andropov had recently been promoted to an influential post in the Secretariat of the Central Committee of the CPSU: the committee that controlled the KGB. Ever since his days as Ambassador in Budapest he had been a strong advocate of using military force to prevent the loss of Soviet control over the socialist republics and the satellite countries. He was as upset as Serov at Khrushchev's capitulation (as they saw it) in Cuba. So was Kryuchkov who had also moved to the Central Committee after leaving Budapest, thus remaining close to his mentor, Andropov.

All three of these figures – Serov, Andropov and Kryuchkov – were men of action and risk-takers. They had schemed together to persuade a reluctant Khrushchev to invade Hungary and taken part in the subsequent battle. It would have been natural for them to meet, have a few drinks, and discuss the circumstances of the Cuban Missile Crisis. Serov would have floated the idea of taking revenge on Kennedy.

The world would once again be brought to the brink of nuclear war if the Soviet Union were found to be responsible for the death of the President of the United States. That would not have worried Serov, who may even have rejoiced at the thought. But he lived in a world of secrecy and would be confident those responsible for the act would not be discovered.

One can only speculate on these matters, as Serov vanished after Penkovsky's trial.

The Soviet system catered, at will, for lies and deceptions to hide the results of the less wholesome decisions it made. Disgraced senior politicians and officials could be made to disappear. Records could be changed or destroyed. News of anyone or anything could be blacked out or fabricated.

34

WASHINGTON AND LONDON 1963

Following the arrest of Penkovsky and Wynne in October and November 1962, the CIA and MI6 became entangled in arguments about how best to save them from their probable fates – the death penalty for Penkovsky and a long prison sentence for Wynne. Both sides felt it essential to do all they possibly could to save them, if only to show their respective agents how much they cared.

The CIA wanted to send an anonymous letter which would be sent covertly to the KGB and GRU through British channels, threatening public revelation of some of the material passed to the West by Penkovsky. MI6 at first objected strongly to this suggestion but later agreed that there should be some communication with the KGB/GRU. However, MI6's suggestion went much further: they wanted to threaten detailed exposure of several categories of Penkovsky's material and to make an official approach through London representatives of the KGB and GRU. There had never before been direct contact with the KGB/GRU and the CIA objected vigorously that they could not condone official contact with any Soviet intelligence agency.

MI6 proposed, in that case, that they would go it alone and take official unilateral action including the possibility of declaring a substantial number of Soviet intelligence personnel in the UK personae non grata.

This, in turn, was unacceptable to the CIA, both for its very unilateralism, and the inevitability of equal or greater retaliation in a persona non grata war. They would, however, consider the use of a written communication alluding to the possibility of revealing facts given by Penkovsky about official and unofficial representatives of the KGB and GRU abroad. The CIA would also be willing to use a cleared British attorney ostensibly acting on behalf of Mrs Wynne to communicate the message.

Joseph Bulik and George Kisevalter, the CIA half of the team who had debriefed Penkovsky, were angered by the bickering. It was wasting precious time and all of the proposed actions, they thought, were unlikely to help Penkovsky and would not send a strong enough message to potential defectors.

In a joint memorandum to their boss, the Chief of the Soviet Russia Division, dated 14 May, they submitted an elaborate plan that envisaged sending identical letters to two KGB and two GRU *Rezidents* in Bonn, The Hague, Copenhagen and Rome. Four points were chosen to ensure delivery. Each letter said that similar letters were being sent to the other three places, which would dissuade recipients from ignoring them. The content of the letter was intended to embarrass the recipients. A photograph of Penkovsky with Chief Marshal Varentsov would be enclosed. They recommended that their plan 'be carried out without any reference to the British, in the light of the Soviet statement that the CIA "does not give a hoot about the fate of their agents"'. They believed it would 'in no way jeopardise whatever plans the British have for negotiating with the Soviets for the release of Wynne'.

The Bulik/Kisevalter plan was rejected by Angleton but the CIA and MI6 did make a joint effort to embarrass the Soviets and possibly save Penkovsky from a death sentence. The Soviets ignored them.

35

MOSCOW 1963 (PART 2)

Preparations for the trial of Penkovsky and Wynne took six months. Everything – the questions and the expected answers – were carefully rehearsed.

Court proceedings began in open session on Tuesday 7 May 1963 with Penkovsky standing accused of treason and Wynne of assisting him. About 300 selected Soviet citizens and some authorised diplomats and journalists were present.

The trial lasted five days. Penkovsky admitted his guilt and stuck to the script throughout. Wynne maintained he knew nothing of Penkovsky's treachery – if, indeed, Penkovsky *was* passing secrets – and acted, perhaps naively, as an innocent messenger. He strayed from the script, but to no avail.

Penkovsky's behaviour was controlled and professional throughout. He showed no nerves, no fear and little emotion. Much of the detail of the espionage evidence against him had come from Penkovsky himself during pre-trial interrogation. With regard to character and motivation he maintained he was driven solely by his desire for Western luxuries and alcohol, not by any political motive. He had never – he said – had any difference of opinion with the party or the government. He admitted to some dalliances with women, but denied the extensive philandering of which he stood accused. He loved his wife and two daughters.

The court questioned Penkovsky on strained relationships between the CIA and MI6, asking if he had ever met separately with the CIA debriefing team. He admitted that there had been one such meeting, in Paris. It had been very informal, and he claimed that the American team had expressed regret at having to share him with the British.

The third day (Thursday) was a closed session with the public and press excluded. There was also a closed session on the morning of the fifth and final day (Saturday). At no time during the open sessions were the names of any senior Soviet officials such as Varentsov and Serov mentioned.

On the Saturday afternoon both men were found guilty. Penkovsky was sentenced to death by firing squad and Wynne to eight years' detention.

Officially, Penkovsky was executed by gunshot in Lubyanka Prison in Moscow on 16 May 1963. Within a few days, however, it was rumoured that he had not been shot but tied to a stretcher and burned alive as a graphic warning to other potential defectors, and that his ashes had been thrown into a mass grave at Donskoi Monastery cemetery in Moscow. The Soviet authorities did nothing to confirm or deny this rumour.

36

USA 1963

Dallas

In response to Vladimir Kryuchkov's telegram of 18 July 1962, Cuba's Interior Minister Ramiro Valdés had appointed Major Rolando Cubela of Cuban Intelligence (G-2) as Lee Harvey Oswald's case officer. Cubela had contacted Oswald in November and Oswald had embarked upon an overt campaign to gain support for Castro through the Fair Play for Cuba Committee (FPCC). He contrived to work hard on this but in the end his personal contribution was relatively ineffectual. It did, however, give him cover for contact with the Communist world.

He wrote letters to the Information Section at the Soviet Embassy in Washington asking about the availability of Soviet magazines in the United States and subscribed to several of them. He also had a subscription for *The Worker*, the newspaper of the American Communist Party.

A front page story in *The Worker* on 7 October 1962 warned the Kennedy administration and the American people of the need for action against General Edwin Walker and his followers. General Walker had left the US Army in 1961 after being criticised at the highest level for right-wing indoctrination of soldiers under his command. After leaving the military, Walker attempted to launch a political career as a hard-right segregationist and McCarthyite anti-Communist, running for Governor of Texas in 1962 (he finished last in a primary election field of six candidates).

Perhaps it was this article that led Oswald to purchase a Smith and Wesson revolver, using a post-office box address under an assumed name (A. J. Hidell), at the end of January 1963. Or maybe a KGB agent, or a representative of some other group, encouraged him to do so.

Oswald decided – or was instructed by someone else – to kill Walker.

He discovered as much as he could about Walker's daily routines, and reconnoitred his house, creeping round the back of it and taking photographs of the view into Walker's study. His best opportunity, he decided, would be to shoot Walker in his study on a Wednesday evening. Oswald would not be seen at the back of the house and he could make a relatively easy escape by blending into the numbers of good people making their way to the local Wednesday evening church service.

The revolver, however, would not be a suitable weapon for shooting over this distance so, on 12 March, he ordered a Carcano 6.5mm rifle, again using the alias Hidell and the post-office box address.

On Wednesday 10 April, he shot at General Walker, made a safe escape, and hid the rifle near a railway line. Regrettably, from Oswald's point of view, the bullet hit a part of the window frame, leaving Walker with only minor injuries from shrapnel.

Oswald was never suspected of this attempt on Walker's life until after the assassination of President Kennedy. There was plenty of evidence against him because he had left a note for his wife, Marina, before he went out, telling her what to do with herself and their daughter if he failed to return. Marina was also pregnant with their second child at the time. She found the note before he returned and asked him what it was all about. He told her he had shot Walker.

New Orleans
Within two weeks of the assassination attempt on Walker, Oswald moved to New Orleans with his family, leaving no forwarding

address. The decision to move and the actual move took place within a few days. On 18 April – just ten days after the shooting – Oswald wrote to the FPCC reporting that he had handed out some of their leaflets on the 17th and requesting more. He gave his Dallas address, so he appears not to have been preparing to relocate; yet less than a week later, on 24 April, he moved to New Orleans.

It is difficult to understand why he would have made such a precipitate move unless he had been encouraged or instructed to do so. One thing is known: the FBI, who had been able to maintain checks on him in Dallas, lost track of him for two months when he moved to New Orleans. They did not discover his presence in the city until 26 June and did not verify his residence there until 5 August.

In New Orleans Oswald discovered there was no local chapter of the FPCC, so he wrote to the national director offering to start one. He asked for a charter for the new branch and suggested that he rent an office at his own expense. He also asked for advice about buying large quantities of pamphlets and FPCC application forms.

He was not given a charter, though his pamphlets said he had one. The national director advised him not to rent an office, but he went ahead and did so.

He had managed to get a low-wage job in New Orleans, but he had a wife and child to keep and another child on the way. How was he going to be able to afford to rent a small office and pay for printing large quantities of pamphlets?

Oswald used a post-office box address (No. 30061) which was also accessible by A. J. Hidell and Marina Oswald. He used this address correctly for all correspondence and for delivery of the magazines to which he subscribed. However, he intentionally put 'Box 30016' (last two digits transposed) on his pamphlets so that he would neither receive any written expressions of interest nor applications to join the FPCC. He also used the name A. J. Hidell on the pamphlets.

On 19 July Oswald was sacked from his menial job with the Reily Coffee Company. At about the same time, he started to use his real name and correct address on the pamphlets he distributed.

At the beginning of August, he started to play a double-agent role, continuing his overt pro-Castro FPCC activities but behind the scenes posing as an anti-Castro agent.

On 5 August he visited Carlos Bringuier, the New Orleans delegate of the Cuban Student Revolutionary Directorate (DRE), an anti-Castro organisation part-financed by the CIA. Oswald told Bringuier he wanted to help the DRE to depose the Castro regime. He said he had been a Marine and offered to give military training to DRE members and even to go to Cuba himself and join the anti-Castro resistance.

Bringuier declined the offer, saying that his job with the DRE was to disseminate anti-Castro propaganda and information, not to become involved in military activities. Oswald persevered, promising to give Bringuier a Marine training manual, and also offering a financial donation. Bringuier refused to accept any money on the grounds that the DRE in New Orleans did not have a permit to collect money.

Oswald delivered the Marine training manual the next day, in spite of Bringuier's negative response to his overtures.

On 9 August Oswald went to a corner close to Bringuier's shop and began distributing pro-Castro FPCC leaflets. Word of this reached Bringuier, who came to confront Oswald, accompanied by two friends. There was a scuffle and all four were arrested for disturbing the peace.

Bringuier was convinced that Oswald had gone to that particular corner purely to provoke an altercation with him.

At the police station Oswald was interviewed by Lieutenant Frances Martello, but he also *asked* to be interviewed by an FBI officer. In the interview with Martello he refused to give the names of any members of his FPCC branch, but he did say that only five or so people attended the monthly meetings, held in private homes.

He was then interviewed by FBI agent John Quigley to whom he gave a number of silly answers. He said he had married in Fort Worth; that there had been a branch of the FPCC in New Orleans when he arrived; that he had had telephone conversations with A. J. Hidell and took instructions from him; that he had received his FPCC membership card from Hidell. He even gave the wrong date for his own birth.

In court on 12 August, Oswald was fined $10.

On 21 August Oswald participated in a live debate on Cuban–American relations on WDSU, a local radio station. The programme host was Bill Stuckey. There was a co-host called Slatter and two other participants: Ed Butler, who ran an anti-Communist organisation called 'The Information Council of the Americas', and Carlos Bringuier.

The debate was a disaster for Oswald. He had expected questions about his pro-Castro activities with the FPCC. Instead, Stuckey asked leading questions about his time in the Soviet Union. Oswald eventually admitted that he was a Marxist.

Oswald's usefulness to the FPCC was over. At that time, Castro maintained that Cuba was a socialist country; he kept Communism and the Soviet Union at arm's length. As a self-professed Marxist, Oswald could no longer promote Castro's Cuba.

Bringuier, as the DRE's delegate, reported all of Oswald's strange behaviour in New Orleans to the CIA through his contact at Bill Harvey's *JM/WAVE* station in Miami, but this would have been just one of many reports they received from the variety of anti-Castro organisations financially supported by the CIA. It may not have been forwarded to headquarters and thence to Oswald's file.

Oswald's five-month stay in New Orleans had been surreal. Why had he been so anxious to get there, deciding to go and arriving in the course of less than a week? Why had he set up a branch of the Fair Play for Cuba Committee and then put a false name and address on the leaflets? He clearly had not wanted to recruit any members and this was borne out during the interview with police Lieutenant Frances Martello when he had been unable to name any members and said that only five people attended monthly meetings. Why had he asked to be interviewed by an FBI agent and then told him a pack of lies that he knew would be uncovered?

Why had he gone to Bringuier's store pretending to be anti-Castro and then inspired a confrontation with Bringuier over the distribution of FPCC leaflets? He would have known that Bringuier's DRE organisation was supported by the CIA and that Bringuier would file a report on him.

Who had fed Stuckey, the programme host at Radio WDSU, all of the detailed background about Oswald's connections with the Soviet Union so that he could ask pertinent questions on the live programme? Oswald had kept calm throughout this surprising line of questioning and, on the whole, had given truthful answers that could have damaged the FPCC's image; that was not natural for Oswald who regularly lost his temper and was never averse to telling lies.

Oswald's encounters with Bringuier had a lasting effect on the man. Bringuier campaigned for the rest of his life to prove that Fidel Castro was responsible for the assassination of President Kennedy, and the articles he wrote nearly always cited Oswald's activities in New Orleans as evidence.

Oswald was simply not capable of orchestrating such a series of events and actions of his own volition, and none of them were accidental. Someone, or some organisation, was pulling Oswald's strings.

The aim could only have been to generate total confusion about Oswald, what motivated him and where his life was heading.

The FPCC, as a pro-Castro organisation, were never enamoured with Oswald's efforts on their behalf. They did not give him money to rent an office, print FPCC pamphlets and pay people to distribute them, only for him to take action that ensured he would not be burdened with a bunch of enthusiastic Castro supporters. The FPCC did not orchestrate any of Oswald's activities in New Orleans.

The FBI found Oswald exasperating. Their scheduled interviews in the past had been stormy events and at one point they had closed his file. In New Orleans, he had *asked* to be interviewed by an FBI agent and then made a total nonsense of the interview. The FBI had no use for him.

The CIA had been copied in on some of the FBI's documentation on Oswald and they would have received a report on him from Bringuier, but these sources would likely have portrayed him as a useless and aggravating eccentric. Besides, the CIA was not permitted to operate within the United States.

Anti-Castro organisations were busy working with the CIA on strategies and training that might lead to the overthrow of his regime. They may have had some interest in Oswald in relation to monitoring his FPCC activities, but they could ill afford to use their limited resources on that task and would have left it to the FBI/CIA.

That left the KGB. They had the resources and the ability to control Oswald. He had spent nearly three years in the Soviet Union, returning to America with a Soviet wife and a child. He had declared himself a Marxist. He was regularly in correspondence with the Soviet Embassy in Washington, usually asking for information about Communist newspapers and magazines. The only rational explanation for Oswald's sudden, unpremeditated departure for New Orleans is that the KGB asked him to go there. They then orchestrated his sometimes bizarre conduct. The KGB were more likely than any other organisation to have given an anonymous tip-off to the radio station about Oswald's Soviet Union connections. They must have warned him they were doing so, because he did not falter in answering questions that would otherwise have caused him to lose his temper, lie, or both.

There is also the conundrum of the KGB's Vladimir Kryuchkov

sending a telegram to Cuba's Interior Minister, Ramiro Valdés, suggesting that *Cuban* Intelligence might wish to contact Oswald in the United States. It would have been easier and more fitting for KGB agents to do so themselves. The telegram set a false trail.

The KGB have always claimed that Oswald was of no interest to them: he did not have the right background, intelligence or mental stability to be of any real use. Were that true, they would not have sent a telegram at ministerial level to Cuba.

✝
✝

There was clearly no future for Oswald in New Orleans, at least not as an FPCC agent. Marina was eight months pregnant and their relationship was deteriorating. She told Oswald she was going to live with her friend Ruth Paine in Irving, not far from Dallas. Marina and Ruth had been close friends for some time and Ruth was now separated from her husband and living alone. The invitation to Marina was not extended to Oswald on the pretext that there was not enough room for everyone, but Marina knew Ruth did not like or trust him.

Oswald decided to apply for visas for himself and his family to return to the Soviet Union, stopping in Cuba for a while on his way there. If this decision were an attempt to save his marriage it is strange he did not discuss it with Marina or even inform her of it. It is more likely to have been a suggestion or an instruction from the KGB.

By now, Oswald was well versed in the red tape of passports and visas: where to apply, how to apply and how long it was likely to take. He would have known, for example, that as an American citizen residing in America he would have to apply to the Soviet Embassy visa section in Washington for a visa to enter the Soviet Union.

Instead, he went to the Soviet Consulate in Mexico City. Perhaps this was down to his not particularly intelligent and often confused mind, but would he not have telephoned the consulate first to check that it was possible to obtain a visa from them, or to ask for a blank visa application form that he could complete before travelling that considerable distance in an uncomfortable bus? Perhaps he was instructed to go to Mexico City.

On 17 September he visited the Mexican Consulate in New Orleans and obtained a fifteen-day tourist visa for Mexico. He set off for Mexico City by bus on 26 September. Marina had already gone to Irving to stay with Ruth Paine.

‡

For more than a month before this there had been reports that President Kennedy would make a campaign visit to the electorally crucial State of Texas, then consumed by internal strife among the Democratic Party establishment. On the day of Oswald's journey to Mexico City, 26 September, the *Dallas Morning News* announced that the President would be visiting Texas on 21 and 22 November and that Dallas might be on the itinerary.

37

MEXICO CITY 1963

The CIA were strong on the ground in Mexico City, led by their energetic station chief, Winston 'Win' Scott. Their main preoccupation was to infiltrate pro-Castro groups and generate anti-Castro sentiment. Notoriously, they 'set up' some prominent pro-Castro Cubans who, although innocent, were charged with treason and imprisoned.

Some of the success of the CIA's operations must be attributed to their infiltration of the Cuban Embassy and Consulate in Mexico City. With inside help they had rigged up surveillance cameras outside the consulate and tapped the telephone lines.

Silvia Duran, an attractive round-faced 26-year-old Mexican, was married to Horacio Duran Navarro, fourteen years her elder. Both were strong Communist sympathisers. Silvia had come to the attention of the CIA when, the previous year, she had had an affair with Carlos Lechuga, the Cuban Ambassador in Mexico. Lechuga was promptly posted to New York as Ambassador to the United Nations and Silvia found a job as a receptionist at the Cuban Consulate in Mexico City.

Oswald arrived on the morning of Friday 27 September 1963, and was at the Cuban Consulate by 11 a.m. Silvia Duran was on the visa applications desk. He asked her for a transit visa for Cuba and offered abundant evidence of his support for Fidel Castro, including his Fair Play for Cuba Committee membership card. He admitted at the outset that he was a member of the American Communist Party and that he had lived in the Soviet Union for several years.

Duran asked him for his final destination, explaining that he would need to put this on the application form. He would also have to provide proof that he would be admitted there and that he had the necessary travel documentation. He would need four passport photographs to go with his application.

His final destination was the Soviet Union but he did not yet have a visa. She said he would need to get the Soviet visa first and directed him to the Soviet Consulate, just two blocks away.

Oswald returned to the Cuban Consulate at 12.15 p.m. with the passport photographs, but he had not yet been to the Soviet Consulate. Duran helped him to complete a transit visa application form but reiterated that he had to have his Soviet visa before any action could be taken on it.

He arrived at the Soviet Consulate just after 12.30 and was initially dealt with by Vice-Consul Valery Kostikov, a sturdy, round-faced man in his mid-thirties. CIA records showed that he worked for Department Thirteen of the First Chief Directorate of the KGB: the department responsible for executive action, including sabotage and assassination. There were two other consular officials: Consul Pavel Yatskov and Vice-Consul Oleg Nechiporenko, both of whom were also KGB officers.

Kostikov listened for a while to Oswald's story and to his request for a visa to go to the Soviet Union, and decided after a few minutes that it would be better for Vice-Consul Oleg Nechiporenko to deal with him. Nechiporenko, a slim, dapper man with a carefully trimmed black moustache, was several years younger than Kostikov. He wore thick-rimmed spectacles with dark lenses.

According to a book published under Nechiporenko's name thirty years later, Oswald created a poor impression and was certainly not KGB agent material.[†] He listened to Oswald whining about FBI harassment rendering him unemployable. He

---

[†]   See Oleg Nechiporenko, *Passport to Assassination* (Carol Publishing Group, 1993). Translated from Russian by Todd P. Bludeau.

wanted to return to the Soviet Union for the sake of his family and his sanity. Nechiporenko studied the large bundle of documents that Oswald produced – all of them supporting Oswald's story – and led him through the requirements for a visa application. Oswald told him that his earlier visa application to the Soviet Embassy in Washington had been rejected. Now, he was afraid of being arrested by the FBI if he went to the embassy in person.

When Nechiporenko explained that his visa application would take at least four months to process, and that it would have to be dealt with through the Washington Embassy because Oswald was a United States resident, he became agitated. He expected better treatment in the light of his history in the Soviet Union and marriage to a Soviet citizen. His frustration boiled over. He threw one of his tantrums and stormed out.

It was a stifling hot day but he managed to cool down, at least mentally, before returning to the Cuban Consulate just before four o'clock. There, he again saw Silvia Duran and lied to her, saying that the Soviet Consulate had granted him a visa.

Thinking this unusual, she asked him to whom he had spoken. He could not remember the exact name but gave an approximate pronunciation that enabled her to establish, when she phoned the consulate, that it had been Kostikov.[†]

Kostikov confirmed that he had spoken to Oswald, but said he had not yet been granted a visa, and in any case it would take four months to process an application.

Duran reproached Oswald for lying to her, and informed him he could not have a visa for Cuba unless and until he had one for the Soviet Union. Yet it appears that she must have had some sympathy or compassion for this man in his present, lonely predicament, for she invited him out that evening.

[†] Nechiporenko recorded that throughout his interview with Oswald, Oswald had never asked for his name and he had never given it. Hence, it was only an approximation of Kostikov's name that Oswald gave to Duran.

Married consular officials do not, willy-nilly, invite unknown customers out for the evening. Duran's dalliance of a year before had been with a foreign ambassador, not a lying rascal like Oswald.

There has been much confusion and speculation about the role played by the Cuban Consulate in Mexico City in general, and Silvia Duran in particular, but there can be little doubt that if Duran befriended Oswald, then she did so at the behest of one of the security services: the CIA, the KGB or the Cuban G2.[†] The last of these should not be discounted. Cuban G2 officers attended the Soviet spy school in Minsk as part of their training and Oswald had a friendly relationship with some of them during his time there. He sometimes told Marina that he would like to go to Cuba, and even join the Cuban government.

†
†

The following morning, Oswald was in better spirits after his night out with Silvia and decided to have another go at persuading the Soviet Consulate to be more forthcoming over his visa application. He arrived early at the consulate, at about nine o'clock. It was Saturday and the main door was locked, so he rang the bell. A security guard answered, let him in, and led him to Consul Pavel Yatskov's office. Yatskov, perhaps forty, his hair turning grey, looked more the part of a stereotypical Russian of the 1960s than his colleagues. Tall and slim, with a rugged face, he often wore his jacket on his shoulders without using the arms.

He was the only officer present, but Kostikov and Nechiporenko arrived separately, a little later. They had gone to the consulate to change into their sports gear for a serious volleyball match: the embassy's diplomatic and consular sections against the military attaché and trade mission sections. Essentially,

---

† Some lines of research say that Oswald and Duran had an intimate relationship.

this was the KGB against the GRU: a needle match if ever there was one.

By the time the other two consular officers had arrived, Oswald had repeated his story of the previous day at least two more times. He became emotional, pleading for a visa. He burst into tears. He lost his temper, this time placing a loaded revolver on the desk and wailing that he was watched so closely by the FBI he had to carry this weapon with him all the time for his own personal safety. He pleaded for a visa because his life in the United States was so miserable.

Yatskov unloaded the weapon and put it back on the desk.

Oswald eventually accepted that he would not get a Soviet visa soon and, as his immediate problems could not be solved by fleeing to the Soviet Union, he decided not to bother even completing the visa application form.

Dejected, he left the Soviet Consulate at 10.30 a.m. Yatskov, Nechiporenko and Kostikov, jointly or collectively, had spent one-and-a-half hours with Oswald. They missed their vital volleyball game and the GRU team beat the KGB, which was an institutional humiliation.

Yatskov and Kostikov immediately drafted a record of the meetings with Oswald for the embassy's *Rezident*. They also enci-phered it and sent it as a telegram to the KGB's Moscow centre. Nechiporenko later called this telegram a life preserver that they had thrown to themselves.

It would be timely to remember that at this point Oswald was little more than a John Doe. No one, with the possible excep-tion of whoever was manipulating him, could have imagined that this was the person who, one day, would kill the President of the United States. He was not a figure that commanded particular attention.

Even the most conscientious consular officer, of any national-ity, would not give up his or her Saturday morning to grant an interview for a visa that could not in any case be granted for at least four months. He or she might do so for distressed national subjects who had been robbed of their passports and money and needed to travel the same or the next day, or those who had suffered an accident or fallen seriously ill, but not for a routine visa application.

If John Doe rang the bell of a closed consulate on a Saturday morning he would be turned away and told to come back on Monday morning. If, extraordinarily, he were to be granted a visa interview, there could be no question of any more than one officer conducting that interview. The interview having been conducted, the visa application would be sent to the home headquarters by diplomatic bag: it would never warrant the immediate sending of a cypher telegram.

One can smile at the 'seriousness' of the KGB v. GRU volleyball match, but it was a serious matter for the players. None of them would have missed it unless obliged to do so by urgent business.

The known details – and there are many – of the two interviews at the Soviet Consulate originate from Soviet sources. No one else, apart from Oswald, was present. The Soviet system of the 1950s and 1960s was expert at fabricating information to suit its objectives.

The CIA was definitely interested to know what Oswald was doing in Mexico City. All telephone calls by or relating to Oswald were monitored by the CIA and transcribed. Some of the transcriptions went missing, but recollections by the transcribers suggest that Oswald had been in contact with the Soviet Embassy in Washington before he went to Mexico; or – more likely – the Washington Embassy had contacted him. He clearly expected the Consulate in Mexico City to have been briefed about his arrival. It is possible that Vladimir Kryuchkov or Yuri Andropov in Moscow had instructed the KGB *Rezident* in Washington to pass a message to Oswald asking him to go to the Soviet Consulate in Mexico City to meet Kostikov and Nechiporenko. There would have been no need for the *Rezident* or anyone else to know the purpose of the visit.

The head of the CIA's Mexico City station, Win Scott, was a close friend of James Angleton, the CIA's head of counterintelligence staff from 1954 until he resigned under a cloud in 1975. 'After Scott's death in April 1971, Angleton flew to Mexico City, removed the contents of Scott's safe, and demanded that the family turn over Scott's papers to him'.[†] The papers in Scott's safe must have been of sensational sensitivity, bearing in mind that Angleton retrieved them after Kennedy's and Oswald's deaths.

CIA agents were snooping around and may have discovered something that should be kept from public knowledge at all costs, but the action was with the KGB.

‡

Oswald stayed on in Mexico City until early Wednesday morning, 3 October. He did not return to either the Cuban or Soviet Consulates, though he may have gone out with Silvia Duran several more times.

---

† See John Newman, *Oswald and the CIA* (New York: Carroll & Graf, 1995), p. 369.

38

DALLAS, OCTOBER AND NOVEMBER 1963

Oswald did not return to New Orleans. Instead, on Wednesday 3 October, he boarded a bus bound for Dallas where he found lodgings at 1026 North Beckley. From there, he went to visit Marina, now living with her friend Ruth Paine in Irving, about ten miles (sixteen kilometres) from Dallas. Marina was just two weeks from giving birth to their second child.

He told her he had spent the previous week in Houston and said nothing about Mexico City or his efforts to get visas for the Soviet Union and Cuba.

He said he would look for a job. Ruth Paine, keen not to be saddled with Oswald, said she had heard from a neighbour that the Schoolbook Depository in Dallas had a vacancy that might suit him.

Oswald applied for the job and got it. He worked hard and conscientiously and, at last, had a supervisor who was pleased with him. He stayed in his lodgings during the week and went to Irving at the weekends, taking a lift from a co-worker who lived there. This was acceptable to Ruth.

The arrangement also suited Oswald, who was able to do some research into the forthcoming visit of President Kennedy and plan his course of action without the distraction of his heavily pregnant wife and their daughter, June. He would also be free to make contact with his master or co-conspirator.[†]

---

† The US Select Committee on Assassinations concluded that there was a high probability that *two* gunmen fired at the President.

Marina gave birth to their second daughter on 20 October. Oswald was pleased it had all gone well and was attentive, even loving, to Marina and the baby in hospital, but both Oswald and Marina knew their marriage was still in difficulty.

News of the likely route to be taken by the President leaked into the press on 18 November. The motorcade would make its way from the airport to the Business and Trade Mart for a Presidential luncheon with the local great, good and wealthy.

Oswald's heart would have missed a beat when he discovered the route was along Main Street, with a right turn into Houston Street and then left into Elm Street. The Schoolbook Depository where he worked was right on the junction of Houston and Elm. From a window he would be able to see the motorcade turning into Houston Street and driving straight towards him. It would still be in his view after taking the sharp left turn at the Depository and along Elm Street where it would pass Grassy Knoll before disappearing into an underpass.

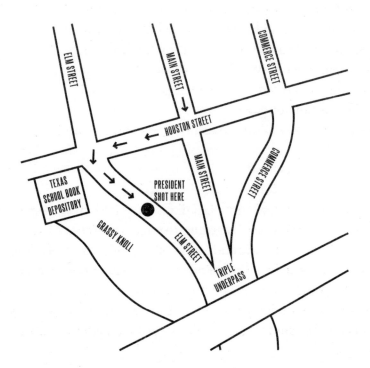

Three options presented themselves. The easiest shot would be from one of the Depository windows as the President's car came towards him along Houston Street, but virtually all of the security people would be looking ahead and they were almost certain to spot someone pointing a rifle from a Depository window. There were also the problems of making an escape, and hiding the rifle which would undoubtedly lead back to him.

Second, he could wait until the car had turned into Elm Street and shoot the President from behind. There would be confusion about where the shot had come from and perhaps the Depository would not immediately be closed off. In any case, it was his legitimate place of employment and if he acted casually enough he would be allowed past any cursory police check.

Third, he could take up a position on Grassy Knoll, which was a raised belt of grass running along the right-hand side of Elm Street. There would be a lot of people standing and sitting there, but there was also a sturdy fence at the back, separating the Knoll from a car park and commercial buildings. If he took up a position behind the fence he would have a clear shot at the President and those watching the motorcade would have their backs to him. However, he might be seen by someone in the commercial buildings or in the car park. He would have to run fast to evade any pursuers.

He chose – or was told to use – the second option.

‡

One can only imagine how he might have felt on the morning of Friday 22 November. He awoke from a fitful sleep, full of fear, and trembling as he drank his breakfast coffee. But eventually he forced himself into a state of grim determination. He *had* to succeed; whether he was doing it for himself, or because he was under orders with dire consequences for failure and rich rewards for success. He knew there would never be a better opportunity than this.

Perhaps his thoughts were altruistic: that the world would be a better place after the deed was done. Was he really so devoted to Communism and did he hate America so much?

He would have to try to act as if everything were normal throughout the day, especially after the event.

He had selected a small, unoccupied room on the sixth floor, on the left of the building as one looks out from it. He put the rifle together, checked it thoroughly, and hid it behind some boxes in the room.

At 11.50 a.m. Oswald entered his chosen room without being seen. Most of the other workers in the Depository grouped together in larger rooms, or went outside to get a closer view of their President. He opened the window about 18 inches (45cm) and knelt on the floor to get his height and position right.

The motorcade was due to pass by at a few minutes after 12 noon but Air Force One arrived late at Love Field, and the President asked to have his car stopped so that he could exchange greetings, first with a group of nuns, and then with a group of schoolchildren. It was an interminable wait. What was Oswald thinking? Why do these things never happen right on schedule? Had the authorities been forewarned and changed their plans? Did he have a clean handkerchief at hand to wipe away his perspiration?

He was breathing quickly now; frightened, terrified, but not petrified: he must not freeze. He *had* to do it.

Oswald would not have been told that there was another gunman to ensure the President's death. The other shooter probably fired from behind the fence on Grassy Knoll.

The motorcade turned into Houston Street at 12.29 and made its way towards Oswald. He wiped his forehead and then his clammy hands. He strained to see which car held the President and which seat he was occupying, and then ... his mind-set moved smoothly into an ethereal state. There was silence. He could no longer hear the cheering and the shouting. Everything happened in *his* time. He felt he could stop the motorcade if he wished, but there was no need for that. His hands were on the rifle at floor level, he glanced to his right for final confirmation that he would have a clear shot. He was calm now.

The President's car swung hard left into Elm Street. He raised the rifle and took careful aim at a point ahead of his moving target. The President's demure wife, Jacqueline, was in his sights. He changed his aim smoothly, targeting the President's head and squeezed the trigger, as he had been taught in the Marines.

Everything was happening in slow motion. Everything was clear. The first shot was a bit low. He renewed his aim with great care. In real time it took less than two seconds. He fired twice more in quick succession.

Bits of the President's skull and brain flew off in different directions, one of the larger pieces, perversely, landing backwards on the flat back of the car. Jacqueline Kennedy turned around and picked it up. She was screaming, but Oswald heard nothing.

He put the rifle carefully back behind the boxes and walked quickly down the stairs to the canteen on the second floor. He must not panic. This was a moment of danger, when a sense of reality was beginning to return. Normal sounds filled his ears.

There was already a policeman in the canteen. Act normally. Tell him you work here. Ask him what's happening. Ask him why the police are here. Ask if you can go outside to see what's happening: that's what a normal person would do.

The policeman had no orders to prevent anyone from leaving the building. FBI officers on the scene outside were in turmoil, worrying about the President – whose car had now gone off at speed to the nearest hospital – and the other VIPs. Some had, however, started to give orders to control traffic and pedestrians and to investigate what exactly had happened.

Just over three long minutes after the shooting Oswald left the building by the front door. The building was sealed moments later.

He caught a bus to his lodgings where he spent a few minutes collecting some of his papers, including his passport, and a few other personal items, but nothing bulky or heavy. The enormity of what he had done must have been hitting him hard by now, though he would have been relieved it was all over.

He caught another bus that took him nearly a mile further away from the scene of his crime, and got off to walk to a local cinema: the Texas Theatre. Had this all been carefully planned and rehearsed? Was he going to meet someone in the cinema, or immediately afterwards? Someone who would assist his escape to a safe place? That is what they would have told him, but he was too naive to realise he could not be allowed to live to tell the tale.

‡

Officer J. D. Tippit of the Dallas Police, on a routine patrol along 10th Street, saw Oswald walking purposefully along the road. On seeing the police car Oswald hesitated, half turned as if to run away, but then – remembering to keep calm – he continued to walk in the same direction as before. The hesitation had been enough to make Tippit suspicious, so he stopped the car with a view to questioning Oswald, not about the assassination of the President but simply to satisfy himself that he was not up to something sinister. It was 1.15 p.m.

Oswald panicked. He drew his revolver and shot officer Tippit dead.

Several people had witnessed this from a distance and one of them watched Oswald walk quickly towards the Texas Theatre. Still in a panic, he rushed in without paying. The cinema receptionist called the police. The police, suspecting it might be the man who had shot their colleague, arrived in force in several patrol cars.

In the ensuing scuffle in the cinema Oswald drew his gun, but did not fire. He punched one of the policemen and kicked out violently, but was eventually overpowered. It was 1.50 p.m.

Oswald was taken to Dallas jail where he was charged with the murder of Officer Tippit. Within half-an-hour of his arrest he was also suspected of murdering President Kennedy.

This news was transmitted quickly through police channels. The messages to the FBI, and later the CIA, mentioned that Oswald claimed to have been forced into his actions by the Mafia. Senior FBI and CIA officers called for the files on Oswald and were distressed to find he had not been considered a threat.

Oswald was questioned for several hours in Dallas jail. He had no lawyer present and no notes were taken.

✝

On Sunday morning, 24 November, Oswald was to be moved from the city jail to the county jail. The press were informed and the time was changed from early morning to 'after ten o'clock' to accommodate their deadlines and broadcast schedules. Jack Ruby was informed of this by one of his many sources; probably a policeman.

About twenty press, radio and television representatives were given passes to enter the basement area of the city jail. They were all well known to the police and most of them were nodded into the building without even showing their passes. Ruby was equally well known and was also nodded through.

Prisoners were normally transferred by police car from within the secure basement area. A sturdy roller gate was lifted to allow the car to drive up a ramp onto the street. However, this was the man accused of assassinating the President. A thousand or more people were gathering in the street and things could turn nasty; so they hired an armoured van which, unfortunately, was too high to reverse into the basement. Oswald would have to be led from the elevator, along the level basement area where the car would normally be parked, and up part of the ramp to the van, which had been reversed as far as the gate.

The twenty authorised reporters – and Ruby – and at least the same number of police officers waited for the handcuffed and strongly escorted Oswald to emerge from the lift.

Questions were shouted, camera bulbs flashed, reporters

jostled for position, police tried to keep a clear path to the waiting van.

It was a simple matter for Jack Ruby to step forward and fire off a single pistol shot into Oswald's stomach. Oswald died within two hours in the hospital to which President Kennedy had been taken two days earlier.

✚

Jack Ruby was a complex man.

Jacob – known as Jack – was the fifth of eight children born to Joseph and Fanny Rubenstein in a Chicago Jewish neighbourhood. Both parents were penniless Polish immigrants. Juvenile courts decided the parents were unfit to bring up the children and some of them, including Jack, spent up to five years in foster homes.

In 1947 Jack and two of his brothers legally changed their family name to Ruby.

Jack developed into a tough character, determined always to be able to defend himself. For most of his early life – starting even when he was still at school – he dabbled in small personal businesses run from street corners or door-to-door. At one stage he was proud to be selling busts of President Roosevelt, whom he greatly admired.

He always dealt in cash, which he kept in his pockets or – after he prospered a little – in his car. Not surprisingly, therefore, he was often in trouble with the tax authorities. He owed $40,000 in taxes at the time he murdered Oswald.

There is no evidence that he attempted to bribe or seek favours from policemen, but he did give them discounted rates at his clubs. All bar and club owners did that sort of thing. Many policemen patronised his clubs and, naturally, he got to know them and they him.

The Warren Commission on the Assassination of President Kennedy believed 'that the evidence does not establish a significant link between Ruby and organized crime. Both State and Federal officials have indicated that Ruby was not affiliated with organised criminal activity and numerous persons have reported that Ruby was not connected with such activity.'[†]

Ruby was, however, an inveterate gambler and was well known and accepted in gambling circles, which would have included many people in organised crime.

He was 5ft 9in. (152cm) tall and weighed 12st. 7lb (175lb; 80kg). He was generally a mild, soft-spoken, fashionably dressed man known for his generosity to friends and those in need. However, he had a vicious temper when riled and often resorted to physical violence. He kept himself fit and strong, regularly working out in the gym.

His temper led him, at times, to attack people who offended his Jewish origins – though he was not, himself, religious – the military, or even the President. At other times he would be violent with his staff and cabaret performers if they displeased him. Those he attacked nearly always sustained noticeable physical injury. He served as his own bouncer at his clubs. He once put a heavyweight boxer in hospital. On another occasion he disarmed a man who had drawn a gun on him, beat him almost to death, and threw him down the stairs.

He carried a gun for protection, as he always carried cash, but never used it in fights other than, perhaps, to pistol-whip the occasional unfortunate.

This, then, was nobody's servant. He may have performed a favour for a genuine friend, but he would not have been bullied or bribed into the act of killing Oswald. It was most likely his own personal decision to kill the man who assassinated 'his' President.

On the other hand, would whoever was behind the assassination have allowed Oswald to testify in open court?

The Mafia, the CIA, the Soviet Union, Cuba, or loose cannons

[†]   Warren Commission Report, p. 181.

(or rogues) within these bodies were all front-line suspects. None of them could risk the possibility of disclosure. To a greater or lesser degree, they all suspected each other of commissioning Oswald to do the shooting, and that the responsible party (or parties) would try to implicate others.

Even if Oswald had held his nerve – not shot Officer Tippit – and escaped the hands of the law, it seems unlikely that he would have been allowed to live.

†
†

From a moment after the death of the President, and in the days and weeks that followed, senior officials in the CIA, the FBI, the White House and the new President himself (President Lyndon B. Johnson) delved through files, listened to tapes of telephone conversations, held meetings, made decisions, gave orders and took action.

It is now clear that those decisions, orders and actions did more to change, destroy and 'create' evidence that generated confusion and hid the truth, than to answer the question of who was responsible for the assassination.

The White House press office asked the news media to refrain from speculation about either the Soviet or Cuban governments being responsible for the assassination of President Kennedy. The media, in an atmosphere of national tragedy, honoured the request, much as they would show great restraint towards the grieving Kennedy family in the days and weeks ahead.

It would have been President Johnson's worst nightmare. He had suddenly been thrust into the world's hottest seat with the immediate double task of leading a nation in mourning and establishing himself as a credible President. As a 'Dixiecrat' leader he had to walk a tightrope between a welfareist agenda and the conservative leanings of his supporters in the south, many of whom would have wanted to invade Castro's Cuba. If the nation came to believe that Cuba or the Soviet Union had been responsible for Kennedy's death, Johnson would have been under immense pressure to take physical rather than verbal retaliation. This could have developed into another nuclear stand-off, or worse.

Analysis of the international situation at the time confirms that it would *not* have been in the interests of either the Soviet Union or Cuba to enrage the United States government and people by killing their President.

In 1992 the United States Congress passed the President John F. Kennedy Assassination Records Collection Act. Since then, a multitude of declassified documents, audiotapes of witness interviews and phone calls, and other information on the assassination have been released from government archives. Some of the documents were liberally redacted (sensitive information blacked out). Many more documents and other pieces of evidence have not yet been released, and some files may remain closed in perpetuity.

There are millions of pages of detailed evidence and learned research on events leading up to the assassination; the result is thousands of contradictions, inconsistencies, false trails, gaps and more questions. None of it entirely rules out the possibility that rogue elements in the Mafia, the CIA, or the right-wing political or military communities could have been responsible. Some allege that President Johnson himself was implicated in the assassination.

There is little evidence, however, of research into the possibility that rogue elements in either the Soviet or Cuban governments might have played a central part. From the American perspective it would have been impossible to distinguish between a government-backed conspiracy and a conspiracy led by rogue elements within those governments. The White House had said the subject was off-limits: even if the rogue-elements theory were true the American government did not wish to know.

If either the Soviet or Cuban governments had discovered the assassination was the work of their own rogue agents they would have taken steps to cover it up rather than risk accusations of appointing scapegoats to take the blame for what others would believe was government-sponsored 'executive action'.

‡

The evidence suggests that Oswald's time in New Orleans and, more particularly, his visits to the Soviet Consulate in Mexico City, were orchestrated by the KGB. Oswald had been invited, or instructed, to go to the consulate where he was briefed by Kostikov (the KGB assassin expert) and Nechiporenko.[†] From Mexico, he went straight to Dallas, where he had no home and to where the President would be paying a visit. His job at the Depository was fortuitous, but alternative arrangements would otherwise have been made to shoot from somewhere else along the President's route.

Khrushchev would not, under *any* conceivable circumstances, have authorised or condoned the assassination of President Kennedy with whom he had been fostering a better relationship since the Cuban Crisis.

However, Ivan Serov, since his demotion in March 1963, was no longer part of the inner circles of Soviet leadership. He had lost his position as head of the GRU and no longer took orders directly from Khrushchev, the Politburo or the Central Committee.

In the course of the social meetings he may have had with Andropov and Kryuchkov after his removal from office, Serov may well have raised the possibility of taking revenge on Kennedy. At first it would have been speculative, a 'what if we ...' game. Then one of them could well have mentioned that Valery Kostikov from the KGB's Department Thirteen (sabotage and assassination) was at that time in Mexico City, as was Oleg

---

[†]   Consul Pavel Yatskov appears to have played little or no role in managing Oswald.

Nechiporenko. The game soon became a plan and Andropov and Kryuchkov would be able to put it into action on behalf of Serov.

Thus, they would have identified the Soviet Consulate in Mexico City as the best place from which to operate: there were only three members of staff and they were all KGB officers. Using Mexico City had the added attraction of not involving any of the KGB stations in the United States.

In police investigation terminology, Ivan Serov had the motive and opportunity to arrange to have President Kennedy assassinated. One might go even further and suggest that he had stronger motivation, better opportunity and greater resources to do so than anyone else in the conspiracy line-up.

KGB Chairman Vladimir Semichastny said that at the time of President Kennedy's assassination *the KGB's exclusive concern was to be absolutely certain of its non-involvement in the assassination.*[†] This statement suggests official concern with the possibility of unauthorised KGB involvement.

Semichastny may have discovered, or suspected, involvement by any or all of Serov, Andropov, Kryuchkov, Kostikov and Nechiporenko. He could not, however, act against any of them for fear of global accusation and condemnation of Soviet involvement in the assassination. Indeed, it would be reasonable for even *him* to have been directly involved with this gang of five, because Andropov and Kryuchkov were his close allies. Semichastny did not approve of Khrushchev's actions during the Missile Crisis and, less than a year after Kennedy's assassination, he joined forces with Leonid Brezhnev and Alexander Shelepin to bring Khrushchev down. Andropov and Kryuchkov were later appointed chairmen of the KGB.[‡]

[†] See Oleg Nechiporenko, 'Chapter 7', *Passport to Assassination* (Carol Publishing Group, 1993). Translated from Russian by Todd P. Bludeau.

[‡] Andropov succeeded Semichastny as chairman of the KGB in 1967 and Kryuchkov was appointed chairman in 1988.

Serov was already in disgrace and had been removed from the public eye over the Penkovsky business and the alleged bad performance of the GRU in Cuba, so there was no need to take any further action to keep him out of the news. However, the Soviet propaganda machine, though ruthlessly efficient, was noted for its tendency for overkill, and so it was that they inspired – or at least failed to deny – rumours of Serov's death in 1963 by alcohol abuse or suicide. This adds to the suspicion that Ivan Aleksandrovich Serov's sins were more disturbing than just having served as the superior officer and friend of a traitor.

EPILOGUE

Ivan Serov

In 1965, Serov was expelled from the Communist Party for 'violations of socialist legality' during his time as Deputy Commissar of the NKVD under Beria. Given the long list of Serov's Stalinist atrocities, the vagueness of this charge and the lapse of time since these 'violations' had taken place, the charge appears weak and arbitrary, probably intentionally so. In any case, on Khrushchev's orders following Beria's death, Serov had destroyed all of the records of the outrages perpetrated by Khrushchev and Serov during Stalin's reign of terror, so there would have been little or no original evidence to support the charge.

As there is no record of Serov's whereabouts or activities in 1965, it is not clear whether he was personally informed of his expulsion from the party or whether it was served *in absentia* (or even posthumously).

I have no particular information that suggests Serov took a personal initiative to plot the assassination of President Kennedy, nor have I read or heard of this possibility elsewhere. Such an act would, however, have been in keeping with Serov's life history and personality. He was dedicated – in Stalinist style – to the elimination of all 'enemies of the people'. President John F. Kennedy, the bragging, brash and (to Serov) militant representative of the United States and capitalism, was public enemy number one.

He would undoubtedly have had support from his hard-liner friends Vladimir Kryuchkov and Yuri Andropov (see separate notes on each of them, below), both of whom were in a position to call upon the services of assassination expert Valery Kostikov in Mexico City and other members of the KGB.

What strikes me as odd, however, is the manner in which the Soviet leadership manipulated news of Serov's disgrace and disappearance after Penkovsky's trial, and inspired the most unlikely propaganda about what they portrayed as his appalling leadership of the GRU. Virtually all references state that the GRU became an incredibly corrupt and inefficient organisation during Serov's tenure as its leader.

It was normal in those days for the propaganda machine to distort the truth or tell outright lies, and it was common practice to destroy documents that did not fit in with the wishes of the leadership.

What, exactly, was the Soviet propaganda machine trying to hide?

Victor Suvorov wrote:[†]

Under Serov's leadership, corruption in the GRU attained unbelievable proportions. In 1962 he was dismissed and quietly liquidated.

Serov's was the dirtiest career in the history of the GRU. He displayed a high degree of personal sadism. The years when Serov was chief of the GRU were also the most unproductive in its history. It was the only period when GRU officers voluntarily made contact with Western services and gave them much more valuable information than they took from them.

[†] See Viktor Suvorov, 'Appendix A', *Inside Soviet Military Intelligence* (New York: Macmillan, 1984). Suvorov (real Russian name was Vladimir Rezun) served for many years in the GRU and defected to the West (the United Kingdom) in 1978.

Ilya Dzhirkvelov wrote:[†]

> They say that every malicious act is ultimately avenged. So it was
> with Serov, the head of the KGB, whose hands were red with
> the blood of Soviet people. A specialist in the business of mass
> deportations, a man without honour or conscience, sadistic and
> unprincipled, he was himself thrown out of the GRU following
> the exposure of Colonel Oleg Penkovsky, a British agent with
> whom Serov had been on friendly terms. Shortly afterwards,
> after a heavy drinking bout, he shot himself and was found dead
> in the doorway of a greengrocer's shop on the Arbat.

Jerrold L. Schecter and Peter S. Deriabin wrote:[‡]

> [After Penkovsky's exposure] General Ivan Serov was demoted
> to major general and fired as head of the GRU in March 1963.
> He was supposed to become assistant chief of staff of the Volga
> Military District, but never assumed his new post. Serov began
> drinking heavily and is reported to have committed suicide by
> shooting himself in an alley in the Arbat after he was expelled
> from the Communist Party in 1965, following Khrushchev's ouster.

The website 'GuideToRussia.com' (based in the United States)
records that Serov committed suicide in 1963.

Most important of all, perhaps, is the bald statement in *The
Mitrokhin Archive* that 'Ivan Serov blew his brains out in 1963'.[§]
The Mitrokhin Archive is based on copious notes taken over a
number of years from the KGB's secret intelligence archives
by Vasili Mitrokhin, the KGB defector who was brought out of

[†] See Ilya Dzhirkvelov, 'Chapter 6', *Secret Servant* (New York: Harper &
Row, 1987).

[‡] See Jerrold Schecter and Peter S. Deriabin, 'Chapter 17', *The Spy Who
Saved The* World (New York: Charles Scribner's Sons, 1992).

[§] See Christopher Andrew and Vasili Mitkrokhin, 'Chapter 2', *The Mitrokhin
Archive: The KGB in Europe and the West* (London: Allen Lane, 2000) p. 30.

Russia by MI6 in 1992. Did the KGB try to take Serov off the radar in 1963, the year of Kennedy's assassination?

I have found no evidence to support the contention that the GRU became an incredibly corrupt and inefficient organisation during Serov's leadership. A study of Soviet intelligence operations during the Cuban Missile Crisis found that neither the KGB nor GRU had sources close enough to the Kennedy administration to accumulate effective intelligence reports on its thinking. However, it was the KGB rather than the GRU that came in for serious criticism of its working methods and discipline:[†]

> ... the KGB appears to have performed extremely poorly in this episode. Fursenko and Naftali describe an organisation obsessed with espionage, unable to integrate secret and open sources, either unable or unwilling to synthesize and interpret, ill-informed about Soviet policy, lacking well-placed informants, reduced to the ignominy of hanging around a parking lot at the crack of dawn to keep a journalist under observation, and – if one of the more plausible versions of the Scali-Fomin story is correct – undisciplined to boot.

Serov was in his mid-fifties during the time he was in charge of the GRU. Although one may not agree with his methods or objectives, he had an excellent record of working hard and well, and of getting results. He had taken the initiative – possibly even taking it away from Khrushchev – in Budapest (when he was fifty) and swiftly turned around a difficult situation for the Soviet Union.

Serov was resurrected – if the rumours of his death had been true – in 1971, by none other than Yuri Andropov who was by

---

† See Alexsandr Fursenko and Timothy Naftali, 'Chapter 7' in James G. Blight and David A. Welch (eds), *Intelligence and the Cuban Missile Crisis* (London: Frank Cass, 1998).

then the chairman of the KGB. On 12 February 1971, Andropov reported to the party's Central Committee that Serov was working on his memoirs.[†] He was under KGB surveillance and his dacha was bugged.

What had he been doing during the eight years from 1963 to 1971? Was there a very sound reason why he should be kept – or why he would keep himself – out of the limelight?

Serov eventually died of natural causes on 1 July 1990 at the age of eighty-four. Had he been clinically depressed, or had he taken to excessive drinking, in 1963, it is unlikely he would have lived for another twenty-seven years.

Serov was an excellent drafter of official documents, whether they were reports, proposals or detailed instructions. He could describe incidents, report – or intentionally omit – facts, incorporate innuendos and make coherent proposals; all finely tuned to the requirements of the party or of the specific recipient. This was in large part the reason for his survival throughout Stalin's purges and the vicissitudes of Khrushchev's leadership.

His memoirs – if indeed he had been writing them – would have been a masterpiece. Were they suppressed or destroyed because of their content? There is speculation that they were passed to a member of his family.

The demise of the Soviet Union enabled the publication of some KGB records and led to happy meetings and reunions between former American and Soviet Union intelligence officers.[‡] Strangely, none of this refreshing freedom of information

---

[†]   Nikita Petro, *First Chairman of the KGB: Ivan Serov* (Moscow: Materik, 2005).

[‡]   British MI6 officers, on the whole, maintained their strict code of practice and did not participate in these meetings, which could leave an unbalanced picture. This was particularly so in relation to the 1999 Teufelsberg (Berlin) Conference which brought together many ex-CIA and ex-KGB operational managers and agents to reminisce about Cold War intelligence operations. The conclusions failed to incorporate the full weight of the role played by MI6 in, for example, the Berlin tunnel operation.

appears to have shed any light on the secret life of Serov from 1963 onwards.

The United States Select Committee on Assassinations concluded that there was a 'high probability' that *two* gunmen fired at President John F. Kennedy, but that he was killed by Lee Harvey Oswald's fatal third shot. The committee believed that Kennedy was 'probably assassinated as a result of a conspiracy', but that they were 'unable to identify the other gunman or the extent of the conspiracy'. They did not believe that either the Soviet government or the Cuban government were involved in the assassination; neither did they believe that 'anti-Castro Cuban groups, as groups, were involved', but that the evidence 'does not preclude the possibility that individual members may have been involved'. They believed that 'the national syndicate of organized crime, as a group, was not involved in the assassination' but did 'not preclude the possibility that individual members may have been involved'. The Secret Service, FBI and CIA 'were not involved in the assassination'.

The committee criticised agencies and departments of the US government for inadequate investigation. The FBI 'performed with varying degrees of competency' but 'failed to investigate adequately the possibility of a conspiracy to assassinate the President'. The FBI 'was deficient in its sharing of information with other agencies and departments', and the CIA 'was deficient in its collection and sharing of information both prior to and subsequent to the assassination'. The Warren Commission – which had carried out an earlier investigation into the assassination – failed to investigate adequately the possibility of a conspiracy to assassinate the President. This deficiency was attributable in part to the limited cooperation of numerous government agencies, and their failure to forward relevant documentation to the commission.

Neither the Warren Commission nor the Select Committee on Assassinations appear to have considered the possibility of a conspiracy by a rogue element in the Soviet Union.

Vladimir Kryuchkov

(KGB officer who assisted with Serov's suppression of the Hungarian uprising.)

Kryuchkov was a hard-liner who supported Yuri Andropov, his Ambassador during the Hungarian uprising. When Andropov rose to power (he was appointed chairman of the KGB before becoming the leader of the Soviet Union from 1982 until his death in 1984) he brought Kryuchkov along with him. Kryuchkov led the KGB from 1988 to 1991. At this time he was strongly against Soviet leader Gorbachev's proposed reforms and tried to discredit him. On 19 August 1991, when it became clear that Gorbachev was about to take radical reformist action, Kryuchkov led a coup with, he thought, the full power and might of the KGB. The coup was initially successful but the KGB's support was far from comprehensive and it all fizzled out in three days. Kryuchkov was arrested, found guilty of treason and sentenced to imprisonment. He was released three years later under an amnesty. He died in 2007, aged eighty-three.

Yuri Andropov

(As Soviet Ambassador in Hungary in 1956, he gave strong support to Serov in suppressing the Hungarian uprising.)

After events in Hungary, Andropov was convinced that armed force should always be used when there were signs of collapse of central Soviet Communist Party control over individual Soviet republics, and over the governments of the satellite countries. Just as Serov had been largely responsible for stamping out the Hungarian uprising, so Andropov played a leading role in persuading Soviet leader Brezhnev to send in tanks to stamp out the liberalising influences of the Dubček government in Czechoslovakia to end the 'Prague Spring' in 1968. Andropov created false intelligence to bolster the case against the Dubček government.

He returned to Moscow from Budapest in 1957 to head the Department for Liaison with Communist and Workers' Parties in Socialist Countries. In that capacity he would have had close connections with the Communist Party in Cuba. In 1961 he was (in addition) elected a member of the Soviet Communist Party's Central Committee, which controlled the activities of the KGB through the Politburo.

He was appointed head of the KGB in 1967, a post he held until 1982 when he became the Soviet leader on the death of Leonid Brezhnev.

It was largely upon Andropov's insistence that the Soviet Union invaded Afghanistan in 1979.

Andropov's health started to fail in 1983. On 31 December 1983 he celebrated the New Year for the last time. Vladimir Kryuchkov (see notes, above) together with other friends visited him and they had a drink of champagne. After the others left, Kryuchkov remained alone with him. Andropov raised his glass and told Kryuchkov he wished health and success to all the friends. (One of his closest friends, Ivan Serov, was of course still alive at that time.)

Andropov died on 9 February 1984.

Sergei Kondrashev
(KGB officer who was Blake's spymaster.)

After the Cuban Missile Crisis, Kondrashev's career continued its ascendency. He became Deputy Head of Foreign Intelligence in 1968. Highly decorated, he reached the rank of Lieutenant-General of the KGB before retiring in 1992. He died in 2007.

Colonel Oleg Penkovsky
(GRU officer who spied for the West.)

Neither of the two versions of Penkovsky's execution has been indisputably substantiated. Is it possible he is still alive (born 23 April 1919), hoping to outlive both Fidel Castro and George Blake?

Greville Wynne
(International sales representative for several British companies and part-time MI6 agent. He was Penkovsky's first proper

contact with the West and regularly thereafter acted as a courier for Penkovsky's material.)

In 1963, after serving less than two years of his eight-year sentence, he was exchanged for Konon Molody (alias Gordon Lonsdale) who, in London in 1961, had been sentenced to twenty-five years for spying, including running the Portland spy ring. Wynne died of throat cancer in London in 1990.

Roderick (Ruari) Chisholm

(MI6 officer in Berlin at the time of the spy tunnel and later in Moscow where he was Penkovsky's spymaster.)

Ruari Chisholm left South Africa (his final posting before taking early retirement) in 1979. He told a number of people he intended to write a book about his espionage exploits. He apparently caught malaria in Tanzania while on his way home and died in Scotland shortly thereafter.

His death certificate records the cause of death as 'Malaria (type not identified)'. It seems strange that a fit 54-year-old man who had all the benefits, advice and care of a government medical team should die of malaria. His death was exactly one year after Bulgarian-born BBC World Service broadcaster Georgi Markov died as a result of a poison pellet delivered through the point of an umbrella.

Janet Chisholm (née Deane)

(Wife of Ruari Chisholm; she was the main contact with Penkovsky in Moscow.)

Janet Chisholm died in 2004 at the age of seventy-five. In spite of many offers for her to talk or write about the role she played in the Penkovsky case, she took her own personal knowledge of these events to the grave.

Sir Howard Smith

(Head of Chancery at the British Embassy, Moscow when Penkovsky was passing secrets to the West.)

I was working at the British Embassy in Moscow in 1961–2, at the same time as the Chisholms and Howard Smith. I have no information to suggest that Smith was working under deep cover for MI6 at that time. It seems to me, however, that there ought to have been someone senior to Ruari Chisholm, particularly as Blake had already informed the KGB of Chisholm's identity as an MI6 officer. In 1978, after thirty-two years as a diplomat, Smith was appointed the 9th Director-General of the British Security Service (MI5), a post he held until 1981. He died on 7 May 1996.

George Blake
(MI6 officer who spied for the Soviet Union.)

Five years after the start of his record 42-year sentence Blake escaped from Britain's famous Wormwood Scrubs prison and managed to reach Moscow where he still lives (August 2012). He continued to help the Soviet/Russian security services on a consultancy and training basis and, during a gala celebration of Blake's eighty-fifth birthday on 11 November 2007, Vladimir Putin honoured him with the Russian Order of Friendship.

William King (Bill) Harvey
(CIA officer involved with the Berlin spy tunnel and later with various CIA activities to oust Fidel Castro and his regime.)

Harvey died as a result of complications from heart surgery in June 1976.

Santo Trafficante
(Mafia godfather who had large-scale gambling interests in Cuba before Castro came to power. He was later involved with fellow godfathers Sam Giancana and Johnny Roselli in attempting to kill Castro on behalf of the CIA. I have used the widely held theory that Trafficante spied for Castro.)

Giancana was killed (shot) in July 1975 just before he was scheduled to testify to the Senate Intelligence Committee on the CIA's alliance with the Mafia to try to kill Castro. A year later Roselli's dismembered body was found in a steel drum in Dumfounding Bay, Florida. He was scheduled for a second appearance before the Senate Intelligence Committee. Many claim that their deaths had been arranged by Trafficante because they had been talking about the Castro and Kennedy plots. Trafficante died of complications following heart surgery on 17 March 1987.

BIBLIOGRAPHY

Andrew, Christopher and Mitkrokhin, Vasili, *The Mitrokhin Archive: The KGB in Europe and the West* (London: Allen Lane, 2000)

Blight, James G. and Welch, David A. (eds), *Intelligence and the Cuban Missile Crisis* (London: Frank Cass, 1998)

Dzhirkvelov, Ilya, *Secret Servant* (New York: Harper & Row, 1987)

Granville, Johanna, *The First Domino* (Texas: Texas A&M University Press, 2004)

Hyde, H. Montgomery, *George Blake Superspy* (London: Constable, 1987)

Kaiser, David, *The Road to Dallas* (London: Belknap Press of Harvard University Press, 2008)

Khrushchev, Sergei, *Khrushchev on Khrushchev*, edited and translated by William Taubman (London: Little, Brown and Company, 1990)

Nechiporenko, Oleg, *Passport to Assassination* (Carol Publishing Group, 1993). Translated from Russian by Todd P. Bludeau.

Newman, John, *Oswald and the CIA* (New York: Carroll & Graf, 1995)

Penkovsky, Oleg, *The Penkovsky Papers* (London: Collins, 1965)

Petro, Nikita, *First Chairman of the KGB: Ivan Serov* (Moscow: Materik, 2005)

Schecter, Jerrold and Deriabin, Peter S., *The Spy Who Saved The World* (New York: Charles Scribner's Sons, 1992)

Stafford, David, *Spies Beneath Berlin* (London: John Murray, 2003)

Stockton, Bayard, *Flawed Patriot* (Washington D. C.: Potomac Books, 2007)

Suvorov, Viktor, *Inside Soviet Military Intelligence* (New York: Macmillan, 1984)

Taubman, William, *Khrushchev: The Man – His Era* (London: Free Press, 2003)

Verrier, Anthony, *Through the Looking Glass: British Foreign Policy in an Age of Illusions* (London: Cape, 1983)

APPENDIX 1

President John F. Kennedy's radio and television address to the American people on the Soviet arms build-up in Cuba, 22 October 1962.[†]

Accession Number: WH-142-001
Title: Radio and television address to the American people on the Soviet arms build-up in Cuba, 22 October 1962
Date(s) of Materials: 22 October 1962

Description: Audio recording of President John F. Kennedy's radio and television address to the nation regarding the former Soviet Union's military presence in Cuba. In his speech President Kennedy reports the establishment of offensive missile sites presumably intended to launch a nuclear offensive against Western nations. The President characterises the transformation of Cuba into an important strategic base as an explicit threat to American security, and explains seven components to his proposed course of action: quarantine all offensive military equipment under shipment to Cuba, increase the degree of surveillance, regard a possible attack launched from Cuba as a Soviet attack, reinforce the Guantanamo Bay Naval Base, call for

---

[†] This transcript is taken from the John F. Kennedy Presidential Library and Museum Website.

a meeting of the Organ of Consultation, call for an emergency meeting of the United Nations Security Council, and demand that Premier Nikita Khrushchev cease his current course of action. In his speech the President famously states, 'Our goal is not the victory of might, but the vindication of right, not peace at the expense of freedom, but both peace and freedom, here in this hemisphere, and, we hope, around the world.'

> Physical Description: 1 audio tape/reel (18 minutes)
> Running Time (Minutes): 18
> Media Type: Audio Tape/Reel
> Digital Identifier: JFKWHA-142-001
> Archival Creator: Department of Defense. Defense Communications Agency. White House Communications Agency. (1962 – 06/25/1991)
> Copyright Status: Public Domain
> Date: 10/22/1962

Good evening my fellow citizens:

This Government, as promised, has maintained the closest surveillance of the Soviet Military build-up on the island of Cuba. Within the past week, unmistakable evidence has established the fact that a series of offensive missile sites is now in preparation on that imprisoned island. The purpose of these bases can be none other than to provide a nuclear strike capability against the Western Hemisphere.

Upon receiving the first preliminary hard information of this nature last Tuesday morning at 9 a.m., I directed that our surveillance be stepped up. And having now confirmed and completed our evaluation of the evidence and our decision on a course of action, this Government feels obliged to report this new crisis to you in fullest detail.

The characteristics of these new missile sites indicate two distinct types of installations. Several of them include medium range ballistic missiles capable of carrying a nuclear warhead for a distance of more than 1,000 nautical miles. Each of these missiles, in short, is capable of striking Washington, D.C., the Panama Canal, Cape Canaveral, Mexico City, or any other city in the south-eastern part of the United States, in Central America, or in the Caribbean area.

Additional sites not yet completed appear to be designed for intermediate range ballistic missiles – capable of traveling more than twice as far – and thus capable of striking most of the major cities in the Western Hemisphere, ranging as far north as Hudson Bay, Canada, and as far south as Lima, Peru. In addition, jet bombers, capable of carrying nuclear weapons, are now being uncrated and assembled in Cuba, while the necessary air bases are being prepared.

This urgent transformation of Cuba into an important strategic base – by the presence of these large, long range, and clearly offensive weapons of sudden mass destruction – constitutes an explicit threat to the peace and security of all the Americas, in flagrant and deliberate defiance of the Rio Pact of 1947, the traditions of this Nation and hemisphere, the joint resolution of the 87th Congress, the Charter of the United Nations, and my own public warnings to the Soviets on September 4 and 13. This action also contradicts the repeated assurances of Soviet spokesmen, both publicly and privately delivered, that the arms build-up in Cuba would retain its original defensive character, and that the Soviet Union had no need or desire to station strategic missiles on the territory of any other nation.

The size of this undertaking makes clear that it has been planned for some months. Yet only last month, after I had made clear the distinction between any introduction of ground-to-ground missiles and the existence of defensive antiaircraft missiles, the Soviet Government publicly stated on September 11, and I quote, 'the armaments and military equipment sent to Cuba are designed exclusively for defensive purposes,' that, and I quote the Soviet Government, 'there is no need for the Soviet Government to shift its weapons ... for a retaliatory blow to any other country, for instance Cuba,' and that, and I quote their government, 'the Soviet Union has so powerful rockets to carry these nuclear warheads that there is no need to search for sites for them beyond the boundaries of the Soviet Union.' That statement was false.

Only last Thursday, as evidence of this rapid offensive build-up was already in my hand, Soviet Foreign Minister Gromyko told me in my office that he was instructed to make it clear once again, as he said his government had already done, that Soviet assistance to Cuba, and I quote, 'pursued solely the purpose of contributing to the defense capabilities of Cuba,' that, and I quote him, 'training by Soviet specialists of Cuban nationals in handling defensive armaments was by no means offensive, and if it were otherwise,' Mr. Gromyko went on, 'the Soviet Government would never become involved in rendering such assistance.' That statement also was false.

Neither the United States of America nor the world community of nations can tolerate deliberate deception and offensive threats on the part of any nation, large or small. We no longer live in a world where only the actual firing of weapons represents a sufficient challenge to a nation's security to constitute maximum peril. Nuclear weapons are so destructive and ballistic missiles are so swift, that any substantially increased possibility of their use or any sudden change in their deployment may well be regarded as a definite threat to peace.

For many years both the Soviet Union and the United States, recognizing this fact, have deployed strategic nuclear weapons with great care, never upsetting the precarious status quo which insured that these weapons would not be used in the absence of some vital challenge. Our own strategic missiles have never been transferred to the territory of any other nation under a cloak of secrecy and deception; and our history – unlike that of the Soviets since the end of World War II – demonstrates that we have no desire to dominate or conquer any other nation or impose our system upon its people. Nevertheless, American citizens have become adjusted to living daily on the Bull's-eye of Soviet missiles located inside the USSR or in submarines.

In that sense, missiles in Cuba add to an already clear and present danger – although it should be noted the nations of Latin America have never previously been subjected to a potential nuclear threat.

But this secret, swift, and extraordinary build-up of Communist missiles – in an area well known to have a special and historical relationship to the United States and the nations of the Western Hemisphere, in violation of Soviet assurances, and in defiance of American and hemispheric policy – this sudden, clandestine decision to station strategic weapons for the first time outside of Soviet soil – is a deliberately provocative and unjustified change in the status quo which cannot be accepted by this country, if our courage and our commitments are ever to be trusted again by either friend or foe.

The 1930s taught us a clear lesson: aggressive conduct, if allowed to go unchecked and unchallenged ultimately leads to war. This nation is opposed to war. We are also true to our word. Our unswerving objective, therefore, must be to prevent the use of these missiles against this or any other country, and to secure their withdrawal or elimination from the Western Hemisphere.

Our policy has been one of patience and restraint, as befits a peaceful and powerful nation, which leads a worldwide alliance. We have been determined not to be diverted from our central concerns by mere irritants and fanatics. But now further action is required – and it is under way; and these actions may only be the beginning. We will not prematurely or unnecessarily risk the costs of worldwide nuclear war in which even the fruits of victory would be ashes in our mouth – but neither will we shrink from that risk at any time it must be faced.

Acting, therefore, in the defense of our own security and of the entire Western Hemisphere, and under the authority entrusted to me by the Constitution as endorsed by the resolution of the

Congress, I have directed that the following initial steps be taken immediately:

First: To halt this offensive build-up, a strict quarantine on all offensive military equipment under shipment to Cuba is being initiated. All ships of any kind bound for Cuba from whatever nation or port will, if found to contain cargoes of offensive weapons, be turned back. This quarantine will be extended, if needed, to other types of cargo and carriers. We are not at this time, however, denying the necessities of life as the Soviets attempted to do in their Berlin blockade of 1948.

Second: I have directed the continued and increased close surveillance of Cuba and its military build-up. The foreign ministers of the OAS, in their communique of October 6, rejected secrecy in such matters in this hemisphere. Should these offensive military preparations continue, thus increasing the threat to the hemisphere, further action will be justified. I have directed the Armed Forces to prepare for any eventualities; and I trust that in the interest of both the Cuban people and the Soviet technicians at the sites, the hazards to all concerned in continuing this threat will be recognized.

Third: It shall be the policy of this Nation to regard any nuclear missile launched from Cuba against any nation in the Western Hemisphere as an attack by the Soviet Union on the United States, requiring a full retaliatory response upon the Soviet Union.

Fourth: As a necessary military precaution, I have reinforced our base at Guantanamo, evacuated today the dependents of our personnel there, and ordered additional military units to be on a standby alert basis.

Fifth: We are calling tonight for an immediate meeting of the Organ of Consultation under the Organization of American States, to consider this threat to hemispheric security and to invoke articles 6 and 8 of the Rio Treaty in support of all necessary action. The United Nations Charter allows for regional security arrangements – and the nations of this hemisphere decided long ago against the military presence of outside powers. Our other allies around the world have also been alerted.

Sixth: Under the Charter of the United Nations, we are asking tonight that an emergency meeting of the Security Council be convoked without delay to take action against this latest Soviet threat to world peace. Our resolution will call for the prompt dismantling and withdrawal of all offensive weapons in Cuba, under the supervision of UN observers, before the quarantine can be lifted.

Seventh and finally: I call upon Chairman Khrushchev to halt and eliminate this clandestine, reckless and provocative threat to world peace and to stable relations between our two nations. I call upon him further to abandon this course of world domination, and to join in an historic effort to end the perilous arms race and to transform the history of man. He has an opportunity now to move the world back from the abyss of destruction – by returning to his government's own words that it had no need to station missiles outside its own territory, and withdrawing these weapons from Cuba – by refraining from any action which will widen or deepen the present crisis – and then by participating in a search for peaceful and permanent solutions.

This Nation is prepared to present its case against the Soviet threat to peace, and our own proposals for a peaceful world, at any time and in any forum – in the OAS, in the United Nations, or in any other meeting that could be useful – without limiting our freedom of action. We have in the past made strenuous efforts to limit the spread of nuclear weapons. We have proposed the elimination of all arms and military bases in a fair and effective disarmament treaty. We are prepared to discuss new proposals for the removal of tensions on both sides – including the possibility of a genuinely independent Cuba, free to determine its own destiny. We have no wish to war with the Soviet Union – for we are a peaceful people who desire to live in peace with all other peoples.

But it is difficult to settle or even discuss these problems in an atmosphere of intimidation. That is why this latest Soviet threat – or any other threat which is made either independently or in response to our actions this week – must and will be met with determination. Any hostile move anywhere in the world against the safety and freedom of peoples to whom we are committed – including in particular the brave people of West Berlin – will be met by whatever action is needed.

Finally, I want to say a few words to the captive people of Cuba, to whom this speech is being directly carried by special radio facilities. I speak to you as a friend, as one who knows of your deep attachment to your fatherland, as one who shares your aspirations for liberty and justice for all. And I have watched and the American people have watched with deep sorrow how your nationalist revolution was betrayed – and how your fatherland fell under foreign domination. Now your leaders are no longer Cuban leaders inspired by Cuban ideals. They are puppets and agents of an international conspiracy which has turned Cuba against your friends and neighbors in the Americas – and turned it into the first Latin American country to become a target for nuclear war – the first Latin American country to have these weapons on its soil.

These new weapons are not in your interest. They contribute nothing to your peace and well-being. They can only undermine it. But this country has no wish to cause you to suffer or to impose any system upon you. We know that your lives and land are being used as pawns by those who deny your freedom.

Many times in the past, the Cuban people have risen to throw out tyrants who destroyed their liberty. And I have no doubt that most Cubans today look forward to the time when they will be truly free – free from foreign domination, free to choose their own leaders, free to select their own system, free to own their own land, free to speak and write and worship without fear or degradation. And then shall Cuba be welcomed back to the society of free nations and to the associations of this hemisphere.

My fellow citizens: let no one doubt that this is a difficult and dangerous effort on which we have set out. No one can see precisely what course it will take or what costs or casualties will be incurred. Many months of sacrifice and self-discipline lie ahead – months in which our patience and our will will be tested – months in which many threats and denunciations will keep us aware of our dangers. But the greatest danger of all would be to do nothing.

The path we have chosen for the present is full of hazards, as all paths are – but it is the one most consistent with our character and courage as a nation and our commitments around the world. The cost of freedom is always high – and Americans have always paid it. And one path we shall never choose, and that is the path of surrender or submission.

Our goal is not the victory of might, but the vindication of right – not peace at the expense of freedom, but both peace and freedom, here in this hemisphere, and, we hope, around the world. God willing, that goal will be achieved.

Thank you and good night

APPENDIX 2

This Appendix contains the text of exchanges of letters between President Kennedy and Chairman Khrushchev between 22 and 27 October 1962. Although these exchanges ran in parallel with United Nations negotiations and secret discussions at official and even private level, it is these letters that represent the full head-of-state negotiations and details of the settlement. They also draw a stark picture of how close to the brink both men went.[†]

Letter from President Kennedy to Chairman Khrushchev

Dated 22 October 1962

DEAR MR. CHAIRMAN

A copy of the statement I am making tonight concerning developments in Cuba and the reaction of my Government thereto has been handed to your Ambassador in Washington. In view of the gravity of the developments to which I refer, I want you to know immediately and accurately the position of my Government in this matter.

---

† The text of this correspondence has been taken from the US Department of State website http://www.state.gov/www/about_state/history/volume_vi/exchanges.html.

In our discussions and exchanges on Berlin and other international questions, the one thing that has most concerned me has been the possibility that your Government would not correctly understand the will and determination of the United States in any given situation, since I have not assumed that you or any other sane man would, in this nuclear age, deliberately plunge the world into war which it is crystal clear no country could win and which could only result in catastrophic consequences to the whole world, including the aggressor.

At our meeting in Vienna and subsequently, I expressed our readiness and desire to find, through peaceful negotiation, a solution to any and all problems that divide us. At the same time, I made clear that in view of the objectives of the ideology to which you adhere, the United States could not tolerate any action on your part which in a major way disturbed the existing over-all balance of power in the world. I stated that an attempt to force abandonment of our responsibilities and commitments in Berlin would constitute such an action and that the United States would resist with all the power at its command.

It was in order to avoid any incorrect assessment on the part of your Government with respect to Cuba that I publicly stated that if certain developments in Cuba took place, the United States would do whatever must be done to protect its own security and that of its allies.

Moreover, the Congress adopted a resolution expressing its support of this declared policy. Despite this, the rapid development of long-range missile bases and other offensive weapons systems in Cuba has proceeded. I must tell you that the United States is determined that this threat to the security of this hemisphere be removed. At the same time, I wish to point out that the action we are taking is the minimum necessary to remove the threat to the security of the nations of this hemisphere. The fact of this minimum response should not be taken as a basis, however, for any misjudgement on your part.

I hope that your Government will refrain from any action

which would widen or deepen this already grave crisis and that we can agree to resume the path of peaceful negotiations.

Sincerely,

JFK

Telegram from Chairman Khrushchev to President Kennedy.

Dated 23 October 1962

Mr President.

I have just received your letter, and have also acquainted myself with text of your speech of October 22 regarding Cuba.

I should say frankly that measures outlined in your statement represent a serious threat to peace and security of peoples. United States has openly taken path of gross violation of Charter of United Nations, path of violation of international norms of freedom of navigation on high seas, path of aggressive actions both against Cuba and against Soviet Union.

Statement of Government of United States America cannot be evaluated in any other way than as naked interference in domestic affairs of Cuban Republic, Soviet Union, and other states. Charter of United Nations and international norms do not give right to any state whatsoever to establish in international waters control of vessels bound for shores of Cuban Republic.

It is self-understood that we also cannot recognize right of United States to establish control over armaments essential to Republic of Cuba for strengthening of its defensive capacity.

We confirm that armaments now on Cuba, regardless of classification to which they belong, are destined exclusively for defensive purposes, in order to secure Cuban Republic from attack of aggressor.

I hope that Government of United States will show prudence and renounce actions pursued by you, which could lead to cata-strophic consequences for peace throughout world.

Viewpoint of Soviet Government with regard to your statement of October 22 is set forth in statement of Soviet Government, which is being conveyed to you through your Ambassador in Moscow.

N. Khrushchev

Letter from President Kennedy to Chairman Khrushchev

Dated 23 October 1962

Dear Mr Chairman:

I have received your letter of October twenty-third. I think you will recognize that the steps which started the current chain of events was the action of your Government in secretly furnishing offensive weapons to Cuba. We will be discussing this matter in the Security Council. In the meantime, I am concerned that we both show prudence and do nothing to allow events to make the situation more difficult to control than it already is.

I hope that you will issue immediately the necessary instructions to your ships to observe the terms of the quarantine, the basis of which was established by the vote of the Organization of American States this afternoon, and which will go into effect at 1400 hours Greenwich time October twenty-four.

Sincerely, JFK.

Letter from Chairman Khrushchev to President Kennedy

Dated 24 October 1962

DEAR MR. PRESIDENT

I have received your letter of October 23, have studied it, and am answering you.

Just imagine, Mr President, that we had presented you with the conditions of an ultimatum which you have presented us by your action. How would you have reacted to this? I think that you would have been indignant at such a step on our part. And this would have been understandable to us.

In presenting us with these conditions, you, Mr President, have flung a challenge at us. Who asked you to do this? By what right did you do this? Our ties with the Republic of Cuba, like our relations with other states, regardless of what kind of states they may be, concern only the two countries between which these relations exist. And if we now speak of the quarantine to which your letter refers, a quarantine may be established, according to accepted international practice, only by agreement of states between themselves, and not by some third party. Quarantines exist, for example, on agricultural goods and products. But in this case the question is in no way one of quarantine, but rather of far more serious things, and you yourself understand this.

You, Mr President, are not declaring a quarantine, but rather are setting forth an ultimatum and threatening that if we do not give in to your demands you will use force. Consider what you are saying! And you want to persuade me to agree to this! What would it mean to agree to these demands? It would mean guiding oneself in one's relations with other countries not by reason, but by submitting to arbitrariness. You are no longer appealing to reason, but wish to intimidate us.

No, Mr President, I cannot agree to this, and I think that in your own heart you recognize that I am correct. I am convinced that in my place you would act the same way.

Reference to the decision of the Organization of American States cannot in any way substantiate the demands now advanced by the United States. This Organization has absolutely no authority or basis for adopting decisions such as the one you speak of in your letter. Therefore, we do not recognize these decisions. International law exists and universally recognized norms of conduct exist. We firmly adhere to the principles of international law and observe strictly the norms which regulate navigation on the high seas, in international waters. We observe these norms and enjoy the rights recognized by all states.

You wish to compel us to renounce the rights that every sovereign state enjoys, you are trying to legislate in questions of international law, and you are violating the universally accepted norms of that law. And you are doing all this not only out of hatred for the Cuban people and its government, but also because of considerations of the election campaign in the United States. What morality, what law can justify such an approach by the American Government to international affairs? No such morality or law can be found, because the actions of the United States with regard to Cuba constitute outright banditry or, if you like, the folly of degenerate imperialism. Unfortunately, such folly can bring grave suffering to the peoples of all countries, and to no lesser degree to the American people themselves, since the United States has completely lost its former isolation with the advent of modern types of armament.

Therefore, Mr President, if you coolly weigh the situation which has developed, not giving way to passions, you will understand that the Soviet Union cannot fail to reject the arbitrary demands of the United States. When you confront us with such conditions, try to put yourself in our place and consider how the United States would react to these conditions. I do not doubt that if someone attempted to dictate similar conditions to you – the United States – you would reject such an attempt. And we also say – no.

The Soviet Government considers that the violation of the freedom to use international waters and international air space is an act of aggression which pushes mankind toward the abyss of a world nuclear-missile war. Therefore, the Soviet Government cannot instruct the captains of Soviet vessels bound for Cuba to observe the orders of American naval forces blockading that Island. Our instructions to Soviet mariners are to observe strictly the universally accepted norms of navigation in international waters and not to retreat one step from them. And if the American side violates these rules, it must realize what responsibility will rest upon it in that case. Naturally we will not simply be bystanders with regard to piratical acts by American ships on the high seas. We will then be forced on our part to take the measures we consider necessary and adequate in order to protect our rights. We have everything necessary to do so.

Respectfully,

N. Khrushchev

Letter from President Kennedy to Chairman Khrushchev

Dated 25 October 1962

Dear Mr Chairman:

I have received your letter of October 24, and I regret very much that you still do not appear to understand what it is that has moved us in this matter.

The sequence of events is clear. In August there were reports of important shipments of military equipment and technicians from the Soviet Union to Cuba. In early September I indicated very plainly that the United States would regard any shipment of offensive weapons as presenting the gravest issues. After that time, this Government received the most explicit assurances from your Government and its representatives, both publicly and privately, that no offensive weapons were being sent to Cuba. If you will review the statement issued by Tass in September, you will see how clearly this assurance was given.

In reliance on these solemn assurances I urged restraint upon those in this country who were urging action in this matter at that time. And then I learned beyond doubt what you have not denied – namely, that all these public assurances were false and that your military people had set out recently to establish a set of missile bases in Cuba. I ask you to recognize clearly, Mr.

Chairman, that it was not I who issued the first challenge in this case, and that in the light of this record these activities in Cuba required the responses I have announced.

I repeat my regret that these events should cause a deterioration in our relations. I hope that your Government will take the necessary action to permit a restoration of the earlier situation.

Sincerely yours,

John F. Kennedy.

Letter from Chairman Khrushchev to President Kennedy

Dated 26 October 1962

Dear Mr President:

I have received your letter of October 25. From your letter, I got the feeling that you have some understanding of the situation which has developed and (some) sense of responsibility. I value this.

Now we have already publicly exchanged our evaluations of the events around Cuba and each of us has set forth his explanation and his understanding of these events. Consequently, I would judge that, apparently, a continuation of an exchange of opinions at such a distance, even in the form of secret letters, will hardly add anything to that which one side has already said to the other.

I think you will understand me correctly if you are really concerned about the welfare of the world. Everyone needs peace: both capitalists, if they have not lost their reason, and, still more, Communists, people who know how to value not only their own lives but, more than anything, the lives of the peoples. We, Communists, are against all wars between states in general and have been defending the cause of peace since we came into the world. We have always regarded war as a calamity, and not as a game nor as a means for the attainment of definite goals, nor, all the more, as a goal in itself. Our goals are clear, and the means to attain them is labor. War is our enemy and a calamity for all the peoples.

It is thus that we, Soviet people, and, together with US, other peoples as well, understand the questions of war and peace. I can, in any case, firmly say this for the peoples of the Socialist countries, as well as for all progressive people who want peace, happiness, and friendship among peoples.

I see, Mr President, that you too are not devoid of a sense of anxiety for the fate of the world[†] understanding, and of what war entails. What would a war give you? You are threatening us with war. But you well know that the very least which you would receive in reply would be that you would experience the same consequences as those which you sent us. And that must be clear to us, people invested with authority, trust, and responsibility. We must not succumb to intoxication and petty passions, regardless of whether elections are impending in this or that country, or not impending. These are all transient things, but if indeed war should break out, then it would not be in our power to stop it, for such is the logic of war. I have participated in two wars and know that war ends when it has rolled through cities and villages, everywhere sowing death and destruction.

In the name of the Soviet Government and the Soviet people, I assure you that your conclusions regarding offensive weapons on Cuba are groundless. It is apparent from what you have written me that our conceptions are different on this score, or rather, we have different estimates of these or those military means. Indeed, in reality, the same forms of weapons can have different interpretations.

You are a military man and, I hope, will understand me. Let us take for example a simple cannon. What sort of means is this: offensive or defensive? A cannon is a defensive means if it is set up to defend boundaries or a fortified area. But if one

---

†   Garble in the source text. It was subsequently corrected to read 'not with-out an'.

concentrates artillery, and adds to it the necessary number of troops, then the same cannons do become an offensive means, because they prepare and clear the way for infantry to attack. The same happens with missile-nuclear weapons as well, with any type of this weapon.

You are mistaken if you think that any of our means on Cuba are offensive. However, let us not quarrel now. It is apparent that I will not be able to convince you of this. But I say to you: You, Mr President, are a military man and should understand: Can one attack, if one has on one's territory even an enormous quantity of missiles of various effective radiuses and various power, but using only these means. These missiles are a means of extermination and destruction. But one cannot attack with these missiles, even nuclear missiles of a power of 100 megatons because only people, troops, can attack. Without people, any means however powerful cannot be offensive.

How can one, consequently, give such a completely incorrect interpretation as you are now giving, to the effect that some sort of means on Cuba are offensive. All the means located there, and I assure you of this, have a defensive character, are on Cuba solely for the purposes of defense, and we have sent them to Cuba at the request of the Cuban Government. You, however, say that these are offensive means.

But, Mr President, do you really seriously think that Cuba can attack the United States and that even we together with Cuba can attack you from the territory of Cuba? Can you really think that way? How is it possible? We do not understand this. Has something so new appeared in military strategy that one can think that it is possible to attack thus. I say precisely attack, and not destroy, since barbarians, people who have lost their sense, destroy.

I believe that you have no basis to think this way. You can regard us with distrust, but, in any case, you can be calm in this regard, that we are of sound mind and understand perfectly well that if we attack you, you will respond the same way. But you too will receive the same that you hurl against us. And I think that you also understand this. My conversation with you in Vienna gives me the right to talk to you this way.

This indicates that we are normal people, that we correctly understand and correctly evaluate the situation. Consequently, how can we permit the incorrect actions which you ascribe to us? Only lunatics or suicides, who themselves want to perish and to destroy the whole world before they die, could do this. We, however, want to live and do not at all want to destroy your country. We want something quite different: To compete with your country on a peaceful basis. We quarrel with you, we have differences on ideological questions. But our view of the world consists in this, that ideological questions, as well as economic problems, should be solved not by military means, they must be solved on the basis of peaceful competition, i.e., as this is understood in capitalist society, on the basis of competition. We have proceeded and are proceeding from the fact that the peaceful co-existence of the two different social-political systems, now existing in the world, is necessary, that it is necessary to assure a stable peace. That is the sort of principle we hold.

You have now proclaimed piratical measures, which were employed in the Middle Ages, when ships proceeding in international waters were attacked, and you have called this 'a quarantine' around Cuba. Our vessels, apparently, will soon enter the zone which your Navy is patrolling. I assure you that these vessels, now bound for Cuba, are carrying the most innocent peaceful cargoes. Do you really think that we only occupy ourselves with the carriage of so-called offensive weapons, atomic and hydrogen bombs? Although perhaps your military people imagine that these (cargoes) are some sort of special type of weapon, I assure you that they are the most ordinary peaceful products.

Consequently, Mr President, let us show good sense. I assure you that on those ships, which are bound for Cuba, there are no weapons at all. The weapons which were necessary for the defense of Cuba are already there. I do not want to say that there were not any shipments of weapons at all. No, there were such shipments. But now Cuba has already received the necessary means of defense.

I don't know whether you can understand me and believe me. But I should like to have you believe in yourself and to agree that one cannot give way to passions; it is necessary to control them. And in what direction are events now developing? If you stop the vessels, then, as you yourself know, that would be piracy. If we started to do that with regard to your ships, then you would also be as indignant as we and the whole world now are. One cannot give another interpretation to such actions, because one cannot legalize lawlessness. If this were permitted, then there would be no peace, there would also be no peaceful coexistence. We should then be forced to put into effect the necessary measures of a defensive character to protect our interests in accordance with international law. Why should this be done? To what would all this lead?

Let us normalize relations. We have received an appeal from the Acting Secretary General of the UN, U Thant, with his proposals. I have already answered him. His proposals come to this, that our side should not transport armaments of any kind to Cuba during a certain period of time, while negotiations are being conducted – and we are ready to enter such negotiations – and the other side should not undertake any sort of piratical actions against vessels engaged in navigation on the high seas. I consider these proposals reasonable. This would be a way out of the situation which has been created, which would give the peoples the possibility of breathing calmly. You have asked what happened, what evoked the delivery of weapons to Cuba? You have spoken about this to our Minister of Foreign Affairs. I will tell you frankly, Mr President, what evoked it.

We were very grieved by the fact – I spoke about it in Vienna – that a landing took place, that an attack on Cuba was committed, as a result of which many Cubans perished. You yourself told me then that this had been a mistake. I respected that explanation.

You repeated it to me several times, pointing out that not every-body occupying a high position would acknowledge his mistakes as you had done. I value such frankness. For my part, I told you that we too possess no less courage; we also acknowledged those mistakes which had been committed during the history of our state, and not only acknowledged, but sharply condemned them.

If you are really concerned about the peace and welfare of your people, and this is your responsibility as President, then I, as the Chairman of the Council of Ministers, am concerned for my people. Moreover, the preservation of world peace should be our joint concern, since if, under contemporary conditions, war should break out, it would be a war not only between the reciprocal claims, but a world wide cruel and destructive war.

Why have we proceeded to assist Cuba with military and economic aid? The answer is: We have proceeded to do so only for reasons of humanitarianism. At one time, our people itself had a revolution, when Russia was still a backward country. We were attacked then. We were the target of attack by many countries. The USA participated in that adventure. This has been recorded by participants in the aggression against our country. A whole book has been written about this by General Graves, who, at that time, commanded the US Expeditionary Corps. Graves called it 'The American Adventure in Siberia.'

We know how difficult it is to accomplish a revolution and how difficult it is to reconstruct a country on new foundations. We sincerely sympathize with Cuba and the Cuban people, but we are not interfering in questions of domestic structure, we are not interfering in their affairs. The Soviet Union desires to help the Cubans build their life as they themselves wish and that others should not hinder them.

You once said that the United States was not preparing an invasion. But you also declared that you sympathized with the Cuban counter-revolutionary emigrants, that you support them and would help them to realize their plans against the present Government of Cuba. It is also not a secret to anyone that the threat of armed attack, aggression, has constantly hung, and continues to hang over Cuba. It was only this which impelled us to respond to the request of the Cuban Government to furnish it aid for the strengthening of the defensive capacity of this country.

If assurances were given by the President and the Government of the United States that the USA itself would not participate in an attack on Cuba and would restrain others from actions of this sort, if you would recall your fleet, this would immediately change everything. I am not speaking for Fidel Castro, but I think that he and the Government of Cuba, evidently, would declare demobilization and would appeal to the people to get down to peaceful labor. Then, too, the question of armaments would disappear, since, if there is no threat, then armaments are a burden for every people. Then too, the question of the destruction, not only of the armaments which you call offensive, but of all other armaments as well, would look different.

I spoke in the name of the Soviet Government in the United Nations and introduced a proposal for the disbandment of all armies and for the destruction of all armaments. How then can I now count on those armaments?

Armaments bring only disasters. When one accumulates them, this damages the economy, and if one puts them to use, then they destroy people on both sides. Consequently, only a madman can believe that armaments are the principal means in the life of society. No, they are an enforced loss of human energy, and what is more are for the destruction of man himself. If people do not show wisdom, then in the final analysis they will come to a clash, like blind moles, and then reciprocal extermination will begin.

Let us therefore show statesmanlike wisdom. I propose: We, for our part, will declare that our ships, bound for Cuba, will not carry any kind of armaments. You would declare that the United States will not invade Cuba with its forces and will not support any sort of forces which might intend to carry out an invasion of Cuba. Then the necessity for the presence of our military specialists in Cuba would disappear.

Mr President, I appeal to you to weigh well what the aggressive, piratical actions, which you have declared the USA intends to carry out in international waters, would lead to. You yourself know that any sensible man simply cannot agree with this, cannot recognize your right to such actions.

If you did this as the first step towards the unleashing of war, well then, it is evident that nothing else is left to us but to accept this challenge of yours. If, however, you have not lost your self-control and sensibly conceive what this might lead to, then, Mr President, we and you ought not now to pull on the ends of the rope in which you have tied the knot of war, because the more the two of us pull, the tighter that knot will be tied. And a moment may come when that knot will be tied so tight that even he who tied it will not have the strength to untie it, and then it will be necessary to cut that knot, and what that would mean is not for me to explain to you, because you yourself understand perfectly of what terrible forces our countries dispose.

Consequently, if there is no intention to tighten that knot and thereby to doom the world to the catastrophe of thermonuclear war, then let us not only relax the forces pulling on the ends of the rope, let us take measures to untie that knot. We are ready for this.

We welcome all forces which stand on positions of peace. Consequently, I expressed gratitude to Mr Bertrand Russell, too, who manifests alarm and concern for the fate of the world, and I readily responded to the appeal of the Acting Secretary General of the UN, U Thant.

There, Mr President, are my thoughts, which, if you agreed with them, could put an end to that tense situation which is disturbing all peoples.

These thoughts are dictated by a sincere desire to relieve the situation, to remove the threat of war.

Respectfully yours,

N. Khrushchev

Letter from Chairman Khrushchev to President Kennedy

Dated 27 October 1962
[This was a follow-up to his letter of the day before, without wait-ing for a response from President Kennedy.]

DEAR MR. PRESIDENT,

I have studied with great satisfaction your reply to Mr Thant concerning measures that should be taken to avoid contact between our vessels and thereby avoid irreparable and fatal consequences. This reasonable step on your part strengthens my belief that you are showing concern for the preservation of peace, which I note with satisfaction.

I have already said that our people, our Government, and I personally, as Chairman of the Council of Ministers, are concerned solely with having our country develop and occupy a worthy place among all peoples of the world in economic competi-tion, in the development of culture and the arts, and in raising the living standard of the people. This is the most noble and necessary field for competition, and both the victor and the vanquished will derive only benefit from it, because it means peace and an increase in the means by which man lives and finds enjoyment.

In your statement you expressed the opinion that the main aim was not simply to come to an agreement and take meas-ures to prevent contact between our vessels and consequently a deepening of the crisis which could, as a result of such contacts spark a military conflict, after which all negotiations would be superfluous because other forces and other laws would then come into play – the laws of war. I agree with you that this is only the first step. The main thing that must be done is to normalize and stabilize the state of peace among states and among peoples.

I understand your concern for the security of the United States, Mr President, because this is the primary duty of a President. But we too are disturbed about these same questions;

I bear these same obligations as Chairman of the Council of Ministers of the USSR. You have been alarmed by the fact that we have aided Cuba with weapons, in order to strengthen its defense capability – precisely defense capability – because whatever weapons it may possess, Cuba cannot be equated with you since the difference in magnitude is so great, particularly in view of modern means of destruction. Our aim has been and is to help Cuba, and no one can dispute the humanity of our motives, which are oriented toward enabling Cuba to live peacefully and develop in the way its people desire.

You wish to ensure the security of your country, and this is understandable. But Cuba, too, wants the same thing; all countries want to maintain their security. But how are we, the Soviet Union, our Government, to assess your actions which are expressed in the fact that you have surrounded the Soviet Union with military bases; surrounded our allies with military bases; placed military bases literally around our country; and stationed your missile armaments there? This is no secret. Responsible American personages openly declare that it is so. Your missiles are located in Britain, are located in Italy, and are aimed against us. Your missiles are located in Turkey.

You are disturbed over Cuba. You say that this disturbs you because it is 90 miles by sea from the coast of the United States of America. But Turkey adjoins us; our sentries patrol back and forth and see each other. Do you consider, then, that you have the right to demand security for your own country and the removal of the weapons you call offensive, but do not accord the same right to us? You have placed destructive missile weapons, which you call offensive, in Turkey, literally next to us. How then can recognition of our equal military capacities be reconciled with such unequal relations between our great states? This is irreconcilable.

It is good, Mr President, that you have agreed to have our representatives meet and begin talks, apparently through the mediation of U Thant, Acting Secretary General of the United Nations. Consequently, he to some degree has assumed the role of a mediator and we consider that he will be able to cope with this responsible mission, provided, of course, that each party drawn into this controversy displays good will.

I think it would be possible to end the controversy quickly and normalize the situation, and then the people could breathe more easily, considering that statesmen charged with responsibility are of sober mind and have an awareness of their responsibility combined with the ability to solve complex questions and not bring things to a military catastrophe.

I therefore make this proposal: We are willing to remove from Cuba the means which you regard as offensive. We are willing to carry this out and to make this pledge in the United Nations. Your representatives will make a declaration to the effect that the United States, for its part, considering the uneasiness and anxiety of the Soviet State, will remove its analogous means from Turkey. Let us reach agreement as to the period of time needed by you and by us to bring this about. And, after that, persons entrusted by the United Nations Security Council could inspect on the spot the fulfilment of the pledges made. Of course, the permission of the Governments of Cuba and Turkey is necessary for the entry into those countries of these representatives and for the inspection of the fulfilment of the pledge made by each side. Of course it would be best if these representatives enjoyed the confidence of the Security Council as well as yours and mine – both the United States and the Soviet Union – and also that of Turkey and Cuba. I do not think it would be difficult to select people who would enjoy the trust and respect of all parties concerned.

We, in making this pledge, in order to give satisfaction and hope of the peoples of Cuba and Turkey and to strengthen their confidences in their security, will make a statement within the framework of the Security Council to the effect that the Soviet Government gives a solemn promise to respect the inviolability of the borders and sovereignty of Turkey, not to interfere in its internal affairs, not to invade Turkey, not to make available our territory as a bridgehead for such an invasion, and that it would also restrain those who contemplate committing aggression against Turkey, either from the territory of the Soviet Union or from the territory of Turkey's other neighboring states.

The United States Government will make a similar statement within the framework of the Security Council regarding Cuba. It will declare that the United States will respect the inviolability of Cuba's borders and its sovereignty, will pledge not to interfere in its internal affairs, not to invade Cuba itself or make its territory available as a bridgehead for such an invasion, and will also restrain those who might contemplate committing aggression against Cuba, either from the territory of the United States or from the territory of Cuba's other neighboring states.

Of course, for this we would have to come to an agreement with you and specify a certain time limit. Let us agree to some period of time, but without unnecessary delay – say within two or three weeks, not longer than a month.

The means situated in Cuba, of which you speak and which disturb you, as you have stated, are in the hands of Soviet officers. Therefore, any accidental use of them to the detriment of the United States is excluded. These means are situated in Cuba at the request of the Cuban Government and are only for defense purposes. Therefore, if there is no invasion of Cuba, or attack on the Soviet Union or any of our other allies, then of course these means are not and will not be a threat to anyone. For they are not for purposes of attack.

If you are agreeable to my proposal, Mr President, then we would send our representatives to New York, to the United Nations, and would give them comprehensive instructions in order that an agreement may be reached more quickly. If you also select your people and give them the corresponding instructions, then this question can be quickly resolved.

Why would I like to do this? Because the whole world is now apprehensive and expects sensible actions of us. The greatest joy for all peoples would be the announcement of our agreement and of the eradication of the controversy that has arisen. I attach great importance to this agreement in so far as it could serve as a good beginning and could in particular make it easier to reach agreement on banning nuclear weapons tests. The question of the tests could be solved in parallel fashion, without connecting one with the other, because these are different issues. However, it is important that agreement be reached on both these issues so as to present humanity with a fine gift, and also to gladden it with the news that agreement has been reached on the cessation of nuclear tests and that consequently the atmosphere will no longer be poisoned. Our position and yours on this issue are very close together.

All of this could possibly serve as a good impetus toward the finding of mutually acceptable agreements on other controversial issues on which you and I have been exchanging views. These issues have so far not been resolved, but they are awaiting urgent solution, which would clear up the international atmosphere. We are prepared for this.

These are my proposals, Mr President.

Respectfully yours,

    N. Khrushchev

[This letter caused a major problem for Kennedy because the Turks were adamant that the NATO missiles should stay and, in any case, the United States could not unilaterally decide to remove the NATO missiles. Under advice, the President simply ignored the most recent letter and referred instead to the more acceptable terms of Khrushchev's letter of the 26th, thus bypassing the tricky problem of withdrawing the NATO missiles in Turkey.]

Letter from President Kennedy to Chairman Khrushchev

Dated 27 October 1962

Dear Mr Chairman:

I have read your letter of October 26th with great care and welcomed the statement of your desire to seek a prompt solution to the problem. The first thing that needs to be done, however, is for work to cease on offensive missile bases in Cuba and for all weapons systems in Cuba capable of offensive use to be rendered inoperable, under effective United Nations arrangements.

Assuming this is done promptly, I have given my representatives in New York instructions that will permit them to work out this weekend – in cooperation with the Acting Secretary General and your representative – an arrangement for a permanent solution to the Cuban problem along the lines suggested in your letter of October 26th. As I read your letter, the key elements of your proposals – which seem generally acceptable as I understand them – are as follows:

1) You would agree to remove these weapons systems from Cuba under appropriate United Nations observation and supervision; and undertake, with suitable safeguards, to halt the further introduction of such weapons systems into Cuba.

2) We, on our part, would agree – upon the establishment of adequate arrangements through the United Nations to ensure the carrying out and continuation of these commitments – (a) to remove promptly the quarantine measures now in effect and (b) to give assurances against an invasion of Cuba. I am confident that other nations of the Western Hemisphere would be prepared to do likewise.

If you will give your representative similar instructions, there is no reason why we should not be able to complete these arrangements and announce them to the world within a couple of days. The effect of such a settlement on easing world tensions would enable us to work toward a more general arrangement regarding 'other armaments', as proposed in your second letter which you made public. I would like to say again that the United States is very much interested in reducing tensions and halting the arms race; and if your letter signifies that you are prepared to discuss a detente affecting NATO and the Warsaw Pact, we are quite prepared to consider with our allies any useful proposals.

But the first ingredient, let me emphasize, is the cessation of work on missile sites in Cuba and measures to render such weapons inoperable, under effective international guarantees. The continuation of this threat, or a prolonging of this discussion concerning Cuba by linking these problems to the broader questions of European and world security, would surely lead to an intensification of the Cuban crisis and a grave risk to the peace of the world. For this reason I hope we can quickly agree along the lines in this letter and in your letter of October 26th.

   John F. Kennedy

INDEX

Also available from Biteback

SMERSH
VADIM J. BIRSTEIN

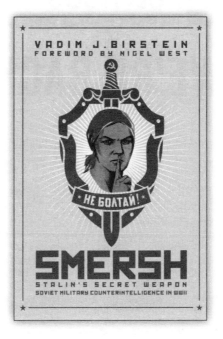

In the early James Bond novels 007 is pitched against Smersh,
a top secret Soviet agency. Bond's creator Ian Fleming took
his inspiration from true life, but the real Smersh was far more
savage than Bond's fictional nemesis.

Vadim Birstein makes comprehensive use of recently released
Russian military archives in Moscow and speaks to survivors
and victims of Smersh to tell, for the first time, one of the
darkest stories in Soviet Russia's history.

528pp hardback, £25
Available from all good bookshops or order from
www.bitebackpublishing.com

REEZE.